Divided Libraries

Divided Libraries

*Remodeling Management
to Unify Institutions*

T. D. WEBB

McFarland & Company, Inc., Publishers
Jefferson, North Carolina, and London

Library of Congress Cataloguing-in-Publication Data

Webb, T.D.
Divided libraries : remodeling management to unify institutions /
T.D. Webb.
p.   cm.
Includes bibliographical references and index.

ISBN 978-0-7864-6478-4
softcover : acid free paper ∞

1. Academic libraries — Administration.   2. Academic libraries —
Relations with faculty and curriculum.   3. Libraries and colleges.
4. Academic libraries — Aims and objectives.   5. Academic libraries —
Evaluation.   6. Libraries and education.   I. Title.
Z675.U5W396 2012   025.1'977 — dc23   2012024862

British Library cataloguing data are available

Front cover images © 2012 Shutterstock

Manufactured in the United States of America

*McFarland & Company, Inc., Publishers
Box 611, Jefferson, North Carolina 28640
www.mcfarlandpub.com*

TABLE OF CONTENTS

Introduction

Teaching and Learning in Libraries

In the new train station at Kuala Lumpur, there is a bookstore named Nile Books. In the bookstore's front window, a sign reads *Better be unborn than untaught.*

All over the world, and throughout all the millennia, people have sought books, or their forerunners, to gain knowledge and education. Ever since writing emerged and tablets, incunabula, scrolls, and books were invented, the written word has been like manna to those who seek learning and wisdom. Even without the benefit of academic institutions, instructors, or teachers, books and libraries — as well as bookstores like Nile Books — have transferred their knowledge to anyone willing to read and study and escape the bondage of ignorance. Long before there were universities, as we now know them, people obtained knowledge directly from books, and libraries were seats of learning.

What librarian is not discouraged, then, by modern university administrators who idly allow their libraries to wither under the burden of shrinking budgets and struggle with staffing inadequacies and deteriorating facilities, and who pay lip service to their libraries, yet fail to realize that in the modern era libraries remain seats of learning. Given the highly qualified library staff now available and the vast and growing array of packaging for information and knowledge, libraries have the capacity to become preeminent places of learning, research, and *teaching*.

Despite this potential, libraries remain divided from their constituencies and their governing bodies, be they students, faculties, university administrations, municipal governments, or ordinary citizens. I believe that librarians themselves bear much of the guilt for these divisions. Furthermore, the current dialogue in the library profession regarding the future of libraries and librarianship, the reformation of scholarly communication, the education of library professionals, and the very mission of librarianship itself leaves me with dread that the changes that need to be made in our profession will again be put off, and the divisions within librarianship will not be ameliorated because some university leaders still hope their libraries and their energetic librarians will fade away.

Maverick

In 1987, *American Libraries* labeled me an automation "maverick" because of my skepticism about promoting "open systems" at the expense of integrated systems following

1

an *AL* automation symposium. At that time, a complete, fully integrated system did not really exist, in my view. I was not fully satisfied with any vendor-supplied integrated library system. Furthermore, I did not appreciate the way library systems vendors designed their systems and treated their clients, nor the differences of opinions that arose in negotiations with our vendors.

I can especially tell when I participate in consortia that I am more of a maverick now than ever before. I seem to see library priorities very differently than do my colleagues. Many library leaders engage in grandstanding, go berserk, and contrive something new just because we can! and not because it will benefit our clientele and colleagues. Everywhere I look in librarydom, I see libraries divided: divided from their missions, divided from their users, divided from their administrative overlords, divided from each other, divided from the information marketplace, divided from innovation and variant technologies, on and on. Carlson found that "many institutions are bureaucratically segmented ... departments are short of time and talent, and I wince at Susan Metros' description: 'Unfortunately, we're still in our separate silos'" (Carlson 2003).

Chapter 8 will tell the truth about another unfortunate library throwback still in place: Library directors are often especially full of themselves. Some are controlling and overbearing, with a distinct absence of civility to their support staff. Maybe it is trickle-down from university administrators who are not keen on libraries or librarians, as with the rogue chemist. This book has several documented instances:

I heard recently from a former colleague that a university librarian is under siege from the library staff because the UL is draconic, extremely rude, and has wreaked upheaval in the library. Faculty are also working on a letter of no confidence to bring to the Faculty Senate. So far, no real change.

My former colleague sensed, however, that the UL is doing precisely what the university administration wants her to be doing — saving money, getting rid of old-timers, and the university administration will ignore all letters of no confidence. The UL doesn't have to be nice or communicate well to get the job done — the VP over the library evidently has little or no faith (or perhaps no understanding) about librarians. His values seem not to correlate at all with those of most of the beleaguered librarians. Big surprise.

Medieval Hangovers

Sometimes I think we librarians have not yet moved fully into the 21st century, and maybe not even the 20th century. We may be stuck in the 19th century. Hell, we may even be medieval. Think about it: We are now serfs for the publishing conglomerates who commandeer research from our institutions, and then extort our library budgets at a pirate's ransom for us to buy back the research our faculties conduct and publish, thus ruining the stability of academic institutions and higher education.

Another medieval throwback: Many libraries are building giant, remote cave-like Qumrans equipped with robotic automated retrieval systems (ARS) technology, supposedly to store and retrieve little-used books. Yet if those books are that little-used where they are now, very few will likely ever want to read any of them once they are shelved in their remote caves, at the enormous costs of building and operating these book catacombs, including a huge staffing boondoggle. Why do we feel that we should build something just because we can!?

The ARS "strategy" is growing fast. Instead, librarians should be making a much stronger effort toward more digital restructuring of scholarly communication among universities and their libraries. This will cut the ground from under the publisher/pirate middlemen and accelerate the growth of research. For my money, I would spend library budgets on open access (OA) institutional repositories and do away with costly ARS caverns and build solutions.

We should move our chess pieces toward the wholly digital domain, but under the control of libraries, not outlaw publishers. These are the days of the jackal, crooked monopolies, dwindling resources for schools, universities, research, and academe itself. These, too, are the days of open access, digital academic presses (DAPS), Kindles, iPads, and wave after wave of ever more sophisticated information platforms. There will be a huge market shakeout soon enough. Will librarians be ready for it? We have not been too successful in the past at separating the disruptive technologies from the sustaining ones, such as CD-ROM, towers, daisy chains, lame online library systems, and so on.

In another throwback form of library operations, many library managers act like dictators who hardly care or qualify to understand the needs, sensitivities, and underutilized talents of their subordinates, and mistreat them angrily, with an absence of civility, or even cavalierly, which may be the most offensive treatment. Over and over, I also see shameful divisions among librarians who demean and criticize their non-professional subordinates, but then turn right around and bend over backwards to extend their services to their clientele. This makes no sense to me. More about this in Chapter 2.

A Struggling Open Access Breakthrough

The open access movement seems to be entering a cascade phase in which many university faculty are demanding open access and greater control of their publications along with reasonable costs for very current research. Yet, many librarians are not striving enough to achieve OA to end the Enronic reign of publisher robber-barons; many librarians have little interest in returning control of scholarly communication to academe by creating institutional repositories of faculty research, and digital academic presses as outlets for obscure research that will nonetheless be of great interest to many diverse groups; many librarians are not seriously considering the important step of earning Ph.D.s, seeking promotion and tenure, conducting energetic research and publication, and volunteering for involvement in university committees and other relevant associations. More about OA, DAPS, and Ph.D.s in later chapters.

Some Good Vibes

I remain heartened that OCLC's *Perceptions of Libraries and Information Resources* (2005) found that "85 percent of all respondents *agree*, or *agree completely*, that the library is perceived to be a place to learn." Yet I also remain disillusioned by my 35-year career because I see the profession wobbling, despite the generally good response of loyal library users. There are lots of cross-currents in libraries now, and lots of divisions within libraries and between libraries and their publics.

More heartening news: at this writing, over 20 U.S. universities unilaterally have begun to offer doctoral degrees in librarianship, with not so much of a tip of their mortarboards to ALA. Think of that! ALA may try hard to make progress, but in reality it is becoming inert, leaving librarianship to the mercy of the winds of change and the native intelligence of librarians that can be greatly honed to lift libraries and librarianship to a new place, maybe even building a new professional organization for librarians. Librarianship is in bouleversement, and we all need to look for seams of divisions that might be made to come together.

Ironically, one of the largest disruptors in librarianship *is* the ALA. Many librarians seem to be living in a mythical world of their own imaginary missions and unrealistic realities instead of becoming fully committed to their mission to educate students, and to the missions of their institutions. ALA is not as counterproductive as the robber publishing conglomerates that are destroying libraries and universities through their avaricious monopolies, but our "professional" organization at least needs to move from the 19th century to the 21st.

The purpose of this book is to identify, diagnose, and remedy the divisions in and between libraries and librarianship. It is a summation of my 35 years of experience as a librarian and library director. Although librarianship is now more vibrant than at any other time, libraries remain divided from ordinary citizens, their institutions, and their primary mission as educators. Libraries are still at risk, and librarians are seen as ancillary citizens in academe. This book lays plans for resolving these negative situations.

I lay full blame on ALA for the shabby way many faculty disrespect librarians. We're caught between ALA's weaknesses and the skepticism of the faculty, including administrators, most of whom were faculty in previous lives. We could chalk it up to "faculty culture," and "librarian culture," but that's neither the long nor the short of this.

The truth is that faculty and university administrators do not consider us colleagues. Yet we hold onto Mother ALA tightly because we somehow feel that we have our own national professional association like other professions and occupations. It appears to give us stature, while in fact our "stature" is of our own fabrication. For instance, where is the benefit if our ALA supposes that learning for librarians only needs to go to mid-level, but not beyond to the doctoral sphere? By so doing, we cannot help but embarrass ourselves. It is an ALA insanity *not* to encourage, much less expect, librarians to earn doctoral degrees. Although librarians certainly do not lack the necessary intelligence, ALA wants librarians to stay barefoot and outrageously less productive than we can, should, and must be. I count this to be the most damaging division between librarians and our "colleagues" in academe.

Another outcome of ALA's superficial structure, training, professionalism, and library education is the way many librarians demean and criticize their non-professional subordinates, but extend themselves to the library users and other stakeholders. No library stakeholders are more important than the library subordinate staff. This management error would be controllable if library "managers" had the needed learning to activate and utilize their support staff members' management skills, but few take the opportunity to learn how to manage and elevate their subordinates effectively. This is another way ALA holds librarians back from their full potential as educators, managers, and colleagues in academe, and in public libraries as well.

Denise Covey × 1

Covey (2002) says, "Libraries evolve on different paths ... and offer different services or venues for service. Given the context of rapid, constant change and diversity [and frequently faltering assessment practices], the new measures initiatives are essential and commendable." She adds, "The lack of community agreement about appropriate new assessments acts as an impediment to investing in assessment." Here, another division in libraries; nothing new about that. She continues, "An organizational culture is an aggregate of subcultures, which can benefit librarians. To change library culture into a culture of assessment, library administrators must understand and modify the frame of reference of library personnel to bring it into alignment with the beliefs, behaviors, and assumptions of the new culture ... libraries appear to be unwilling, unable, or unaware of the need to: articulate the beliefs, behaviors, and assumptions of a culture of assessment; assess the beliefs, behaviors, and assumptions of the existing culture; identify gaps between the current and desired frame of reference; and develop action plans to *close the gaps*" (emphasis added) — or, in the present study, end the divisions in libraries, library schools, universities, colleges, public libraries, and so on. The thing to do: tip over the silos.

As a cultural anthropologist, I've studied modernization, ethnicity, community development, culture change, and culture loss. I've lived among ethnic minorities in China and the Pacific for years. In anthropological terms, my observations are that librarians are considered and treated as a subculture in academe, with lower social capital than that of professors, administrators, and even students. They will not take us on as wards or squires. No one above us will deign to raise us. We must do that ourselves. Universities are still medieval, after all, with fiefdoms, lords, and combats — scholarly, that is, but sometimes vicious, nevertheless. I also rely heavily on symbolic librarianship (Webb 2000).

Having professed these views in no direct way links me to the "intracultural reciprocity" gambit of Crowley and Ginsberg (2003) to save American librarianship. They argue that globalization "will make it impossible for many librarians, information specialists, and knowledge managers to secure acknowledged rights to manage information provision and analysis on the basis of their educational credentials." They add that librarianship in the 21st century may well live or die, not on the basis of superior information expertise, but on the grounds of its ability to combine such expertise with support of a spectrum of values prized by significant subcultures within the broader national culture. But it seems to me that they are trading the educational mission of librarianship for another, even narrower one-lane road to the preservation of librarians and libraries. More about globalization in Chapter 7.

We need an essential strategy because even though many college and university instructional faculty work well with librarians as educators and are delighted to engage them for library instruction to their students, a large portion of faculty still see librarians as an academic subculture, like counselors and mentors.

Covey × 2

Covey observes, "Libraries continue to gather traditional input and output data to show their potential to provide service and the actual service they provide. These are meaningful data, but the more purposeful, effective data these days are outcomes and performance measures that show what good libraries do and how well they perform given their human and financial resources." She adds, "Measures of efficiency, effectiveness, quality, usability and what difference the libraries make are much needed — and very persuasive — in an era of accountability" (2005). Yet even Covey misses the main point that libraries need to assess and then raise their effectiveness in the teaching and learning of students. This will certainly help students in their disciplines, and will also accelerate the mission of their universities. This assessment method must rely on *quantitative* correlations between student library usage and their performance in the classroom, and *not* mainly qualitative assessment devices like LibQual, which derives its results simply from student surveys adapted from customer satisfaction surveys. By themselves, touchy/feely student satisfaction surveys won't work. Students don't earn their good grades because they like their teachers, their student friends, or the easiness or difficulties of their courses. Their overall success in learning is measured by the GPA. Only by finding a strong qualitative, empirical connection between students' library usage and their overall academic performance can we statistically and quantitatively correlate their academic progress in the form of grade point averages and their library usage. More about this in Chapter 3.

The best way to demonstrate the impact librarians can muster in their institutions is to raise the levels of student learning. Colleges and universities presently have serious conditions about the "new 3Rs," that is, student *r*ecruitment, *r*etention, and *r*egular progress to graduation. Studies have shown that these measures can be remedied by the skills librarians have at their disposal.

Regarding Student Learning

Everything you will read in this book revolves around this basic motivation: excellent student learning driven by librarians with a seamless connection to the faculty. According to Lee Hisle, "Reference librarians must be teachers themselves, in formal information-literacy programs or in one-on-one sessions with faculty members and students who need help navigating an increasingly complex digital environment" (2005). But to make this method work, librarians must track the performance of the students they teach, and correlate these data to the students' grades in their fields of study.

The moral of this is that library employees, professionals, and so-called support staff don't get as much respect as they deserve from faculty and university administrators. So by all means we must make our libraries places of power learning, respect, meaningful student assessment, professionalism, and equality.

Great Public Libraries

This book talks mainly about academic libraries, but there is much here that I hope will interest public libraries, as well, especially in terms of supervision, library education, information technology, librarians as educators, and leadership at all levels. I was very fortunate to have started my career in a fine public library system, and the chapter on management herein (Chapter 8) may come closest to the comparative operations of public libraries.

Whither Learning?

I have long believed that the basic purpose of higher education is to make ordinary people better, people who are more aware of the sensitivities of others, more understanding and sympathetic toward the human condition. I was surprised when a librarian at a very prestigious and well-known U.S. university that was originally founded to be a religious institution firmly disagreed with my premise, and did not agree with my lofty expectations for college students. Instead, he insisted that students seek higher education across the board to find careers and earn lofty salaries. Despite that librarian's views, I have not lost my humanistic ideal.

1

LIBRARIANS AS EDUCATORS

In the Proper Context

I am particularly disappointed that I don't recall ever hearing any university administrators make statements that librarians are educators and teachers, even after I coached some of them a bit. Admitting that librarians are educators and teachers seems to be an alien concept to administrators that might confuse and perhaps demean the academic faculty and maybe put them on edge, something academic administrators are loath to do. Surely, college and university administrators and faculty must have gone to their university libraries at least a few times when they were students. How did they fail to observe that librarians led them to and through the steps of finding, evaluating, and validating sources suitable to their academic pursuits? What did they expect to encounter in the stacks if not a meticulously assembled high-quality collection of information, learning, knowledge, and wisdom, with depth and breadth of coverage in countless subjects, all arranged in a systematic and logical transition from subject to subject?

Such a collection is a monumental educational engine that was carefully assembled by librarians and faculty for the education of students and for faculty research.

Jargon and Jive

I could almost stand up and cheer, however, when I find journal articles that directly refer to librarians as educators or, even better, assume that readers already appreciate the fact that librarians are bona fide educators, without being beaten over the head with it. I am very glad that articles and papers of this genre are increasing in number. Even some teaching faculty, after having worked in a collaborative way with librarians, concede that library staff are indeed teachers. Yet although many librarians now see themselves as educators, there are still many who have not connected the dots between their library schooling, their library practice, and their mission as educators.

The term *library educator* is not new, however. In 1980, while addressing the subject of faculty culture, Stephenson said, "Library educators must be sensitive to ... their own faculty members. They need to be sensitive to them and still have the maturity to put up with overbearing academic-intellectual egos and with the attitudes of superiority that most individual faculty members exhibit." Hardesty (1995) adds astutely, "A sensitivity to faculty and our own values is essential. The burden, fairly or not, remains on librarians."

In 1996, Stoffle, Renaud, and Veldof wrote, "Librarians must build new paradigms and frames of analysis, including *new language*. They must accept that *they are educators* and knowledge managers first and foremost" (emphases added). I applaud the title of *educator* applied to librarians, but I am not keen on *knowledge manager*, partly because all academics are knowledge managers by virtue of their grasp of the subtleties of their disciplines and their imparting that knowledge to their students, but also *knowledge manager* does not imply that there is a second party who is to receive the knowledge, namely, the students and the faculty as well.

Such nicknames and other misnomers like "caretakers" of books or "stewards" of knowledge are out of place. These labels make me think of cemetery groundskeepers, or imply that librarians work in butleries. In 2001, Lynch and Smith, in a content analysis study of wording changes in library recruitment ads, make a stronger point that instruction is now essential to reference work: "Instruction has become an integral part of every reference job, and some responsibility for collection development has emerged as an important component of these jobs." Hisle (2005) makes two good interconnected points: (1) Today's reference questions "tend to be more complex, albeit fewer in number"; and (2) "Reference work helps drive collection development and efforts to increase information literacy, by demonstrating what materials the users need and what instruction they must have to work with those materials." He adds that "reference librarians typically must be teachers themselves, in formal information-literacy programs or in one-on-one sessions with faculty members and students who need help navigating an increasingly complex digital environment."

Hisle (2005) recognizes that "reference librarians need new skills to work with the new pedagogies." This concurs with Lillard and Wales (2003), who seek a "balance between values of traditional LIS education and the role that information science plays." Their solution relates to improvements needed in graduate library schools: "With both an intimate working knowledge of higher education and an appreciation of the practitioner's role, academic librarians are in *a particularly strong position* to collaborate with library educators in ways that will strengthen LIS education and the profession as a whole" (Lillard and Wales 2003, emphasis added). We should surely hope so, but the "particularly strong position" even as of this writing, is hardly yet in place, and will not be settled until librarians accept the need to pursue doctoral-level terminal degrees.

MURL

Hisle, Lillard, and Wales make way too much good sense; I predict it won't ever happen in my lifetime. After receiving an M.A. in interdisciplinary humanities, I was looking for an educational position in an art museum, but there were no openings, so I began teaching humanities at the college level part time. Later, I started working full time as a library assistant, but I continued my part-time college teaching too. My first library was, at that time, designated a "major urban research library," or MURL, another inflated bit of jargon that lasted in the profession I think for only a few weeks. I was hired as a library assistant before I enrolled in library school, and when I decided to commit to the profession and get an MLS, I found that my courses were just barely in touch with the world inside the real library where I had been working.

As Todd Gilman observed, "Nobody said that library school is bad.... The curriculum is just not very rigorous, with a few exceptions" (qtd. in Oder 2003). Gilman is right. Based solely on a year or so as a working cataloger, I "examined-out" of cataloging class, which made me the first person in my library school ever to accomplish this feat. Only about 20 percent of my LIS education and my diploma came from my LIS alma mater. The other 80 percent was earned on the job. My doctoral education at least doubled my knowledge pertinent to my library career in terms of writing, research, scholarly communication, self-discipline, and scholarly pursuits, all of which are essential for librarians to assist students — undergrads as well as graduate students. And let's not forget the faculty.

From the start of that first job, I found library work comfortable, but I was puzzled by the cells of cadres and radicals in library school, not so much, though, in a working library. I found it especially odd that ALA felt it was necessary for librarians to compose their own Bill of Rights. I thought the original was quite adequate, thank you very much. In my exit interview after graduation, the dean of my library school was not happy when I declined to genuflect to ALA by not joining and paying dues. Nor could I identify any of the ALA initialisms she threw at me from behind her desk. I'm sure she knew I heard her sigh to herself, "What is librarianship coming to?" That is exactly where this book is going.

Over thirty years later, things have not changed much. David Durant (2005) wrote of the ALA's radicalism, "To protest the ALA's growing politicization, I allowed my membership to lapse and have no intention of renewing it." I remain proud to say that I never started paying ALA dues.

More Jargon

We librarians need not confuse our educational mission with new job titles that are not germane to teaching, learning, and research. We have already burdened our students and faculty colleagues with jargon that few of them even care to learn or understand (Hutcherson 2004), and now that some of us fancy ourselves as information or knowledge managers, the patter deepens and aligns librarianship with information marketeers, which will erode our mission as educators. Gilman (2006) is spot on when he says: "Some professors may object to the call for 'information literacy'— a phrase that has become the mantra of some academic librarians in their efforts to teach research skills. And the term can rankle. It risks sounding elementary, or condescending, or alarmist, or perhaps seems like an affectation by which librarians seek to mystify and aggrandize what they do via jargon." Gilman prefers the term *research education*, which nevertheless may also profoundly rankle professors.

Crowley and Ginsberg contend (2003) that the 21st century could bring the disappearance of U.S. librarianship "not on the basis of superior information expertise, but on the grounds of its ability to combine such experience with support of a spectrum of values prized by significant subcultures within the broader national culture." These authors argue that changing terminologies, among other forms of deprofessionalization, could figure largely in the very survival or disappearance of librarianship. They disclaim, and so do I, terms like *information manager, knowledge resource analyst, information professional,* and other descriptors as substitutes for *librarian,* much less *educator.* Such a glut of sobriquets for *librarian* would bewilder anyone working inside or outside librarydom.

The observations of Crowley and Ginsberg remind me of an interview I once had with a candidate for a reference librarian position. She was an experienced, trained librarian, but she had been working in the business sector, where her title was *knowledge management officer.* I was nonplussed when she said that. I had no practical idea what the term really meant. The term itself, and her narrow job duties as well, must have bothered her, too, because she was very eager to redirect her career to academe.

She explained that she conducted research training and provided reference service, all within the narrow field of high-power accounting. The current salary marked on her application form was very generous, but she said her firm did not consider her a professional because she did not bring revenue into the firm directly. The corporate deprofessionalization of her work clearly was not to her liking. She would have been excellent in our library, but I could not even come close to matching her salary and bonus expectations. I suspect she stayed put.

Librarian Values

Echoing Michael Gorman, Crowley and Ginsberg (2003) state that the redefinition of librarianship, especially in the corporate world, but also in academe, "narrows the librarian's professional focus from culture, education, information, and entertainment to information alone. Information, however, is the very same area where millions of others, with considerable differences in academic preparation, are now asserting competence."

To me, this trend is growing because the academic community, including librarians themselves, do not fully comprehend, much less announce, what librarians really do in academe: Teach! Educate! Research! A major reason for this lack of recognition is the prolonged division between academic librarians and the teaching faculty. We speak different terminologies. To me, information and data are the purposive building blocks of culture, education, civility, justice, and other qualities that make people better and more aware of sensitivities of others, and more understanding and sympathetic to the human condition.

To the admonition of Stoffle, Renaud, and Veldof above, I add that if librarians are indeed educators — and I insist that we are — the "new language" librarians need to learn should *not* be some terminology peculiar to our profession, such as "blended librarians" (Bell and Shank 2004, Shank 2006) or other aliases that might increase "conflict-generating identity ambiguity" among librarians (Weaver-Meyers 2002). While I'm not keen on "blended librarianship," I fully support Bell and Shank (2004) when they say, "We must also add to our traditional role a new capacity for collaboration to improve student learning and outcomes assessment...," two of my favorite topics in librarianship.

Taking the "new language" line of thought in a different and more promising direction, Young and Blixrud (2003) advocate that librarians adopt, learn, and apply the language of teaching and learning to the processes of librarianship. The authors also encourage the library profession to devise or adopt valid student learning outcomes, performance indicators, and measures of effectiveness (read: *assessment*) comparable to those being applied in the students' classrooms that can be used to assess library instructional programs as well.

Adams, Fister, and Bell (2005) announce categorically, "Librarians teach," and give examples of librarians' most commonly recognized contributions to teaching and learning: research strategies, citation standards, information ethics, non-credit or for-credit courses, and other programs that satisfy the demand of academic institutions and accrediting bodies that students learn to "define an information need, locate relevant information, evaluate it, and use it effectively and correctly ... this process is what librarians have been prepared to teach."

I would more likely respond, "That is what they *should* be prepared to teach." This is certainly a worthy disciplinary focus for librarians, but we must also be sure that we are guiding students through their respective disciplines, majors, and minors. Through our teaching, we should be leading them to *their* academic objectives, not just to citation standards and database searching.

We must see the mission of librarianship as a double discipline: We teach students how to locate, evaluate, and use data, information, and research knowledgably, but these tasks are to be anchored in many subject disciplines, the content areas through which our students must navigate and learn. Rather than hitch librarianship to information technology in an attempt to forward librarianship cum information literacy as a discrete field in education to substantiate our claim to be educators, or to effect a rapprochement with teaching faculty, we should also be moving in another direction leading back into the disciplines that are our users' scholarly fields of study, in which they will receive their degrees and diplomas. These subject degrees are the ultimate outcomes and missions of the educational institutions that hire librarians.

Librarianship has a double mission within education. Our total teaching content must not be information literacy exclusively. This would only limit librarianship to its current state of teaching. Our approach to the future means a radical expansion of library education along with subject awareness, if not discipline specialization.

Competence, Literacy, and Fluency

In addition to the proliferating articles that focus squarely on the educational mission of librarianship, hordes of authors and librarians have staked out information literacy as the teaching domain of librarians. The terms *information literacy*, or *competence*, or *fluency*, have often been used interchangeably and indiscriminately. Adams, Fister, and Bell (above), pattern *information literacy* after ALA, chapter and verse, but I won't belabor the point; I will use *information literacy* in this book because it seems to have become the preferred term. But my own preference is the term *information fluency*. It implies the ability to multitask various information operations using several knowledge and information technologies effectively, which is the objective of the Information and Communication Technology Literacy Assessment, or ICT, created by the Educational Testing Service (ETS) in 2003. I would expect all university students to be information fluent when they graduate. I believe students should already be information literate, as Adams, Fister, and Bell construe the term, when they arrive in college, just as they should be reading and math literate, although this is hardly true on today's university campuses. The term *information competence* might be the appropriate learning objective for high school students and below.

Information literacy, and especially information fluency, also include the component of information ethics. In the high-tech environment of modern teaching, learning, research, and publication, a sensitivity and respect for information ethics is essential. Librarians see themselves as scrupulous protectors of the ethical use of information, namely, thoroughness and honesty in gathering data and reporting findings; eschewing plagiarism; conscientious application of knowledge to bring about good, not harm; and providing liberal information access to all who seek it. Librarians also have an implied and equally strong belief that knowledge and learning have a salubrious, ennobling effect on human beings, and that to benefit fully from this effect, every individual must be guaranteed free access to the accumulated abundance of information and knowledge without fear of compromise or retaliation (Webb 2000). Librarians can do much to infuse the ethical use of information in their institutions by increasing their role in teaching students the correct way to conduct scientific study, engage critical thinking skills, and share their research through logical exposition and presentation. The proliferating technologies of modern academic libraries can clearly increase the reach and effectiveness of librarians in promoting information ethics.

Adams, Fister, and Bell (2005) take a wrong approach, I think, to controlling plagiarism. They assume students are prone to plagiarize nefariously, and they advocate helping faculty devise better writing assignments that make plagiarism more difficult. Programs like Turnitin and its ilk can catch an information thief who may not even know s/he has committed a crime, not to mention an unforgivable sin against the academy. In writing classes I have taught at the university level, including research writing classes, I learned that most students simply do not know how to research, organize, and write a good paper, much less what *plagiarism* means. I suspect that most students do not knowingly commit plagiarism, and once they understand and appreciate the exhilarating processes of discovery and self-expression, why would they want to plagiarize?

Finding good data, developing one's original insights into those data, organizing them into a reasoned, written argument strengthened with appropriate support from scholarly sources, and presenting the work orally or in writing, is nothing less than invigorating and habit forming. It is the duty of librarians, along with academic faculty, to instruct students in these activities.

Maybe I'm the one who is naïve, but I've had many students thank me at the end of a semester for teaching them how to think and how to write and how to discover new knowledge and how to articulate their discoveries. I think the best way to reduce plagiarism, even in the modern domain of cut-and-paste, is to teach students to understand the logic and appeal of the scientific method, and of combining inductive and deductive reasoning to produce good writing for their GPAs, and for their qualitative satisfaction for completing their courses.

Years ago, one of my students was a woman who returned to college as a third-year student. Her goal was to finish her B.A. degree, which was interrupted when she started a family. She was an intelligent, attentive student, but very much intimidated, as were all the other students, by the assignment to research and write a lengthy term paper complete with scholarly citations. She became a good writer and took very careful notes in class. She then shared those notes with her high-school daughter who was terrified about her own term paper. My student earned an A. At the end of the semester, she told me she had given her class notes to her daughter, who followed all the notes and used them for her high school paper, and also scored an A. Many similar instances demonstrated to me that by following instructions and learning the habits of good reading, research, and writing, many, if not most, students will not feel a need to plagiarize.

This is not to say that writing is easy for college students. On the contrary, scholarly writing is actually related to rocket science. It is a controlled process requiring detailed observation and data gathering, going back and forth between inductive and deductive reasoning, assuring meaningful sequencing, developing hypotheses, weighing competing outcomes, and allowing the readers to replicate the writer's findings according to the data gathered and presented in the paper.

I once worked for a smart provost who took the educational approach to plagiarism rather than the punitive one. Like myself, he simply believed that students were generally ignorant of plagiarism and its unethical nature. He organized a faculty group under the direction of a librarian (not me) to develop examples, resources, and primers to control plagiarism. His campaign also included a plagiarism website for the library's home page that would also link to every faculty syllabus page. The objective was to saturate the campus with a heightened awareness of the ethical and unethical use of information. My own lengthy experience as a classroom instructor supports applying the educational approach to information ethics before we in academe resort to the punitive.

Information Literacy and Ethics

It is true that the strategies of infusing information literacy in university curricula with meaningful outcomes are becoming increasingly common. For example, the California State University system has been a very active and vocal proponent of information literacy for years, and CSU librarians have been avid developers of robust programs to teach and measure students' acquisition of information literacy within discipline-based courses, as well as in library instruction workshops. On April 4, 2005, the Educational Testing Service in Princeton announced that 3,000 students from all 23 CSU campuses were among the first 8,000 nationwide to beta test the ETS ICT Literacy Assessment.

This was a two-hour, standardized, interactive, simulation-based instrument to assess students' ability to "find, use, evaluate and communicate information ethically and legally," in short, to demonstrate that students "are critical consumers and ethical producers of information" (ETS 2005). Given the nature of the exam, the ICT could serve as an entrance or exit exam for university students, or an aptitude test for potential employees in businesses that need top ICT performers.

If and/or when the ICT becomes a university entrance or exit exam, the test would also be a boon for librarians because the results would presumably contribute largely to the mission of their various institutions. Librarians have already staked their claim on the teaching of information literacy, and now have an equal claim on the ICT itself. I was working at the University Library of CSU, Sacramento (CSUS), when this auspicious event took place. Now CSUS librarians have significant buy-in from the university administration for information literacy as an expectation for graduation, and the faculty senate endorsed information literacy as a cross-curricular emphasis.

The halo effect on academic librarians everywhere could be accelerated if the ICT proves in the long run to be a valid measuring device. At CSUS, certain faculty departments decided to design and administer their own information literacy programs according to the critical student outcomes they developed for their specific curricula. The librarians assisted these departments in developing their discipline-based information literacy exams. Information competency is now a graduation requirement at CSUS, and the librarians incorporate ICT training in their instructional activities, while the responsibility for determining the competency requirements and reporting their students' outcomes belongs to the academic departments. This is probably as it should be, but the level of close collaboration between librarians and faculty should be continually rising.

As a result of developments such as these across the country, information competency, literacy, or fluency might some day become a common established measure of librarians' impact on the teaching and learning effectiveness of their universities. Until that happens, however, or until we can point to information literacy programs as factors that accurately measure student performance, information literacy scores will continue to be only isolated data unconnected to the standard measures of university effectiveness, and academic libraries will be the less for that.

Consequently, we cannot wait for information literacy alone to lift academic libraries to a teaching level comparable to that of the instructional departments. Nor need we wait. Evidence of the teaching qualities of librarians is already abundant, if we will simply make this fact commonly known among instructional faculty and administrators and bridge that gap. I say again that a stumbling block for librarians is that we do not adequately understand or properly use the language of teaching and learning. Emmons and Martin (2002) demonstrate that information literacy standards now being used by librarian-educators are "remarkably similar" to standards of critical thinking that are commonly applied by instructional faculty. This is not especially new. As early as 1995, Kelly said, "For librarians, the most satisfying and challenging roles are often related to teaching students critical thinking skills and helping them grasp difficult concepts through work at a public service desk."

Macklin (2002), states, "Laziness — and not a lack of critical thinking skills — is what [faculty] tend to blame when students fail to meet their performance expectations in both research and writing." Macklin adds, "Breaking down some of these misconceptions regarding students' learning outcomes would make our jobs much easier and our input into curriculum development invaluable." The correlation between critical thinking and information literacy should be no big surprise to librarians, but it should be trumpeted to all academic faculties and administrators. Someone should turn the tables on teaching faculty and explain that critical thinking in the subject departments is *aka* and *dba* information literacy in library instruction. Part of that announcement should also make clear the fact that the excellent teaching of librarians does not occur only or even mainly in classroom settings.

Doskatsch, quoting Bundy, stresses "the importance of librarians understanding the *language of pedagogy* and engaging curriculum" (emphasis added). She speaks for all of us when she states, "Academic librarians want their contribution to education to be recognized." To succeed in this, librarians should conform to the terminology of teaching and learning: change *information literacy* to *critical thinking*; gain fluency in speaking about and implementing outcomes-based teaching and learning (OBTL); become conversant in student learning styles; master the pedagogical models appropriate for each department and institution. All of this must be handled in collaboration with the teaching faculty. At the present slow forward pace of the graduate library schools, who knows how long it will take them to import these much needed fields of study into their curricula?

Partners and Collaborators

Coincident with the rise of librarianship articles on librarians as educators, there has been a rise in the number of articles that stress the importance of "partnerships" and "collaborations" between librarians and instructional faculty — too many such articles for my taste because this approach does not put libraries in a convincing position of strength (Ducas and Michaud-Oystryk 2003, 2004). Doskatsch (2003) observed that an academic environment of instructional faculty and librarian collaboration "can only exist if there is strong institutional commitment to and support for integration of information literacy into the curriculum." I agree that information literacy must be integrated into university curricula, and this is occurring in many universities. That's great. But Doskatsch's statement appears to limit librarians to information literacy, and I doubt that the growing institutional commitment to information literacy is presently strong enough to give librarians a higher importance in the processes of teaching and learning in academic institutions. In any case, for the present we must accept the fact that information literacy remains a stand-alone subject that is seen by faculty and administrators to be unconnected to other measures of student academic performance, and consequently this does not usually impress academic faculty.

Still, Doskatsch smartly states that librarians must determine their role in the educational mission of their institutions and then communicate their contribution to their universities. To the extent that librarians can effect this communication, librarian interaction with faculty and researchers can enlarge the librarian's grasp of the academic disciplines. After all, librarians are educators, and we share with the faculty one of the most noble, ethical, and critical of callings.

Partnerships and collaborations between librarians and instructional faculty are nothing new. We have been collaborating with faculty for decades, long before our current tack that faculty could benefit from the librarians' technological savvy. Remember the advent of "learning resources centers?" That "new" model for promoting the centrality of the library and closer collaboration with instructional faculty by merging the library's print materials with audio-visual technology arose with much of the same rationale many librarians are now espousing with regard to the digital expertise we can offer teaching faculty. The more things change, the more things stay the same.

Quite a few partnership articles strike me as demeaning to librarianship. Some articles border on sycophancy. Of course partnerships and collaborations are important and necessary, and do much good in strengthening the library's role in teaching, learning, and research, but let's approach our partners in academe more often as equals in these collaborations, and the collaborative projects as interdisciplinary endeavors, not as library "support" for "front-line" instructional faculty. Librarians are on the front lines of learning as much as and more often than many instructors. We don't have to bootstrap librarianship to a level that we ourselves appear to esteem as being above us. We are educators, and we should not only portray ourselves openly in that light, but we must also perceive ourselves as being in that cadre already.

Disruption and Disadaptation

More than once I have recalled the dicta of Piaget (1971) on the guiding principles and operational strategies — sometimes called the *deep structures*— of enduring social institutions (Webb 2000). Deep structures are only dimly perceived under normal circumstances. They become most discernable, however, when an institution is in a state of *disadaptation* or stress. Piaget also said that during periods of stress, *transformations* emerge in institutions as a response to internal or external factors. These transformations, however, may be less than intrinsic to the institution's dynamics and fundamental health, similar to disruptive technologies (Lafferty and Edwards 2004). CD-ROM was just such a flash-in-the-pan disruptive technology. Such transformations can become liabilities to the institution as conditions change over time. Often, however, especially during periods of stress, non-beneficial transformations may be more apparent and can be discontinued or replaced by more timely and productive properties. It seems quite clear that librarianship is, and has been for some time, in a state of disadaptation, but so far, we have only been tinkering with the ungainly transformations that have affected the deep structures of library motives and practice for the worse. As a consequence, the library profession has become increasingly divided from the real purpose of library service: teaching. We can't go on like this very much longer, or library professionals will lose out as educators.

The Proper Context

Currently, the library profession around the world is reassessing not only job duties, but also the fundamental practices and even the mission of librarianship. The reassessment of the library mission supposedly has been necessitated by the massive computerization of knowledge, information, and educational resources; proliferation of vendors who want to control access to those materials; radical alterations to the processes of scholarly communication; sweeping change in the information industry; and gargantuan digitization projects that augur drastic transformations in the ways academic libraries operate and which could conceivably displace libraries as academic and social institutions.

Furthermore, we are surrounded by numerous emerging technologies, many of which will no doubt prove to be disruptive. We cannot, however, presently distinguish the sustaining technologies from the disruptive ones, even though the latter may eventually lead to the disappearance of academic libraries. All of these current conditions are exerting pressure on us, but they are not exactly fundamental to the mission of our profession, and so do not constitute the proper context for deliberating the future of librarianship. Yet many among us are focusing exclusively on these supposed factors of change.

We are educators. Everything we choose to do, especially amid rampant technological shakeouts, must be central to our practice of education. The changes we are now facing in our profession are only in the applications used by librarians in their practice of education. The changes are *not* in the mission of librarianship. The true causal motive underlying our perceived need to reassess our mission is our own continuing failure as librarians to embrace, promote, and perform to the fullest our fundamental role as educators. In the current dialogue regarding our mission, librarians would be self-defeating *not* to focus on the core of our practice: teaching. Given that we are educators, we are obliged to adopt teaching practices, concepts, and language already employed by our peers in the classrooms and laboratories. We must also adopt new library assessment methods equivalent to those of instructional academic departments. Furthermore, if we profess to be educators, we must acquire academic credentials comparable to those of our peers in academe. Beyond that, we must engage in scholarship as do our esteemed colleagues. These topics will be addressed in the subsequent chapters of this book.

The current debates over librarianship need a context shift that will bring us to the crucial issue of the profession: Are we educators or are we something else? Few people realize that librarians are indeed teachers and educators despite abundant evidence that the intellectual and operational processes librarians employ daily in the practice of their profession are quite comparable to the teaching strategies followed by instructional faculty. These processes of teaching constitute the genuine context in which to steer librarianship into the future. We are certainly not simply caretakers of resources; nor are we merely support service providers for teaching faculty. We are educators.

Librarians as Educators

Librarians are educators. Not "instructors" necessarily, not "teachers" in all cases, but in all cases "educators." This extends to non-public-service librarians as well as those in public services. I have clearly observed that the title of educator also extends to library support staff and library administrators. In simplistic, non-structuralist terms, we need to get down to the basic business of librarianship — teaching, and teaching better than ever before.

Here is my evidence that the intellectual processes librarians employ in their profession compare well with the teaching strategies followed by instructional faculty. I came to the conclusion over two decades ago that librarians are educators because I started teaching at the tertiary level before I started working in libraries. I taught almost continuously as a faculty member for several colleges and universities in Arizona and Hawaii from 1976 to 2000, and received tenure and eventually obtained the academic title of full professor. Rising through the ranks of librarianship from library assistant to library director, at the same time I was rising in the academic ranks from lecturer to assistant, associate, and full professor, was a double career that taught me a lot about the progression of respect given to professors and Ph.D.s. These tokens are the coin of the realm in academe. Why should it be otherwise? In colleges and universities the academics are the epitome of the institution, models to be followed by those who aspire to higher education.

In my dual career as a university instructor and librarian, I have observed that the professional duties librarians perform are very comparable to the teaching methods of instructional faculty. Over the years, I developed a number of courses, selected textbooks, wrote dozens of syllabi, composed and administered hundreds of exams, devised countless assignments and reading lists, all of which were intended to give my students — undergraduates and graduates — a solid breadth and depth in the various subjects I taught them, which included literature, English composition, research writing, interdisciplinary humanities, business communications, and cultural anthropology, in which I earned my Ph.D. Librarians, like teaching faculty, regularly design learning outcomes for students, devise teaching strategies, and assess their own effectiveness in teaching library users how to find, evaluate, and utilize information and knowledge successfully, usually in the subject areas of the students' chosen fields of study, depending on the background of the librarians and faculty.

While working at reference desks, in cataloging, in collection development, and in bibliographic instruction, my intentions were the same as those I held when I was teaching in the classroom: to make certain that my students — in the classroom and the library — acquired the learning necessary to find the information and knowledge they needed in their respective fields of study. In other words, my teaching objective was not specifically to make my students good library users, but to make them expert in their academic fields. Librarians address outcomes-based, problem-based, and now evidence-based learning needs of students in most disciplines all the time, and this library learning is *not* ancillary learning (Macklin 2002). Librarians provide highly individualized, outcomes-oriented instruction focused on students' academic needs.

Librarians, however, do not normally use the language of teaching and learning that classroom instructors often use. As mentioned above, instead of *critical thinking,* librarians speak of *information literacy.* Instead of *teaching strategies,* librarians refer to *reference interviews* and *consultations.* Instead of creating *learning objects,* librarians develop *collections*— print, digital, archival, and so on. Whereas instructional faculty prepare their courses in terms of *learning outcomes* designed to assure the fluency of students in their disciplines, librarians think in terms of resources that have adequate *scope, breadth,* and *depth* to meet the peculiar needs of all library users. Alan Bundy, former president of the Australian and Library and Information Association, made this statement: "Librarians need to become conversant as early as their preservice education with pedagogical concepts and how people learn. *They may also need to develop the capacity to teach*" (qtd. in Doskatsch 2003, emphasis added). This last line, though rather a let-down, does not invalidate his points.

Terminology and the opinions of faculty doubters aside, I am convinced that librarians have *clear ideas* of what library users need to learn from them in order to find, evaluate, and properly utilize in their exposition and their practice the specific information and knowledge they need and seek in their disciplines, even if those same librarians do not yet speak the language of pedagogy or of teaching and learning. Those "clear ideas" are the librarian's intended learning outcomes for the users, and the librarian's guidance of users into the library's resources constitutes highly individualized teaching strategies for each user. This level of individual guidance rarely occurs in subject department classrooms.

Yet it occurs at reference desks constantly, and is a brand of one-on-one teaching and learning, as well as pinpoint group information literacy sessions in library labs, that can be crucial for student success in their subject department classrooms. In their study on the impact of reference services, Jacoby and O'Brien (2005) affirm that "the reference interaction can be an effective means of teaching students not only about specific library resources, but also about the process of finding, evaluating, and using information." They add, "Reference services clearly can play a significant role in helping students become confident, independent information seekers," and can result in lifelong learning patterns.

It is no longer enough, however, for librarians to keep their learning objectives in their heads. Librarians must write their learning objectives, refine them, test them, share them, and practice them scrupulously. Our learning objectives must also be compatible with and informed by the learning objectives of the teaching faculty and the disciplinary subjects of library users — students and faculty. This must become a major task in the librarian's regular practice. In this exercise, access to faculty syllabi and teaching tools is like gold.

Anyone who has worked at a reference desk in any kind of library — public, academic, special — knows well that libraries are places of teaching and learning. We need to broadcast that message without hesitation or timidity. I have blared this call to all the administrators and faculty members whose attention I could grab.

Librarians and other library workers such as acquisitions staff who may not deal face-to-face with library users also have learning outcomes and teaching strategies in mind. For instance, a library's collection is the primary source of a university's information literacy program, classroom instruction, and research. The collection is a dynamic, complex learning tool. It also mirrors the growth and culture of the university; the teaching, learning, and research that occur in the departments and faculties; the breadth and depth of the entire academic program; and the commitment of university educators to their respective disciplines and to education overall. Conscientious librarians collaborating with faculty create dynamic collections to provide learning experiences for students in the stacks and databases. Even if students choose not to seek assistance from library staff, the carefully organized library collections can lead them into and through the vibrant, amazing educational experience of library collections.

In a 1988 study at a small liberal arts college, Hardesty found that "most classroom faculty have received little or no formal education on how to select library materials that are appropriate for the undergraduate student or on how to encourage undergraduate student use of these materials" (in Dinkins 2003). Conditions have changed since 1988, but collection development librarians and other types of selectors still assume a major share of building library collections by locating books, journals, and other resources for use by students and faculty in the subjects taught in their universities and colleges.

Just as instructional faculty must make sure their students learn every necessary aspect of their disciplines, including subdisciplines, conflicting opinions within the field, disciplinary methodologies, and so on, bibliographers and collection development librarians in similar fashion clearly do their work according to expected learning outcomes. They seek library materials to cover a subject fully, with all its controversies, variant approaches, seminal works and minor ones, historical treatises, and the most current research in the field. In real terms, book selectors conduct instructional activities much like those of educational faculty — creating new courses, composing syllabi, designing exams and assignments, and compiling reading lists, all to make sure their students can master their fields. Library collections are built the same way by librarians and other library staff.

Hur-Li Lee (2003) described collection development as a dynamic confluence of social processes, including personal ideologies, institutional politics, scholarly disciplines, academic priorities, and the like, instead of the "unconnected tasks or activities" that collection development at times appears to be. Dinkins' study at Stetson University (2003) found, contrary to her hypothesis, that the numbers of books selected by librarians that circulated more than once "were equal to or higher than those of department faculty selections" in the subject areas included in the study. Ducas and Michaud-Oystryk (2003) investigated common teaching faculty interactions with collection librarians. In descending order of frequency, the interactions were (1) recommending titles; (2) consulting with librarians about journal cancellations; (3) collection assessment for new courses and program proposals; and (4) collection review for accreditation purposes. This is a good beginning for our interaction with faculty, but our cooperation with them must be deepened considerably.

The social factors and professional librarian roles in Hong Kong, where I wrote this book, are aligned somewhat differently from those just mentioned. In general, "the role of the librarian ... in collection development might vary considerably. While in large libraries in North America, collection development librarians might be responsible for selecting 90+ percent of what is bought, in Hong Kong they might have to get a faculty member to approve every book" (Ferguson, Nesta, Storey 2007).

In the Au Shue Hung Memorial Library at the Hong Kong Baptist University, where I finished this book, librarians do not normally select books or journals. That duty falls to the "library coordinators," who are faculty members chosen by their colleagues to select books from exhaustive lists compiled by the library's acquisition section. Being a faculty library coordinator is a heavy charge that requires a good deal of training to learn (1) the fully automated selection module; (2) the formulas that allocate the funds from the library for book and journal collections in the respective departments; (3) special budget allocations that may accrue from consortial funding schemes; and (4) other developments related to acquisition and other library conditions. Coordinators must report to their deans and colleagues regularly.

The library also assigns librarians to liaise with the faculty coordinators. These liaison librarians provide information to the coordinators about the book selection portal, advise the coordinators on matters of budget, review e-resources, urge the coordinators to apprise their colleagues of best publishers, update impact factors of research journals, lobby the departments to subscribe to open access journals in the coordinators' respective fields, and other pertinent services. Library coordinators and liaison librarians are not so novel, except when the activity levels are going through the roof to provide learning to their institutions.

One of the main roles of acquisitions librarians is tending the highly refined formulas for book and journal costs based on several budgeting factors that can be adjusted according to the mutual needs of instructional faculty and students. Additional one-time adjustments may also be granted by the university administration in critical circumstances. Special factors can be adjusted, such as the number of enrolled undergraduate and graduate students, number of departmental faculty, relative costs of books across the disciplines, international currency fluctuations, rewards for research excellence, and so on. It is a finely tuned operation that most of the academic community never sees, but no one is ever completely satisfied, of course, and the work never ceases. The acquisitions section also conducts periodic surveys to get student feedback on the books and other resources in their respective fields of study. This is not bean-counting, nor is it new stuff for acquisitions librarians. My point is this: the involvement of acquisitions librarians in their professional work is clearly an educational endeavor, and an act of tutelage by carefully building collections in direct response to the educational mission of the university and the needs of the students and faculty, and what the materials can bear.

Acquisitions staff also meet with vendors to create and adjust acquisition profiles and secure the best possible prices via consortial purchasing. They can save hundreds of thousands of dollars by working in several consortia, and with numerous vendors, to get the best possible library educational resources in many formats. All of these actions are part of the librarians' educational efforts to enlarge and strengthen the collections, which are by themselves key sources of learning.

In their unique way, catalogers likewise use teaching strategies and learning outcomes when they create their descriptions for new library resources with author, title, and other headings that serve as recognizable links from the catalog to relevant materials in the student's field of study. Conceptually simple, library cataloging nevertheless requires the librarian's very close attention to subject matter, the author's level of detail or generality, the fine points of the work in hand, the author's scholarly intention and critical approach, and numerous other features. Systematic classification is a fundamental activity of scientific inquiry, and classification systems are essential to scientific analysis, investigation, observation, comparison, and discovery. Learning how to use a library's classification system to find books is often a student's first encounter with scientific differentiation. As such, a library's classification system is itself a tool for teaching analytical reasoning to library users.

Catalogers also assign materials to their proper subject classifications and call numbers. Using complex classification schedules, catalogers position books on similar subjects in physical and topical proximity to each other, not simply for user convenience, of course, but to facilitate the users' broad acquisition of learning in their given subjects. Meyer (1999) agrees: "The bibliographic structure of online catalogs contains complexities that require professional time with authority control, error corrections, and bibliographic enhancements." He adds, "Easier access leads to extended reading and improved writing [and] added labor results in improved collection development, more attention to detail, and better production control. All of these improve user success"—and that, in my view, *is* teaching.

Young and Blixrud (2003) explain that learning outcomes emphasize "the change that takes place within the student" during a learning experience, and not solely the input from the teacher. I think my own cataloging experience demonstrates quite well a cataloger's sense of learning outcomes that can lead students to find and learn from the materials once they are cataloged. I have said elsewhere (Webb 2000) that librarianship is more an act of faith than a science, but the rigorous methodologies of library classification might well be the most scientific aspect of the library profession.

Reality Show: Champions All

It has been my observation in almost every place I have worked in academe that librarians are considered by instructional faculty to be second-class citizens who cannot quite measure up to the teaching skill levels of instructional faculty. That has never been the case, and the error of such thinking is becoming much clearer on two counts: first, librarians are engaging in more teaching activities than ever before, and are becoming more adept at their craft; second, a good many instructional faculty are, quite frankly, awful teachers.

Here are a few examples of librarian-educators I have observed in some of the libraries I have directed who measure up quite well to their instructional faculty colleagues, and who would be good models for other librarians.

Hugh

Hugh has the breadth and experience needed for general reference, and also subject depth in his fields to provide special reference and research assistance. He is right at home in the classroom. He is equally comfortable with general and specialized reference duties, and with one-on-one reference and research consultations with students who need complex information or research. He works with print and electronic resources equally well. Hugh's instructional style is accommodating. He teaches with the facility that comes from long experience with library resources, but he is also approachable and patient with students no matter what their questions or subjects might be. Students can tell by his manner and teaching style that he knows what he's talking about, and the attention and confidence they give to Hugh carry over into individual reference consultations. It is not in Hugh's nature to be dismissive, and he treats students more as colleagues than learners. Because of his calm but intent teaching style and his expertise with online information resources, he was selected to break new ground by team-teaching an inaugural graduate course on medical informatics in the school of nursing and health studies at his university. Though it was experimental, the course was a great success. I received very positive reports about his teaching from the nursing faculty member who teamed with him and from the dean of nursing.

Maria

Most notable of the characteristics I observed about Maria was her work with the faculty in the science department. Relatively few librarians undertake research and publication at all, even in topics of librarianship. Fewer still are those who undertake scholarship in their subject discipline fields and their faculty liaison responsibilities. Maria does very well in both. In this endeavor she has gone beyond the normal call of duty by inspiring an instructional faculty colleague to see clearly his need to become more engaged in developing the library collection in his discipline. He was not the only one Maria has so motivated. She also coauthors scientific papers with science teaching faculty.

Lisa

Lisa is a cataloger, and having been a cataloger myself, I was impressed with her cataloging productivity, which dramatically dwindled our backlogs. I also applaud her collaboration with several instructional faculty. I admire the expertise she voluntarily developed in reference service and her intention to become expert in that area. I think that above all, I admired her willingness to take over the duties of the head cataloger who became ill. Leadership like this is needed at all levels of an organization, and I find that the most remarkable instances of leadership are those in which persons who did not sign on to be leaders or supervisors rise to challenges and opportunities to do so.

Rachel

Rachel had developed the library's instructional program almost from scratch years before I arrived as director. She had taught the classes; created syllabi and lesson plans; made the teaching schedules for the other librarians; developed online tools as the technology became available; trudged through the snow, rain, and sleet (no kidding) to walk from our library, which was at one extreme end of the campus, to the classroom buildings at the other end; advocated for greater collaboration between instructional faculty and librarians; and created online library newsletters and bulletins. She was tireless. In my second year at this library, I nominated Rachel for teacher of the year in light of her good service over many years at the university. My provost was uncomfortable making a solo decision about recommending a librarian for teacher of the year, so he consulted with the deans. I soon received word that while Rachel had the respect of the campus, it was not appropriate to present the teacher of the year award to a librarian. I sighed and I cried. I might add that when I made the recommendation, I held the title of Library Dean and also Associate Vice President for Instructional Technology, but my opinion was still not good enough for neither the other deans and vice presidents, nor the provost, to recognize a librarian over one of their own faculty members. To this day, I remain outraged over the small-mindedness, prejudice, and cowardice among that faculty, the provost, and the university administration generally.

Mary

Mary, a librarian with a Ph.D., no less, deserves special attention for a course-level portal-type online application she created for faculty and students. She then incorporated the product into WebCT and then migrated it to MOODLE to make the application more flexible for students and faculty. R&D in librarianship continues to be far too scarce. Yet as pedagogy and information technology converge, librarians are in an unprecedented position to customize online learning resources and environments to suit the needs of faculty and their students in ways that standardized, mass-market online products cannot provide. It is a momentous opportunity for the library profession. Mary's work is unique in at least two important ways. First, she reaches a level of interaction with instructional faculty that is almost unmatched elsewhere. Much of this collaboration is one-on-one as she develops new ways to use library e-resources and then teaches faculty to use them with their students. Second, she teaches faculty to map their students' encounter with the library's resources according to the specific learning objectives of the courses involved.

This is excellent. I knew it was more than partnership and collaboration when I listened intently as a professor extolled Mary's creation in a large meeting of faculty and administrators who were discussing ways to engage students in the classroom. The faculty member made an impassioned endorsement of Mary's portal to her faculty peers as a sure-fire way to engage students in the classroom. I cannot think of any higher praise Mary could receive. She is a forerunner and a visionary. Mary's type of work is vital to the progress of 21st-century librarianship. She founded her work on sound principles of scholarly and scientific inquiry and application. She has made her share of breakthroughs and discoveries on which to build new and significant finds.

Bin

I worked with Bin, another R&D visionary, in two different libraries I directed, one in Honolulu, then in Sacramento a few years later. He was a self-taught systems librarian because when he began his librarianship degree, there were no courses on creating online databases, managing servers, html, scripts, and so on. He had no disk space to work with, so he ingeniously "borrowed" some. Bin learned these things on his own because of his vision, his native intelligence, and his intuitive grasp of the emerging fields for online teaching and learning. Bin had earned an MLS, but he was working as a library assistant because the administrators of his first library had no vacant librarian positions, and were unable or unwilling to create a new librarian position. By the time I created a librarian position in my library and hired Bin away from his first library position, he had already constructed a number of impressive projects for various government and university clients.

He was most likely one of a mere few persons in Hawaii who was working with interactive resources. Everyone else was still working in the CD-ROM environment. This was the early 1990s just as the Web, Mosaic, and other revolutionary technologies emerged. It was the beginning of the era of virtual, real-time information retrieval. Bin was already at home in these environments. In a very short time, we secured the most advanced technology available through grants and funding from the new and generous collaborations that Bin brought with him to our library. Once onboard, Bin taught other librarians in our shop the very skills he had learned. In effect, he cloned himself. Our production of online resources in our small library more than tripled.

Diana

Diana provided information literacy classes for the students of a visiting management professor on sabbatical leave from the U.S. The professor was also a senior editor of a scholarly journal. In a letter to her library director, he praised Diana's teaching and the meticulous assistance she provided his students in a major research project involving local and multinational firms in industries ranging widely from computer software to film entertainment. She prepared customized examples of firms and industries the students selected for their projects. Diana began by developing and leading a workshop that was extensive and detailed, said the professor. She also demonstrated the full range of print and e-resources available at her university library. The professor extolled her presentation and her superb teaching of his students to locate and understand the best information resources for each firm and industry, and helping them fine-tune their research. At the end of the sabbatical, the professor expressed his wish that Diana could come to work at his university. He even asked her to give a presentation to his family, who had accompanied him on his teaching sabbatical.

Dianne

Dianne, a head of reference, organized her section and launched "office calls," that is deep collaboration visits to faculty in their offices to provide individualized support for teaching and research needs, including knowledge of new library resources and technologies; support in developing and assessing information-based learning outcomes; and research support, such as literature searches, setting up a notification function for specific journals and research topics, and the like. From this, the reference librarians launched discipline-based blogs to support student learning. The dynamic blogs relate directly to subject matter of the courses, and provide assistance and learning opportunities for the students. The instructors support the blogs, and expect their students to monitor and respond to the weekly information on the blogs. Dianne also collaborated with a faculty member to enhance a class on research methods in literature and linguistics. This collaboration led to an invitation from the faculty member for Dianne to participate in a teaching development grant to produce an online linguistics glossary. Dianne and the reference librarians also agreed to teach more than 100 new introductory technology classes required for all incoming students in collaboration with the Computer Sciences Department. The librarians also conducted another 115 classes in other subject areas in consultation with the faculty. The total number of all classes taught by the librarians increased by 74 percent in one year.

Here is some very sincere feedback from another faculty member:

Dear D,

I am writing to express my deep satisfaction and appreciation of your involvement in two of the courses that I ran this semester.... Tutorial classes given by you and Chris [a fine colleague] were not only appreciated by students, but also proved very effective. The term papers that I received from my students, in which they were supposed to conduct a library review, are already better than last year's honors projects, for which I was appointed a second examiner. I look forward to further cooperation.

Yours sincerely,

A

Conclusion

New initiatives like these demonstrate that librarians are dedicated, hard-working, capable educators willing to accept major teaching responsibilities related to information literacy, research methods, institutional curricula, and graduate attributes, among others.

There are so many, many more accounts of library staff as first-rate, master educators that I feel ashamed for not describing more of them. Yet librarians still have not adequately bridged the divide between us and our faculty and administrators.

In spite of all the good things we can say about librarians as educators, many librarians have limitations or drawbacks as educators, and these drawbacks divide them from their mission. Some of these drawbacks bear repeating: lack of fluency in the language of teaching and learning; lack of training in educational methods and development in personal teaching techniques; shortened academic training, as compared with most university teaching faculty; and weak methods to assess the effectiveness of their teaching and their contributions to the mission of their institutions. These topics will be addressed in the following chapters of this book. This is a pivotal time for librarianship, but I still don't see enough people stepping up to the plate to hit away into extra innings. Librarianship must become deeper and broader. Librarians must learn more than we now know.

Covey (2004) urges librarians to upgrade our traditional assessment methods to the much more effective and powerful data, namely, outcomes and performance measures. These new assessments include student learning outcomes and measurable contributions to the institutional mission. This is an essential strategy because even though many college and university instructional faculty work well with librarians as educators and are delighted to engage them for library instruction to their students, a large portion of faculty still see librarians as second-class citizens in academe.

To reverse the view that we are lesser educators and ineligible for the highest posts in academe, we are obliged to translate our actions into the language of teaching and learning, and not simply by aping such terms as *learning objectives, problem-based learning, teaching strategies, outcomes-based learning,* but by reinvigorating ourselves with the ambition to engage fully in our teaching capacities at the highest academic levels.

The Bottom Line

To work at our peak productivity, we have to know what Ph.D. faculty do, how they communicate with each other, and how they got where they are. We cannot match nor know the highs and lows of faculty Ph.D.'s unless we do what they have done.

2

THE 2004 LIBRARY
SELF-STUDY AT CSUS

Library Self-Studies

From 1988 to 1995, Howard Simmons was the executive director of the Middle States Commission on Higher Education, where he became a champion of libraries and information literacy. In 1992, Mignon Adams interviewed Dr. Simmons to hear his views on libraries, information literacy, and the role of libraries in accreditation processes.

Though not a librarian himself, Simmons was a student helper in his high school library and continued to work in his college library. In both libraries he helped his fellow students use the libraries more effectively because he observed that "most students never developed any strategies in using a library" (Adams 1992). While in college, he even disputed faculty assignments that were restricted to the materials in the reserve section, and asked why any students should be limited only to the reserve collection. He argued that "if students were really to learn, they needed to go beyond the reserve system" (Adams 1992).

These experiences taught him this: "If we are to be serious about improvement in the teaching-learning cycle, then it appeared to me that the library ought to play a pivotal role, particularly since we say that the library is central to the educational mission. And to make it work, librarians need to be empowered." So at Middle States, Simmons emphasized "the integration of information literacy into the curriculum," and involved libraries fully in the higher education accreditation processes by steering colleges and universities to strengthen information literacy and making provisions for such programs in the Middle States accreditation standards (Adams 1992).

This vision of librarianship remains right up to date. If librarians believe, as does Dr. Simmons that education is our field and our mission, then every strategic move forward, every adoption of technology, and every adaptation we make to sustain our educational mission must link to that platform of higher education that instructional faculty have perennially made their singular domain, leaving librarians to a subordinate tier.

Furthermore, U.S. universities are beleaguered by the adverse conditions of falling student retention rates, dwindling enrollments, and prolonged time to graduate among many students. These symptoms of dissatisfaction among students had such a negative impact on the entire California State University system that the chancellor hammered the presidents of the 23 campuses to improve these conditions. Otherwise, planning curricula would be virtually impossible; tuition revenues would be insufficient to provide the needed courses; and resources for higher education in the CSU would dwindle. This wake-up call motivated the CSU Sacramento (CSUS) Library staff to aim its self-study toward remedies for these difficulties.

We at CSUS believed that the library was already having a positive effect on these adverse factors, and if we had methods to confirm this, we could strengthen our position in the processes of teaching and learning, boost the library's budget, and emerge from these adverse conditions with greater success. We took a lesson from Covey (2005), who stated, "Assessment requires persuasion every step of the way." She applied this to change within a library. We applied it toward adjusting the university's perceptions of the library as an agent for positive change in teaching and learning by adopting the brand of CSUS language of teaching and learning, or in Covey's words (2005), "Tell the right story the right way to the right people. Data is only part of the story. The rest is rhetorical argument." It worked for us like a charm.

Self-Studies

In response to the question Adams posed, *What kind of information would you look for in a library's self-study?*, Simmons spoke of collection statistics, the development of the collection over time, including weeding, and how it supported the academic program; number and description of bibliographic instruction classes; networks and online access; and descriptions of the ways "the library interacts with students and faculty to get them to use the resources" (Adams, 1992). He also would expect interaction between the librarians and "other pertinent self-study committees, particularly those concerned with academic review." At CSUS, we did exactly that.

Over the years, I've completed more self-studies intended to assess the effectiveness of my libraries than I care to remember. Simmons' approach is refreshing, and is rather like the 2004 self-study of the CSUS. That self-study being the exception, all the others were wholly unsatisfactory to me because they told nothing very specific about the outcomes of the teaching and learning that took place in those libraries. Those self-studies simply gathered statistics and activity levels that established no measurable connection between the libraries and the mission effectiveness of their respective institutions, and certainly could not report real correlations of meaningful measures of student library usage to their overall learning. Nor did these weak self-studies indicate very much about the caliber of the educators in the libraries and the effect of their teaching on the overall academic performance of students in their respective disciplines.

One objective of the 2004 CSUS library self-study, therefore, was intentionally designed to employ the language of teaching and learning in an organized effort to demonstrate to the CSUS community that the library is a place of almost continuous teaching and learning led intelligently by highly professional library educators at all levels of the library's support, professional, and administrative staff operations.

As discussed in Chapter 1, the CSUS library was a national leader in the development of information literacy and had committed to participate very actively in the nationwide beta testing of the ETS ICT Literacy Assessment in 2003. In the spirit of that important event, the library staff wanted the 2004 self-study to demonstrate to the university's teaching faculty and administrators that the library is a place of teaching and learning, and that librarians are competent, energetic educators.

The California State University system of 23 campuses has a long and outstanding record of teaching. Kevin Starr (2005), California State Librarian Emeritus and eminent historian of California, has much to say about the CSU: "Today, this great university grants nearly half of the state's baccalaureate degrees and a third of the master's degrees. It bestows 65 percent of the business baccalaureate degrees and more than half of the agricultural business and agricultural engineering baccalaureate degrees. And it trains 89 percent of the state's professionals in criminal justice, 87 percent of the teachers and related staff, 87 percent of the social workers and 82 percent of the public administrators. The California State University ... has as its primary mission the education and training of Californians through a fusion program of instruction, applied research and preparation for employment." CSU is the largest university system in the United States. Student enrollments surpass 450,000, while faculty and staff members number more than 48,000, according to Lisa Moske of the CSU Chancellor's Office.

As librarians, education is our field and our mission. It is so in the CSU system, and in all other libraries. This is an essential strategy because even though many college and university instructional faculty work well with librarians as educators and are delighted to engage them on occasion for library instruction to their students, full integration of library instruction into the university curricula is still struggling. Gilman (2006) puts into words my own thoughts: "Many academic librarians feel unloved and underappreciated on their campuses, and the main reason is that they sense they are viewed as second-class citizens by members of the teaching faculty." Well put.

The CSUS 1998 Self-Study

When I arrived at CSUS in 2002, I paged through the library's 1998 self-study. A while later, when I was informed by the CSUS administration that the library would be undergoing a self-study in the near future, I took a deep breath and plunged into the older self-study. As I had expected, it was in much the same typical bean-counting format as all the earlier self-studies I had completed in other universities. It was a hefty document with tons of data and charts and plenty of good words for the library and its staff, but I saw in it no strong connections to the processes and terminology of teaching and learning.

All these typical, near-meaningless data on library activity levels were unconnected to the mission of the university and could say nothing much about any measured effect the library might have had on student academic performance and on the effectiveness of the university. The faculty and external reviews for this earlier self-study were generally favorable, which I was glad to see, but the comments were full of holes simply because the reviewers did not know the right questions to ask, and this was because they really didn't know what librarians do nor how libraries should be assessed.

I also knew I could never willingly compose another such self-study. For me the era of this type of self-study had passed. So for the 2004 self-study of the CSUS library, I persuaded the library staff and the university administration to use for the first time in the library the same obligatory outline and the teaching and learning terminology required in the self-studies conducted by all the other CSUS academic departments. This would accomplish a number of important objectives: (1) the library staff would learn more about the academic departments and the pedagogical language they commonly used; (2) it would make us think more like the teaching faculty by using the same terms, logic, reporting structures, and so forth as used by our teaching colleagues; (3) we would reinforce in our own minds the library's educational mission; and (4) we would be positioned to demonstrate more clearly to the teaching faculty and the university administration that the library is indeed a teaching and learning environment, and that librarians and other library staff are bona fide educators. The fact that CSUS librarians are full tenure-track faculty members and are very active in the faculty senate and its committees was a big advantage for us in undertaking the 2004 self-study. We had a good track record in faculty governance.

A Culture of Learning

The regulations of the CSU Board of Trustees require every academic unit to be reviewed once every six years. Each department prepares a self-study that includes an assessment plan and evaluation of data relevant to the unit's stated goals and desired outcomes. These documents are reviewed by a consultant external to the university and a program review team of university faculty from different departments. The purpose of the library's 2004 self-study was to present the processes and documents that demonstrate CSU Sacramento's commitment to create a culture of learning. The context and structure of this university portfolio of self-studies are in direct response to the needs of specific internal and external organizations and individuals who are interested in the university's efforts to demonstrate its educational effectiveness.

The new self-study model used by CSUS for its academic programs came about in part when the university was invited in 1998 to join the Urban University Portfolio Project (UUPP), a national initiative funded by the Pew Charitable Trusts (http/www.csus.edu/portfolio/index.htm). This project provided support to (1) expand meaningful and focused campus conversations about core learning expectations for the baccalaureate degree; (2) improve efforts to develop a coordinated assessment plan integrating institutional and program activities and processes in the CSUS Strategic Plan; (3) identify hallmarks, best practices, and enabling structures that illustrate the university's commitment to undergraduate education, and removal of impediments or barriers in order to provide the best possible environment for teaching and learning at CSUS; (4) collaborate and consult with other comprehensive public universities committed to these same goals and present our activities to various interested groups and individuals; and (5) develop a maintainable web-based institutional portfolio that supports the CSUS assessment and improvement activities.

The institutional portfolio allows CSUS to communicate more effectively with internal and external stakeholders about who we are, why we are, what we are, what we expect of our students, what our community can expect of us, and what we are working to improve. Covey (2005), articulating the shift in academic libraries from customary input/output data to a culture of assessment, praised the fine work done by California State University at Sacramento to ignite new thinking about performance measures (www.csus.edu/portfolio).

Covey (2005) also makes a good point about gathering data that will persuade stakeholders instead of burying them in data they do not understand and which do not clearly relate to learning and assessment. That was our intention from the very early discussions.

CSUS Library Academic Programs

Performing a self-study of the entire library would have been impossible in the time we were given. Because CSUS academic departments have multiple programs, we chose to describe the library's services and functions as our "academic programs," in accordance with teaching and learning terminology, and selected three programs that would be familiar to the faculty and administrators who would be reading and evaluating our self-study. We believed the readers would be able to see these programs in the light and terminology of teaching and learning. The three library programs we selected for the 2004 self-study were (1) Library Collections and Information Organization (acquisitions and cataloging, including e-resources); (2) Library Instruction and Information Use (information literacy instruction); and (3) Reference Service and Information Access (reference and circulation). Of course, there are several more "academic programs" in the library, but we decided that redescribing three programs according to the specific terminology in the guidelines was a tough enough challenge, and requested that other programs be included in future self-studies. The request was approved.

I am happy to say that throughout the planning for the 2004 self-study, we received strong support from the university administration regarding our effort to employ the new CSUS language of teaching and learning. Adapting our self-study to the features of the new culture demonstrated and greatly deepened the library's determination to integrate is programs into the university's processes of teaching and learning. That had been our objective all along.

The 2004 CSUS Library Self-Study Outline

The CSUS Self-Study Guidelines for all CSUS departments, which included the library in 2004, are below, followed by selected content from the library's self-study arranged in the order of the guidelines.

Program Review Self-Study Guidelines

I. PROGRAM INTRODUCTION/HISTORY
- Describe your program's mission and goals. In what way do program goals respond to community and regional needs?
- Assess the effectiveness of changes made in response to recommendations from the last program review. (Include the list of recommendations.)
- What major state and national trends are occurring in your discipline?
- What responses to changes in the discipline is your department planning and/or implementing?

II. ACADEMIC PROGRAMS
- Describe learning expectations for your academic programs: writing and reading in the major, including descriptions of current writing and reading requirements standards for general expository and discipline-specific writing and reading; any plans for the development of writing and reading skills; plans for the assessment of current requirements and of measures to encourage writing and reading skills; computer/ information competence.
- Indicate on what these expectations are based (judgment of faculty, standards/trends in discipline, expectations of programs at other schools, surveys of students/ alumni, etc.).
- Indicate how expectations are communicated to students.
- How is your curriculum structured (including core requirements, prerequisites, and electives) to achieve your learning expectations?
- Include a matrix that displays learning expectations and how courses contribute to achieving the expectations.
- What teaching strategies has your faculty found to be particularly effective in helping students achieve your learning expectations?
- Describe your department's involvement in and evaluation of distance and distributed education courses.
- Describe your program's assessment plan. Include both assessment of student learning outcomes and surveys of graduating seniors, and graduate students and alumni.
- Using assessment data, analyze the effectiveness of your program, including the ability of students to meet:
  1. The department's learning expectations
  2. The university learning goals
  3. Writing and reading standards in the major
  4. Computer/information competence standards
- Describe how your department maintains consistency in multiple sections of courses.
- Discuss changes needed to enhance or improve the effectiveness of your academic program outcomes.
- If your department and its programs offer General Education and/or Service courses:

1. Provide evidence that courses are meeting the General Education area criteria.
2. From the perspective of the department/programs being served, to what extent do your service courses meet their needs?
3. Describe how your department maintains consistency in multiple sections of General Education courses.

- Explain how your program:
  1. Addresses the increasing cultural diversity of CSUS students in the curriculum, as appropriate.
  2. Accommodates differences in student preparation and access to educational opportunities.
  3. Helps students gain an effective knowledge of how to live and work in our diverse society.

- If your department offers a minor, a concentration, or a certificate program, provide evidence of its contribution to the mission of the department, college, and university, and its viability with respect to enrollment patterns since the last program review and to the resources expended to support the program.

III. STUDENTS

- Student Profile Data for the last six years is available on the Office of Institutional Research website for the items below.
- Enrollment patterns in the majors, minors, concentrations, credentials; gender and ethnic composition; Retention and graduation rates; part- and full-time enrollments; Native and transfer students.
- Student Academic Performance
  1. Grading distribution
  2. GPAs
  3. Students on probation
  4. WPE pass rates
  5. Preparation for upper division/graduate coursework (no comparison data available under this heading)
- Student Academic Support
  1. Describe how the department provides academic and career advising. Are faculty and students satisfied that the advising needs of students are met? (Data from SNAPS — Student Needs and Priorities Survey — and Program Assessment Questionnaire is available on the Office of Institutional Research website). If data indicate a need for response, describe your action plans.
  2. What support does your department provide for students in need of extra assistance? To what extent are your faculty and students satisfied with the support available at the department level? At the university level? If your analysis reveals a need for changes, describe plans.
- Student Professional Development
- What opportunities does your department provide to socialize students into the discipline or provide them with professional opportunities?

IV. FACULTY
- Faculty Profile
- Data on faculty are available on the website. Include analysis regarding: full- and part-time faculty; gender and ethnic composition; student-faculty ratio; class size.
- Assess faculty profile for the ability to offer the curriculum and to support program goals. Describe plans for addressing any identified issues.
- Faculty as Teachers
  1. Analyze data available from the College Outcomes Survey (COS) and Program Assessment Questionnaire (PAQ) to identify any issues that need action. Describe plans for addressing issues.
  2. Describe how the faculty are involved in professional development activities to improve and enhance their teaching effectiveness.
  3. To what extent are faculty using "best practices" in their roles as teachers? How are faculty offering students a variety of learning experiences to address the diversity of student learning styles?
  4. Comment on your faculty's' innovations in pedagogy and their knowledge of current trends in their academic specialties.
  5. Describe the department's process for evaluating teaching effectiveness. How are data used to enhance or improve teaching?
- Faculty as Scholars
  1. Describe the department's specific expectations for scholarly/creative activities
  2. Describe scholarly and creative activities of faculty in the last six years (vita).
  3. Analyze the extent to which faculty meet the department's expectations for scholarly/creative activities. Identify issues needing improvement and describe action plans.
- Faculty Service to the University and Community
  1. Describe faculty involvement in service to the university and community in the last six years.
  2. Analyze the extent to which the faculty meet the department's expectations for service. Identify issues in need of improvement and describe action plans.

V. GOVERNANCE PROCESS AT THE PROGRAM, COLLEGE, AND UNIVERSITY LEVELS
- Describe faculty involvement in planning, developing, and implementing department policies.
  1. Indicate the role of the chair/coordinator in department governance.
  2. Indicate whether the department has a formalized set of rules or procedures for departmental governance (if so, include such guidelines as an appendix to the self-study).
- Describe student involvement in the departmental governance process.
- Comment on the relationships of your department/programs with your college and the university.

VI. INSTITUTIONAL SUPPORT/RESOURCES
- Please describe adequacy of support, strengths, and concerns about the following resources and services:
- Library
  1. Curriculum support offered by the collection.
  2. Services provided by library for faculty and students.
- Computer/Technology
  1. Technology/resources for meeting program and faculty needs.
  2. Services provided by media center and computer center for faculty and students
- Student Support Services (e.g., Admissions and Records, Advising Center, Learning Skills Center, Union, Multicultural Center, Educational Opportunities Program, Writing Center).
- Faculty Support Services (e.g., Center for Teaching and Learning, Computing, Communications, and Media).
- Physical Facilities and Equipment
- Financial Resources (faculty, staff, operating expenses)
  1. Enrollment and faculty numbers support the curriculum.
  2. Program staff.
  3. Total operating expense budget (include statement about processes used for effective use of budget).

Note: This is the end of the CSUS Self-Study Guidelines for all CSUS departments, which the library adopted for its self-study. The following sections in this chapter and Chapter 3 include the library's self-study submission to the faculty panel, the external reviewer, and the CSUS administration.

As is common elsewhere, the CSUS library self-study comprises composition of the self-study, a faculty review, and an external review. In the face of this challenging self-study, the library staff organized a steering committee for the overall self-study, and committees for each of three library academic programs we selected for the study.

Furthermore, in addition to the sections in the formal outline, we chose to add two more sections to our self-study. One was almost identical to the Faculty section and described the outstanding expertise, service, credentials, and contributions of the non-faculty employees of the library. The committee for this added section was composed of non-faculty employees. There was some difficulty devising a term for the non-faculty library staff because all the job titles and related terms that are commonly used for these classifications were frankly demeaning to their excellent work. As a result, the committee for this added section devised the term "Library Personnel/Non-Faculty (LP/NF)." It was clear from the data gathered by this self-study committee that the LP/NF, like the faculty, are also fine educators. Among the LP/NF are persons who have advanced degrees in subject areas, foreign languages, librarianship, law, and others.

The second section we added was a Student Employee Profile. The library employs the largest number of students at CSUS. They are industrious, committed, intelligent, and indispensable to virtually all library operations. Their contributions could not go unacknowledged.

The self-study outline required us to provide an overview of each of the library's three selected academic programs, namely, the mission and goals of the program; major state and national trends in our discipline and how our curriculum structure and course offerings compared to those of similar programs in other disciplines; and what response to changes in the discipline our department was planning and/or implementing.

More specific details were also required of each program, such as describing learning expectations for each program; how the expectations are communicated to students; how our curriculum is structured; creating a matrix to display learning expectations and how courses contribute to achieving the expectations; teaching strategies we found particularly effective in helping students achieve our learning expectations; describing how our programs maintain consistency in multiple sections of courses; and discussing changes needed to enhance or improve the effectiveness of our program outcomes.

These are questions not normally asked and answered as part of a library assessment, and they required a great deal of thought for us to translate the library's academic programs to fit into the outline neatly. But in the end, we were happily surprised how well the library's programs meshed with the standard self-study instrument for instructional departments. The process forced us to use the concepts and language of teaching and learning to describe for faculty and administrators the teaching and learning components of the library.

The self-study review panel of six instructional faculty from different CSUS departments applauded our self-study, although they, too, were unaccustomed to thinking about the library as having academic programs, or about librarians as educators. Of the three programs included in the library self-study, our academic programs on library instruction and information use (information literacy instruction), and reference service and information access (reference, circulation) fit most easily into the panel's perceptions of teaching and learning strategies. The panel, however, did not quite grasp the legitimacy of the program of library collections and information organization (acquisitions, cataloging), but they did not dispute the matter.

With the data before them, the panel members were happy to announce that the self-study was a success. University administrators were equally congratulatory about our ambitious effort to describe the library in terms of teaching and learning. We opened some eyes and minds both inside and outside the library. The rest of this chapter includes portions of the self-study describing the library's three academic programs.

Library Self-Study for Program Review
Spring 2004

SECTION I. PROGRAM INTRODUCTION/HISTORY

A. Describe your program's mission and goals (undergraduate, graduate, general education). In what way do program goals respond to community and regional needs?

The library's current mission statement reads, "The primary purpose of the CSUS library is to support the quest for knowledge as well as the information needs of the students, faculty, and staff. The library also serves as a major regional information resource center" (Rev. 1996). One finding of this self-study is that the current mission statement does not promote the library as "an active learning environment for students, staff and faculty," and that our mission statement should be "more aligned with the university mission."

Specifically, the current mission statement does not envision the library as a venue for teaching and learning in its own right. The faculty (librarians) and non-faculty personnel of the CSUS library clearly perceive themselves as educators, and see the library as a center of dynamic teaching and learning activities that supplement and extend the university's classroom instruction. Through its academic programs, the library creates an active environment for teaching and learning processes that are more individualized, more individual-dependent, and more pointed toward the individual student's personal learning needs than is normally possible in the classroom.

Unlike customary library self-studies that mainly describe a library's functions and express its success in numbers of books purchased and circulated, number of instructional sessions conducted, and so forth, this self-study will describe the library's activities and services in the language of teaching and learning. This is to demonstrate to the university community that all library personnel are educators and that teaching and learning occur in the CSUS library almost continuously.

In a second departure from customary library practice, this self-study proposes to develop entirely new library assessment measures for the CSUS library that will be linked directly to the university's measures of effectiveness. A final innovation of this self-study is the inclusion of a section that analyzes data concerning our non-faculty library personnel, whose numbers and contributions to the library's success are too substantial to overlook.

Our major goals for the coming program review period are to (1) integrate the library more fully into the processes of teaching and learning across the university; (2) expand the library's digital initiatives, including activities such as information resource development, online publishing ventures, and creation of new forms of scholarship and scholarly communication; and (3) develop methods to demonstrate empirically the effect of the library's academic programs on the goals and effectiveness of the university. These goals for the library are in keeping with the needs of the university and with the observable trends in librarianship.

SECTION II. ACADEMIC PROGRAMS

Although the library will be reporting in the self-study as a single "department," the library provides teaching and learning programs on the scale of a college-level entity, with a dean (who is also considered a department chair), two associate deans, and a number of discreet programs not unlike the multiple programs that characterize the colleges. The library's self-study, therefore, will focus on its three primary "academic programs"— **Library Collections and Information Organization**, **Library Instruction and Information Use**, and **Reference Service and Information Access**. Largely through these three academic programs, the library utilizes teaching strategies that engage various learning patterns to support the full range of CSUS curricular offerings.

LIBRARY COLLECTIONS AND INFORMATION ORGANIZATION

A. Describe learning expectations for Collections as a program:

The specific goal applicable to collections is to "Select, acquire, manage, assess, and preserve the collections and resources needed to support the instruction, research and co-curricular programs of the university." Collections are the underpinnings of the library and its instruction and reference services, and are also a direct resource to CSUS students, faculty, and staff for study, research, and recreation.

The CSUS library collections are developed by librarians and processes that comprise the Collection Development Program. This program is largely subject-oriented and involves reviewing library materials published and unpublished, current and retrospective, in all formats including materials in electronic format for possible inclusion in the library collections. Additions typically are made through purchase, solicitation, or donation. In recent times libraries also have engaged in developing unique collections through the utilization of digitization and the Web. Criteria considered by librarians making selection decisions include: usefulness to CSUS students, faculty, and staff; applicability to the CSUS curriculum; value provided for cost; usefulness of available formats; quality and/or importance of contents; duplication of contents in the existing CSUS collection. Collection development also involves ongoing review and maintenance of the existing collection for currency; continued appropriateness and usefulness to the library's patrons, and lasting value. De-selection (withdrawal) of materials from the collection occurs as needed. In addition, a core collection of electronic databases funded by the Chancellor's Office is also available to CSUS library users.

1. Specify expectations for:

a. Collection Development Program:

To support and enhance student learning in the classroom and in the library by developing collections that reflect the breadth and depth of literature in the disciplines

(1) To provide sources that serve to teach students in the use of primary sources for research and study

(2) To provide access to a broad range of information on a subject, from the very general and introductory to the more advanced levels of research

(3) To provide research tools (e.g. tutorials, pathfinders, etc.) that assist students in learning the research process, such as how to trace a citation and locate the actual resource

(4) To support the development of critical thinking skills through exposure of students to collections that reflect a diversity of perspectives, from conservative to radical points of view

(5) To provide collections that allow students to trace the evolution of ideas over time and cross-culturally

(6) To provide resources that serve as teaching tools for CSUS student teachers

(7) To support the CSUS academic faculty in their teaching and research

b. Describe the impact of collection development for writing and reading

(1) Making available library materials for students at different reading levels, year-in-school levels, and subject mastery levels. Collections support undergraduate to doctoral studies.

(2) Providing materials for students who want to improve their English language skills

(3) Assisting with improvement of foreign language skills through the use of print, audio, and visual materials made available in the language of the culture being studied

(4) Helping students develop writing skills and gain an understanding of the writing process. Typically this might involve cultivating the ability to gather and apply information from a variety of writing styles and exposition to specific problem-solving tasks.

(5) Giving students the opportunity to learn about their own culture and heritage, as well as other cultures, from the perspective of fiction and non-fiction writings

2. Indicate on what these expectations are based.

Development of the collections is based on a number of factors including consultations with instructional faculty; librarians' knowledge of the academic curriculum and library resources needed to meet the curriculum needs in each discipline; reference and instructional interaction with CSUS students primarily, but also with CSUS faculty and staff; analysis of the use of the collections; analysis of interlibrary loan requests; patron surveys and suggestions; evaluation by subject experts in the field, as in accreditation visits; comparisons with peer institutions; and recommendations of experts in the field.

3. Indicate how expectations are communicated to students

Effective use of the collection is communicated to students through instruction sessions, subject guides, reference assistance, and the organization of the collections that allow the students to browse through an array of materials on one topic.

B. How is your curriculum structured?

The CSUS collections are in an open stack arrangement that makes the materials directly accessible to CSUS students, with the exceptions of reserve, media, and special collections. With these few exceptions the majority of the collections are physically organized by Library of Congress call number, a nationally accepted library classification scheme that arranges library materials by subject matter. The curriculum collection used by the Teacher Education program is organized by the Dewey classification scheme to replicate the organizational scheme most commonly used in K–12 U.S. school libraries and many public libraries.

The collections also offer different formats to allow for different learning styles. The media collection includes a large collection of 16mm films, audio cassettes, CDs, slides, and videos. Multimedia materials are also part of the library's curriculum collection. The library is also providing increasing online access particularly to reference and journal literature. The online portion of the collection is available 24/7 on campus and from remote sites.

The library also offers an impressive and growing collection of special collection and archival materials that provide our students primary sources in such areas as regional, state, and national history and politics; social movements; women's studies, and others.

C. What teaching strategies has your faculty found to be particularly effective in helping students achieve your learning expectations?

Making the collections easily accessible, understandable, and appropriate to student needs is a primary focus of the assistance, instruction, documentation, and online help the library provides. Successful strategies librarians use to help students with the large collection at CSUS include hand-outs, e.g. bibliographies and subject guides; electronic assistance through the library website and the CSUS online catalog; access strategies taught in formal instruction classes and during reference interviews; links from electronic citation sources directly to full-text journal literature through SFX, a commercial serials management software program recently implemented at CSUS library. Also, through tours, signage, documentation, library home page pointers, instruction classes, and reference interviews, students learn to use resources not in the CSUS library print and electronic collections, and are taught how to identify and obtain these materials.

D. Describe the Collection Development Program's involvement (if any) and evaluation of distance and distributed education courses

The Library Collection directly contributes to distance and distributed education courses. One example is the access to videotape copies of distance education classes that are offered in the schedule. These are available for viewing in the Library Media Center.

Furthermore, the acquisition, review, and maintenance of materials and the development of services for the distance and distributed education collection have been promoted by the recently created Department for Online Curriculum Library Services (OCLS).

E. Describe your program's assessment plan

The library's assessment plan has utilized the following approaches in gathering data about its collections use and needs:

1. Selectors conduct and prepare comprehensive reviews of individual subject areas in the collection. These reports lead to recommendations, most of which are then implemented, thereby strengthening the collection.

2. All program reviews, including consultants' reports, are reviewed for comments and recommendations about the collections. This information is then distributed to appropriate decision makers for discussion and action.

3. One comprehensive review of the collections was conducted in the late 1990s utilizing statistical data available from the library's online catalog. Variables considered were: age of the collection, distribution of volumes, distribution of monies spent, and circulation. More analysis and recommendations need to be developed in this area.

4. The library has conducted user surveys, which included patron satisfaction with the collection.

5. Questions about library services are also included in campus and CSU–wide instruments such as SNAPS and CASPER (Computer Assisted Student Phone Entry Registration) surveys.

6. Weaknesses in the collection are also identified through an annual review of the borrowing activity requested by our patrons through the library's interlibrary loan unit. This is one approach by which materials that the patrons need are identified and then added to the collection.

7. The library also investigated the possibility and cost of doing a collection comparison to peer academic libraries through OCLC, but no action was taken.

8. Online database and print periodical usage statistics are reviewed and serve as factors for canceling and/or adding specific titles.

F. Using assessment data, analyze the effectiveness of your program including the ability of students to meet: (1) the department's learning expectations; (2) the university's learning goals; (3) writing and reading standards in the major; (4) computer/information competence standards.

See discussion in Chapter 3 regarding the Review Committee's comments on this section.

G. Describe how your department maintains consistency in multiple sections of courses.

The library attempts to maintain consistency and equity in the Collections Program in number of ways.

1. The annual library materials budget is allocated to the selector for each CSUS academic department/program by a formula in which various factors are given weight. Major factors in the formula are student undergraduate and graduate FTEs and degrees granted in each of these departments/programs. With these factors the number of students in departmental classes are taken into account as well as the number of undergraduate and graduate students who have majored in a subject.

2. The library also strives for equity in its reserve collection. The library purchases multiple copies of books to place on reserve based on a student per class formula (i.e., 1 copy per 15 students). Use of the reserve operation, which allows for the temporary placement of materials on reserve (including purchase for such placement), is available for use by all CSUS professors.

3. As new complex items are introduced to the collections, such as subject databases, the subject librarian typically provides documentation and training so that all librarians have a consistent understanding of this new item in the collection.

4. The library also strives for consistency in buying power by requesting additional funds to cover the inflation cost increase in library materials. The university administration has been very supportive over the last several years and has provided the requested additional funds needed to allow the library to maintain a consistent buying power particularly of periodical and other serial subscriptions. The dramatic effect of budget cuts and inflation on library materials in the 1990s was described in a CSU–wide library directors' report. The university administration has also been very supportive in allowing the library to ameliorate these negative effects by providing additional one-time lottery monies to fill important gaps in the collection.

H. Discuss changes needed to enhance or improve the effectiveness of your academic program outcomes.

1. **Changes needed related to Teaching and Learning:**
   a. Improve and increase outreach and information about collections and access to academic faculty.
   b. Explore ways to improve the Library Liaison Program.
   c. Examine samples of student research papers to learn more about how students are and are not using the library collection.
   d. Introduce a graduate research class to teach graduate students about library resources available to them in their subject area.
   e. Update the CSUS Library Collection Policy.
   f. Continue the review of the library materials allocation formula to determine whether any further adjustments or updating are needed.

2. **Changes needed related to Evaluation and Assessment of the Collection:**
   a. More fully implement collections assessment strategies and analysis.
   b. Conduct a survey of CSUS alumni about research and information competence skills gained through use of the library collections and instruction.
   c. The coordinator for collections should send a written response about action taken as a result of comments and recommendations pertaining to collections in academic department program reviews and accreditation reports.
   d. Provide a standardized template for collections information prepared by selectors responding to accreditation reports and program reviews. Selectors then can add additional information as requested or needed.
   e. Find funds to complete the OCLC assessment of the CSUS Collection related to education.

3. **Changes needed to improve Access to the Collection:**
   a. Provide improved focus on new books and new library materials with, for example, a more prominent and eye-catching "new book list" and electronic display of selected book jackets.
   b. Enhance access to the collections with tables of contents, links to full-text material, and summary information in the online catalog.
   c. Include in the online catalog library materials currently not included, e.g., maps, special collections.
   d. Develop a strategy to complete within a maximum of 5 years the conversion of the remaining manual card catalog.
   e. Investigate and put into place ways that would make access to our collections easier for our students and other users.
   f. Investigate what library materials, particularly in the area of periodicals and reference materials, can appropriately be transferred to an electronic format only, and which materials warrant the additional expense of maintaining both the print and electronic versions.
   g. As part of the Collections Program, decide what parts of the collection warrant digitization because of their uniqueness or value to teaching and/or research.
   h. Revisit the usefulness of classifying the CSUS print periodical collection.
   i. Enhance interlibrary loan access by implementing patron access to unmediated requests and electronic delivery of articles to requestors' computers.

    j. Enhance access to collections through improved access via the library website.

    k. Complete implementation of serials management software (SFX) and library portal software (Metalib).

    l. Enhance methods and funding strategies for the library to scan or otherwise provide electronic access to copyrighted print articles for reserve or other purposes.

I. If your department and its programs offer General Education and/or Service Learning courses:

1. Provide evidence that courses are meeting the General Education area criteria.

The Collections Program is meeting the General Education area criteria. Specifically how this is done is addressed in many other parts of this report. The library takes General Education and service courses into account in its library materials formula.

2. To what extent do your service courses meet their needs?

See II. B–G. above.

3. Describe how your department maintains consistency in multiple sections of General Education courses.

See II. B–G. above.

J. Explain how your department/program:

1. Addresses the increasing cultural diversity of CSUS students in the curriculum as appropriate.

The library collection uniquely highlights the tremendous diversity of our students and our society. Library holdings generally reflect the past and present knowledge of peoples and cultures throughout the world, and all subject librarians include multicultural materials in their collection areas as appropriate. The collection development process is driven by the CSUS curriculum and by student and faculty needs. Because collection development is ongoing, selectors are able to quickly incorporate curricular changes into their selection processes. In addition, the library requested and received funding for an Ethnic Studies and Multicultural Librarian position a few years ago in order to bring additional expertise and resources to this important area of collection development.

2. Accommodates differences in student preparation and access to educational opportunities.

The library offers a sizeable collection of language materials as well as materials at different levels of difficulty for students who are at different levels of preparation in a subject.

3. Helps students gain an effective knowledge of how to live and work in a diverse society.

Beyond the curriculum requirements the library provides significant resources to increase understanding of different cultures and understanding among people. These materials are available in fiction and non-fiction and various formats.

K. If your department offers a minor, a concentration or a certificate program, provide evidence of its contribution to the mission of the department, college and uni-

versity, and its viability with respect to enrollment patterns since the last program review and to the resources expended to support the program:

The library collection supports minors and concentrations through its library materials allocation process. The library also supports certificate programs, for example, gerontology, adult learning disabilities, supervisory skills, organizational leadership, etc., offered through College of Continuing Education (CCE).

LIBRARY INSTRUCTION & INFORMATION USE

A. Describe learning expectations for Library Instruction as a program

In the simplest terms, library instruction, formally known as "Information Competence" is the ability to find, evaluate, use, and communicate information in all of its various formats, and our learning expectations are based on these four ideas. The Library Instruction Program at CSUS is available to all students, faculty and staff. It consists of guided, self-guided and virtual tours; library lectures customized for class visits; a formal Information Competence Program using WebCT that is integrated into the General Education program; hands-on instruction for classes in labs; drop-in workshops for individuals; subject guides on the library website and as handouts; outreach to campus and off-campus groups.

Generally, library faculty members teach similar concepts, but adapt each presentation to the learning goals established in conjunction with the course instructor. The program is adapted at each level to meet the needs of users. Library instruction sessions for upper division and graduate level courses focus on the special resources available for those disciplines. Those for lower division classes tend to focus on the research process and interdisciplinary research tools.

1. Specify expectations for:

a. Library Instruction Program:

The primary learning objectives of the instruction program at the CSUS library are all the related research skills necessary for both undergraduate and graduate students to be able to successfully meet their information needs, whether they be in the classroom or in their daily lives. Primary focus is given to finding, evaluating and using information in all of its various formats.

The CSUS Baccalaureate Learning Goals (Fall 1999/Spring 2000) has an entire section on Information Competence listed under Expectations for Undergraduate Learning, including the ability to:

(1) Locate needed information using a variety of resources, including journals, books, and other media

(2) Use basic computer applications such as word processing software, e-mail, the Internet, and electronic databases

(3) Learn, understand, evaluate, and apply appropriate technologies to information processes, communication needs, and problem-solving in productive and sustained ways in both professional and personal settings; distinguish and make judgments among available information resources.

b. Writing and reading in the major

The concepts of "Information Competence" were incorporated into classes long before the term was coined. Learning to successfully navigate the research process provides students with the information necessary to thoughtfully complete assignments. Currently more than 300 classes a year come to the library to participate in the Library Instruction Program, which reaches over 13,000 students annually. Classroom faculty who have their students participate in a library instruction session are convinced that they see a better product, i.e., bibliographies, research papers, fewer websites used as references, more scholarly journals.

Individual librarians have conducted pre- and post-tests on specific parts of the research process that indicate learning is occurring. In one biology class (Bi0160) a question which indicated the student's ability to determine if the library owned a core journal rose 73 percent after the Library Instruction session.

c. **Computer/information competence**
See #2 immediately below.

2. **Indicate on what these expectations are based**

California librarians have been teaching research and critical thinking skills to our students for decades. In 2000, Information Literacy Standards in Higher Education were approved by the ACRL supporting the basis for lifelong learning. Information literacy provides the intellectual framework, and according to the guidelines, "initiates, sustains and extends lifelong learning through abilities which may use technologies but are ultimately independent of them."

As the world of information has become more complex and more accessible through the Web, the need for these skills became even more critical. The CSUS Faculty Senate adopted the Computer Literacy/Information Competence General Policy and Requirements (10/30/97) recommended by the Graduation Requirements subcommittee of the Curriculum Committee, which states that: Before graduation, CSUS students will be expected to demonstrate their abilities to:

a. Acquire, process, communicate, and critically evaluate information using current electronic technologies. A fundamental understanding of computer operations, experience with contemporary user interfaces and basic word processing skills are expected at entrance. Students will acquire and demonstrate competence in the use of computers and networks to access databases and retrieve information. Students will also develop competence in the use of computer systems for effective communication.

b. Use advanced computer skills appropriate to the requirements of a major and related careers.

c. Adapt to changing technologies and to assess the social issues and ethical choices resulting from those changes. http://www.lib.csus.edu/services/instruction/indiv/libinst/infocomp.htm. Other sources for standards include:

- *Information Literacy Competency Standards for Higher Education*, January 2001, http://www.ala.org/acrl/ilcomstan.html
- The *Information Literacy Competency Standards for Higher Education Standards, Performance Indicators, and Outcomes* http://www.ala.org/acrl/ilstandardlo.html.

- *Objectives for Information Literacy Instruction: A Model Statement for Academic Librarians,* http://www.ala.org/acrl/guides/objinfolit.html ACRL 2001.

3. Indicate how expectations are communicated to students

CSUS has no semester-long course in information competence, so library faculty have learned to distill and crystallize information concepts and deliver them in concise 50- or 75-minute lessons. Many use PowerPoint presentations or Web pages to guide the class in learning research and information skills. The Information Competence assignment clearly states, "At the end of this project you will be able to:"

- define a research topic
- determine your information requirements for your research question
- locate and retrieve relevant information
- use the technological tools for accessing information
- evaluate information
- understand the ethical, legal, and socio-political issues surrounding information and information technology

B. How is your curriculum structured (including core requirements, prerequisites, and electives) to achieve your learning expectations?

Learning in the library's academic programs, including the Library Instruction Program, occurs when students come to the library to use its services and resources, or when they access the library's online resources and services. The more students use the library's resources, the more they can be expected to learn.

Include a matrix that displays learning expectations and how courses contribute to achieving the expectations.

Competencies	Learning Expectations	Services to achieve expectations
Determine nature and extent of needed information	• Define a research topic • Understand different types of information and their uses (popular v. scholarly, primary v. secondary sources) • Use literature reviews and general reference works to get overview	Information Competency courses Drop-in workshops Subject specific workshops Subject guides
Access information effectively and efficiently	• Expand search strategies using Boolean operators, truncation, proximity searching, etc. • Understand difference between keyword vs. subject searches • Use controlled vocabularies and thesauri • Navigate electronic database interfaces • Understand how to use library catalog and LC Classification System	Information Competency courses Drop-in workshops Subject specific workshops Library tours

Competencies	Learning Expectations	Services to achieve expectations
Evaluate critically the sources and content of information	Understand how to evaluate using the following criteria • Authority • Accuracy • Currency • Bias	Information competency courses Drop-in workshops
Use information effectively to accomplish a specific purpose	• Create a bibliography • Write research papers, prepare oral reports, etc.	Subject specific workshops
Understand economic, legal, ethical and social issues in the use of information and technology	• Use style guides to cite other's works • Understand the difference between free v. fee based access • Understand copyright restrictions and plagiarism	Information competency courses Drop in workshops

C. What teaching strategies has your faculty found to be particularly effective in helping students achieve your learning expectations?

In the past 6 years we have moved from a passive to active learning environment, based in part on the findings of the Boyer Commission Report on Reinventing Undergraduate Education. Over the past years technology has had a significant impact not only on what the library faculty teaches, but also on how we teach. Where librarians once used transparencies on overheads or demonstrated complex searching with a computer and projection system, our students are now able to follow along and perform searches themselves in our library instruction labs.

This has dramatically changed the students' understanding of the complex, multi-step tasks that are involved in finding relevant information for their research topics. Most students find that they learn better by actually doing a task rather than just being told how to do it.

This change of instruction mode also caused us focus on the most important tasks, and so many of the more subtle aspects of searching cannot be covered in the limited time we have for many classes. That is one of the reasons we developed the 2-hour drop-in workshop series *Demystifying Library Databases* and *Search Engine Strategies*. These sessions are available to anyone and are offered during the middle 10 weeks of each term.

D. Describe your department's involvement in (if any) and evaluation of distance and distributed education courses.

The library has a significant support role for the entire distance and distributed education program. For several years one of our librarians was assigned half-time to support the resource needs of our remote users registered as distance students.

We now have an Online Curriculum Library Services (OCLS) department that supports distance and distributed education on campus, and which plays an important role working with individual distant student and faculty information requests. OCLS also works closely with the Center for Teaching and Learning in various collaborative efforts. In addition, OCLS is developing resources that will help faculty integrate course-specific library resources into their web-based courses (LOCUS project).

The Library Media Center (LMC) also is one of the partners of the CSUS Distance and Distributed Education (DDE) Program. The LMC videotapes the lectures of the video-based courses offered via satellite and web streaming technologies. The Campus Circuit TV (CCTV) courses are distributed to the remote Sacramento regional residents via cable television. Faculty, staff, students, and community users can view all videos and CCTV course videotapes in the LMC. The LMC also provides off-air recording service of cable broadcast studio lectures for viewing the following day based on the DDE's semester schedule. Commercially produced education videos used in conjunction with a distance and distributed education course may also be viewed in the LMC. In an effort to promote innovation and increase participation of its services, the Library Media Center created the Online Media Reserve Form, enabling CSUS faculty to reserve the media items for their classes on 7-day and 24-hour basis.

The Library Media Center has provided the video supporting services of Distance and Distributed Education since 1999. In the past three years, 23,721 DDE videos were circulated by the LMC.

E. Describe your program's assessment plan. Include both assessment of student learning outcomes and surveys of graduating seniors, and graduate students and alumni.

The Library Instruction Assessment Program was developed by the Library Instruction Committee in the spring of 1999 (http://www.lib.csus.edu/services/instruction/indiv/libinst/assess.htm).

Data is collected each year and included in the Instructional Services unit Annual Report. A five-year summary of this data shows that the totals have grown significantly in reflection of the increased teaching role of the library faculty. Not only has the number increased, but the content we teach has become much more complex and critical to the students' learning in this age of information and networking.

	Number of Sessions	Number of Students Taught	% Change
1997/1998	1,231	9,906	
1998/1999	1,059	10,341	+ 4.40%
1999/2000	1,189	10,346	+ 0.04%
2000/2001	1,405	10,982	+ 6.10%
2001/2002	1,351	13,673	+24.50%

F. Using assessment data, analyze the effectiveness of your program including the ability of students to meet: (1) the department's learning expectation; (2) the university learning goals; (3) writing and reading standards in the major; and (4) computer/information competence standards.

Information competence for Communication Studies — General Education Area A1.

This program is specifically designed to address the information competencies defined in 1995 by the CSU Information Competence Task Force. It has gone through a variety of iterations and now is fully functional in WebCT and it integrated into the basic subjects in Area A1 of the General Education program. For a full description of the assignment go to: http://library.csus.edu/services/inst/ICCS/infocomp/welcome.htm.

The Communication Studies Department (COMS) has adopted a WebCT Information-tion Competence for COMS course as a requirement for all COMS 4, *Introduction to Public Speaking,* and COMS 5, *The Communication Experience,* classes.

G. Describe how your department maintains consistency in multiple sections of courses.

Annually the Information Competence Program is offered in over 100 sections of COMS 2, COMS 4 or COMS 5. Students all log into the same WebCT program and take the same pre-test, look at the same tutorial modules, and take the same post-test.

Our drop-in workshop series is also consistent. Although it is taught by a variety of library faculty, they use the same handouts and PowerPoint scripts for their presentations and follow-up with the same online evaluation form.

H. Discuss changes needed to enhance or improve the effectiveness of your academic program outcomes.

1. Identify student groups or populations that we can follow through their academic careers and as alumni to determine how their library instruction experiences impacted their learning, e.g., Work with freshman seminars (ETHN021, GNST021) faculty to identify 50 to 75 students for a longitudinal study. Librarians will meet with the identified students over lunch one or two times a year to discuss how the library has impacted their learning skills and to determine the correlation between library instruction and research skill improvement in the following areas: assignments, adult life situations and the work-place.

2. Partnerships and collaboration with the teaching faculty are becoming ever more important to librarians with teaching responsibilities. CSUS librarians can enhance these partnerships with the following activities:

    a. Integrating team-teaching of information literacy into academic courses;

    b. Developing a one-credit GE stand-alone library instruction course;

    c. Teaching library instruction courses in the academic discipline labs.

3. Create a peer coaching program and train library faculty to work with their colleagues to share teaching methods and strategies and improve their teaching skills.

4. Establish a formal evaluation of librarians as teachers within the library RTP procedures, including such things as class observation, teaching portfolios and student evaluations.

5. Discuss the possibility of integrating the information competence requirements with the GE Advanced Writing Requirement.

I. If your department offers General Education and/or Service courses:

1. Provide evidence that courses are meeting the General Education area criteria.

The Information Competence Program for General Education is delivered entirely on the Web using WebCT course management software. With over 100 sections each year, this library program is the largest user of WebCT on campus.

2. To what extent do your service courses meet their needs?

See Section II. B–G. above.

3. Describe how your department maintains consistency in multiple sections of General Education courses.

See Section II. B–G. above.

J. Explain how the Library Instruction program: (1) addresses the increasing cultural diversity of CSUS students in the curriculum, as appropriate; (2) accommodates differences in student preparation and access to educational opportunities; and (3) helps students gain an effective knowledge of how to live and work in our diverse society.

The CSUS Library Diversity Committee has sponsored staff training and other activities to increase cultural awareness in library employees. We provide resources that go beyond the mainstream (GenderWatch, Ethnic NewsWatch, Chicano Database, Left Index, etc.) and often sponsor thought-provoking exhibits that focus on multicultural issues. Also, the library was seen as the best place on campus to house the MultiCultural Center, the Women's Center and the new Serna Center.

Discussions at the library diversity workshops and elsewhere have focused on accommodating diverse learning styles in our instruction program, and we strive to offer information about the library in multiple formats. Students can choose to come to the library for a guided tour where they can interact with the tour leader; they can take a self-guided, self-paced tour using our checkpoint tour, which many ESL and international students choose; or they can take a virtual library tour on the library's website.

Our instruction sessions usually have handouts or unique Web pages created to supplement and reinforce what the librarians say in class. Users can find paper resource guides for their topics near the reference desk or on the Web, listed under http://library.csus.edu/guides/. These can be printed in large fonts for visually impaired library users.

The overarching goal of the Library Instruction Program is to teach our students the necessary information competence and related skills that will enable them to become independent life-long learners. While we initially focus on helping them succeed academically by providing access to and instruction about the best resources for their class projects, we are also imparting skills that can easily transfer to their personal information needs when they graduate. These include how to write a résumé, find a job, research a new place for relocating, find consumer research before making a major purchase, etc. Students use the Web for numerous information needs beyond the classroom. That's why we teach them how to *critically evaluate information*, both on the Web and in other sources. We teach them to question the authority, accuracy, currency and bias of all their sources.

With the advent of the World Wide Web, information is now available to anyone with a computer and an Internet connection. There are those who are beginning to question the need for libraries, since they think "everything is on the 'Net." The vast store of information and knowledge housed for centuries in our nation's libraries, however, may never be digitized, but much of the periodical literature published since 1980 can now be searched through the use of commercial databases that the library purchases and provides with easy access via the Web. The Web is a marvelous invention that has enabled direct use and interaction with information that has traditionally been available only by visiting libraries. Without information competence skills, however, users can easily get bogged down and overwhelmed by the Internet's vast resources that are not organized or evaluated as traditional library books and journals have always been.

K. If your department offers a minor, a concentration or a certificate program, provide evidence of its contribution to the mission of the department, college and university, and its viability with respect to enrollment patterns since the last program review and to the resources expended to support the program:

See Section II. K above.

REFERENCE SERVICE AND INFORMATION ACCESS

A. Describe learning expectations for Reference Services and Information Access as a program.

The CSU Library Information Competence program clearly states that the learning expectation for all CSU students is "to find, evaluate, use, communicate and value information in all its various formats." The Reference Services and Information Access Program subscribes to this learning expectation. The purpose of reference services and information access at CSUS library is to assist CSUS students, faculty, staff and public users from the Sacramento region to meet their information needs; to teach information and research skills; and to provide equal access for all users in their search for knowledge.

    1. Specify expectations for:

        a. Research, locating and accessing information.

        The CSUS policies pertaining to the General Education Program (CSUS G.E. Policies thereafter) state on page 2 the need for students to gain "the ability to use the tools of research appropriate to a given level or type of activity requiring information one does not already possess, including the ability to find and use common references in libraries, to engage in library research in more specialized areas, to use computers, insofar as these are appropriate and useful to the task at hand, and to seek out appropriate expert opinion and advice."

        In the library and information science field within higher education, we refer to the above abilities as information literacy or information competency. Together with the ability to read, write and orally express ideas, the ability to use mathematical concepts and statistical methods, information literacy or competency is a key requirement for higher education in many U.S. academic institutions. With the increasing use of computer technology and widespread access to the Internet, information literacy becomes an essential skill that all college students must obtain by graduation.

        b. Writing and reading in the major:

        Our walk-in-based reference desk service allows librarians to provide one-on-one and just-in-time instruction and advice for students to complete their assignment or term papers. Appointment-based office consultation service allows librarians to provide in-depth office research assistance for thesis or other major research. These offerings are expected to enhance the development of writing and reading skills. Librarians provide consultation services in the use of style manuals for all majors at CSUS. Librarian guides for using style manuals can be found at http://library.csus.edu/guides/sturmt/style.htm for all style manuals, http://library.csus.edu/guides/blackmer/APAstyle.htm for APA style, and http://library.csus.edu/guides/budge/eography.htm for citing electronic sources.

c. **Computer/information competence.**

Reference librarians help students develop computer/information competency skills through reference desk service and office consultations. Beginning with the reference interview, librarians help students effectively articulate their assignment or project goals, and identify information they need to achieve those goals. Then the librarians instruct the student on the various forms of information resources available to them within the library, electronically and through interlibrary loan. Such instruction includes how to differentiate between forms and formats of information, and how to locate, access, evaluate and properly cite the information. During the process, the student learns how to develop and refine a topic by combining concepts using Boolean search strategies, keyword and subject searches. Throughout the consultation, librarians continually assess the students' computer/ information competency skill level, build on those skills and clarify the student's understanding of the new skills presented (See the Library Instruction section for more details).

Students are expected to become familiar with web-based technologies and to successfully navigate and use online resources.

2. Indicate on what these expectations are based.

Association of College and Research Libraries (ACRL) standards, Library and Information Technology Association (LITA) Technology Trends, and CSUS Strategic Plan Themes, viz., Teaching and Learning, Scholarship, Pluralism, Academic Program, Campus Life, Public Life and Institutional Effectiveness, all of which apply to the library.

3. Indicate how expectations are communicated to students.

Learning expectations are communicated during reference interviews, Library Information Systems Help Desk calls and email communication, and office consultations, as well as during library tours and library instruction. Through a reference interview, the librarian can ascertain the student's information needs as well as their familiarity with the library's resources. Students are also introduced to new information resources during the reference interview as well as taught how to analyze their information needs, identify likely resources, retrieve resources and evaluate their utility. These expectations are also conveyed on the library's website.

B. How is your curriculum structured (including core requirements, prerequisites, and electives) to achieve your learning expectations?

The library offers a number of teaching, learning, research and information access services to all users of the CSUS library. It is through these services that students achieve the learning expectations. The following is a brief listing of the services offered.

1. Reference Desk Service:

The reference desk is often the first and the best place to go when getting started on a research task. Instruction in the form of specific answers to direct questions about academic learning, teaching, research, or information literacy may be obtained at the reference desk. The desk is staffed by librarians, library assistants and student assistants most hours that the library is open. More complicated research questions may be referred to subject specialist librarians for in-depth consultation during their office hours. Ask-A-Librarian is the library's electronic reference service, providing both e-mail and live reference. Currently enrolled students, faculty, and staff of the CSUS may use the service. Questions from others will be answered selectively. Priority is given to questions related to the Sacramento region or to collections and resources unique to the CSUS library. The Ask-A-Librarian service provides brief answers to factual questions. It does not handle inquiries involving extensive research, but can provide sources and strategies.

Because the library's large periodicals collection is split between different floors of the building and available in print, microform, and electronic formats, the periodicals desk personnel provide assistance with verifying and locating periodical materials that are in the CSUS library collection or that can be accessed from CSUS library. For assistance with database searching, identifying articles by subject published in periodicals, and other complex and in-depth research questions, patrons are referred to the reference desk.

2. One-on-One Office Consultation:

Subject librarians often have advanced subject degrees or licenses in their areas of expertise. Office consultation is available by appointment with subject librarians for instruction and assistance with any extensive research problems, including, but not limited to: term papers, theses and dissertations, government or foundation grants, community projects, etc. Through the consultation, students are assisted in formulating a research strategy and taught about the research process and resources.

3. Librarian Subject Guides:

Librarians prepare and regularly update over 100 subject guides to help students locate appropriate sources for conducting research in specific subjects, or answering more general kinds of questions. These guides are available in electronic format via the web and in hard copy free of charge at the reference desk. A list of all of subject guides is available on the pull down menu under "Librarian Guides" from the Library Database and Article Searching page.

4. Users with Disabilities Service:

The library provides a number of services to assist users with physical, visual or learning disabilities. Special computers in the public area include a closed-captioned video magnifying system, ZoomText Xtra Level 2, JAWS for windows screen reading software, large-screen monitors with sound systems, adjustable workstations and chairs, ergonomic keyboards, track ball mouse, arm and wrist supports, and earphones.

Reference desk staff will help users with disabilities retrieve a limited number of books on a walk-in basis. Requests to retrieve large numbers of books can be made in advance by e-mailing the Ask-A-Librarian service. Also, the circulation desk will help users with disabilities photocopy library materials at the self-service rate.

The reference collection contains braille dictionaries and an encyclopedia, and CD sign language dictionaries are housed in the Library Media Center. Most CDs can be run on research stations with CD drives in the library. In addition, every effort is made to both create and provide web-based resources that are designed with accessibility in mind.

For CSUS students with disabilities, more equipment and assistance is available at the High Tech Center, located in the lower level of the library and operated by the Services to Students with Disabilities office.

5. Remote Access to Library Information Resources

The Library Information Systems personnel and reference librarians assist students with off-campus access to the myriad resources available on the Internet. Effective user interfaces to all of the library's electronic resources are designed by the library to provide easy access to electronic resources. The library also provides technical assistance with issues related to web browser configuration software and hardware requirements.

Include a matrix that displays learning expectations and how courses contribute to achieving the expectations.

Competencies	*Learning Expectations*	*Services to achieve expectations**
Determine nature, extent and format of needed information	• Identify and narrow research topic • Identify key concepts • Become familiar with all formats available and when each is appropriate	• Office consultations • Subject guides • Reference Interview • Library Website
Access information effectively and efficiently	• Expand search strategies using Boolean operators, truncation, proximity searching, etc. • Understand difference between keyword vs. subject searches • Use controlled vocabularies and thesauri • Navigate electronic database interfaces • Familiarity with the Web and accessing web resources • Understand how to use library catalog and LC Classification System	• Reference Interview • Ask-a-Librarian • Public Service Desks (ILL/ Document Delivery, Periodicals Desk, Circulation Desk, Reserve Book Room) • Library Website • Remote Access • Proxy Interface Design and Configuration
Understand economic, legal, ethical and social issues in the use of information and technology	• Use style guides to cite other's works • Understand the difference between free v. fee based access • Understand copyright restrictions and plagiarism	• Reference Interview • Library Website

*These services are used in combination to meet the learning expectations.

C. What teaching strategies has your faculty found to be particularly effective in helping students achieve your learning expectations, e.g., information access, service learning, application assignments, etc.?

Through collaboration with teaching faculty, library faculty influence student learning as seekers and users of information through class assignments that can be successfully completed using the resources of the library. Librarians are regularly available to meet with faculty who are designing or revising library-related assignments. This collaboration helps guarantee that assignments refer to the best possible sources and also allows us make arrangements within the library to accommodate the students' information needs. For example, in some cases we may be able to obtain needed items or set materials aside in a special area.

1. A well-designed library assignment can teach students valuable research skills and improve the quality of their papers. Working together with instructional faculty, reference librarians can teach students to:

2. Develop a suitable topic for research, using the library reference collection and other sources to help define the topic and for background information.

3. Develop a list of relevant keywords and phrases to search in the library catalogs and databases.

4. Select and use the most appropriate catalogs, indexes, full-text databases, and Internet search tools to locate relevant and timely materials.

5. Distinguish between popular and scholarly sources and detect signs of bias, whether the material is in printed form or on the Internet.

6. Employ appropriate styles for quoting and citing sources suitable to the discipline in a way that gives proper credit and avoids plagiarism.

7. Prepare an annotated bibliography of information sources on their topics.

8. Starting with a significant event or publication in their discipline, students find out more about the people and issues involved.

9. Prepare a guide that introduces others to information sources in a subject field.

10. Compare how a given topic is treated in several different reference sources, both print and electronic.

11. Analyze the content, tone, style and audience of journals and/or web sites basic to their discipline.

Research, whether in a library or on the Internet, is a complex process that requires and teaches flexibility and adaptability. The reference librarians teach these skills to students in their research. Students benefit from opportunities to reflect on their research strategies and think critically about what they are doing.

D. Describe library's involvement in and evaluation of distance and distributed education courses.

See Library Instruction II.D. Library services operations are closely integrated into the library's distance and distributed education initiatives.

E. Describe your program's assessment plan. Include both assessment of student learning outcomes and surveys of graduating seniors, and gradate students and alumni.

Visiting the library for various academic pursuits should be a learning experience, whether one takes some form of tour, visits the library website, attends a formal library class or interacts with library personnel in the pursuit of information and/or research strategies. For the sake of answering this question, "student learning outcomes" will be broadly defined as benefits received from using one of the library's services.

A formal Survey of CSUS Library Users was conducted during the Fall of 2001. This

pre-tested survey focused on (1) library collection overall quantity, quality and maintenance, (2) library usage by user types and by departments, (3) user service satisfaction,
and (4) library accessibility, e.g., ADA, building and service hours, remote login, etc.
The survey was distributed for two-week periods beginning October 14 and November
4. In all, 4,399 surveys were distributed with 1,178 collected, a 27 percent return rate.
Two previous reference desk surveys were conducted in 2000 (April 2000 and August 4,
2000 reports).

Non-solicited feedback in the form of suggestions in the suggestion box or via electronic feedback is another way the library assesses the quality and effectiveness its programs
and services. Suggestions specifically recommending materials for the library collections
are forwarded to the librarian in charge of the corresponding discipline or format. All
suggestions with names and addresses and/or phone numbers or e-mail addresses receive
personal responses from the associate dean for public services or the most appropriate
library employee. Suggestions serve as a useful ongoing assessment instrument and a
vehicle for improvement.

The ability to access and locate information on the library website is also very important. The library conducts usability studies on the website's interface as well as its navigation and structure.

**F. Using assessment data, analyze the effectiveness of program including ability of
students to meet: (1) the department's learning expectations; (2) the university's
learning goals; (3) writing and reading standards in the major; (4) computer/infor-
mation competence standards**

See Library Instruction and Information Use Program.

**G. Describe how your department maintains consistency in multiple sections of
courses**

The Reference Department offers bi-weekly in-service training for everyone working
on the reference desk. Also, the 4-week-long new employee training ensures a high standard for reference service. Tiered reference service allows librarians at the reference desk
to spend adequate time on research questions, while technical problems are mainly handled
by library assistants and student assistants. There are usually two librarians scheduled at
the reference desk, which allows for observation and assessment of each other during reference interviews. The most complicated questions are referred to the subject specialist
librarians for in-depth consultation.

**H. Discuss changes needed to enhance/improve the effectiveness of Reference and
Information Access outcomes**

Access to library computer workstations needs to increase as the shift to electronic
resources increases. Over the last three years, the library has increased the amount of
public computers from 30 to over 120. The website has also undergone significant enhancements during the past year. The library also needs to continue to research the possibilities
of expanding traditional reference services with other models, such as providing real-time
reference service to anyone connected to the Internet. Many students now come to the
library with a laptop and the library needs to provide access to the library's electronic

resources via wireless technologies through increased wireless access points in the library and through the checkout of laptops with wireless cards.

I. If your department offers general education and/or service courses:

1. Provide evidence that courses are meeting the General Education area criteria.

Reference services are not differentiated according to courses for general education, minor, major, or other standings. Reference services are provided on an individual, as needed basis. Reference librarians are responsible for subject-oriented as well as general information literacy. Working with teaching faculty, librarians also teach students to search and evaluate information in any of their subject areas.

2. To what extent do your service courses meet their needs?

See section J II. I. 1. above.

In addition, partnering with the SJSU Graduate School of Library and Information Science, library school internships are offered in the CSUS library. Graduate interns can work 135 hours at the CSUS library for 3 graduate credit units, or 180 hours for 4 credit units.

3. Describe how department maintains consistency in multiple sections of GE courses.

See section II.G. above.

J. Explain how Reference and Information Access Services: (1) addresses the increasing cultural diversity of CSUS students in the curriculum as appropriate; (2) accommodates differences in student preparation and access to educational opportunities; (3) helps students gain an effective knowledge of how to live and work in our diverse society.

We staff the reference desk with subject specialists and other librarians as well as library assistants from a variety ethnic and cultural backgrounds to reflect the diversity of CSUS. Our communication abilities have been enriched by the addition of multilingual personnel at the reference desk. A majority of our instructional opportunities happen on a one-to-one basis at the reference desk. This allows for individual attention and assessment of the student's needs. We are experienced in determining the level of knowledge a student has concerning his/her search for information as well as different learning and communication styles.

K. If your department offers a minor, a concentration or a certificate program, provide evidence of its contribution to the mission of the department, college and university, and its viability with respect to enrollment patterns since the last program review and to the resources expended to support the program.

The reference services program supports university minor, concentration, and certificate programs within the scope of its regular activities.

SECTION III. STUDENTS

A. Student Profile

The library assumes responsibility to include in its academic programs all CSUS students at all levels, in all majors, in person, via telephone, or over the Internet. Our users also include pre-college students and the general public in the Sacramento area. Our users, therefore, are very diverse, from teenagers to the elderly, of all social, ethnic, and religious backgrounds, and from many different countries.

Statistical data for CSUS students over the last six years in the areas of enrollment patterns in majors, minors, concentrations, and credentials; gender and ethnic composition; retention and graduation rates; part- and full-time enrollments; "native" and transfer students; and other student characteristics are available on the Office of Institutional Research website (http://www.oir.csus.edu/). These data represent the achievement levels of our primary and target user groups.

B. Student Academic Performance

University-wide student academic performance data including grading distribution, GPAs, students on probation, WPE pass rates, preparation for upper division/graduate coursework, etc., are also available on the Office of Institutional Research website (http://www.oir.csus.edu/).

Inasmuch as the library serves all students, all disciplines, and all programs, these university-wide data on student academic performance can provide relevant benchmarks for measuring the library's effect on student learning. The library has an obligation to measure the effectiveness of its academic programs in terms of its direct contribution to the university's overall effectiveness in teaching students. The university chooses its performance measures. The library then must devise ways to contribute to those same performance objectives and to assess and increase its contribution to the university's effectiveness.

Customary measures of library "activity levels" fall short in evaluating a library's positive effect on student learning, and do not allow for any meaningful assessment of a library's academic programs. Surveys, questionnaires, and the like are illuminating, but remain anecdotal and imprecise. Measures of students' information competence taken in library instruction sessions, while quantitative, generally remain isolated data and are not correlated to the students' overall academic success. Furthermore, none of these methods can substantiate the effect of library programs on a university's overall measures of effectiveness as an educational institution, which leaves significant doubts about the effect of library academic programs on the educational mission of their institutions. This must change if academic libraries are to remain relevant in their institutions.

During the years before the next self-study, therefore, the library will work with the University's Office of Institutional Research to develop and implement ways of measuring the overall academic success of students who use the library services compared to students who do not use the library. This will involve longitudinal studies of student cohorts and their respective library usage patterns beginning with their entry into the university and following them throughout their years as students. The variables we intend to study are the same as the university's main assessment measures, such as student retention and graduation rates, years to graduate, grade point averages, and others. Once we have gathered the data and calculated the correlation between our students' library usage and their success in the university, we will devise ways to strengthen the correlation by improving and expanding library programs and services according to what the data tell us.

C. Student Academic Support

1. Describe how the department provides academic advising.

Librarians provide about 500 lengthy office consultation sessions for students and faculty annually. Librarians also provide an advising service for college graduates and graduate students who are interested in pursuing librarianship as a career.

2. What support does your department provide for students in need of extra assistance?

See Sec. II. Reference Services and Information Access. B.4., Users with Disabilities Service, for examples of the extra assistance provided on request to users with disabilities.

Also, library personnel can speak and/or read Spanish, French, German, Hebrew, Chinese, Japanese, Lao, Thai, Latin, Russian, American Sign Language, and other languages. Using these talents, the Library's Foreign Language Assistance Program (FLAP) provides limited translation and interpretation services to library users who need such assistance to use the library's collections and services.

D. Student Professional Development

The library normally employs 110–120 students each year, more than any other single department on campus. Our student employees perform duties that are vital to the success of the library's academic programs and are officially and regularly recognized for their good performance and valuable contributions. Student employees are carefully trained and supervised to be competent, reliable, and productive, and they become highly valued colleagues in the eyes of the regular library employees.

Many students at the library work here for more than two years. Some have stayed after graduation and became full-time library assistants. Several others have gone on to graduate schools of library science and then moved on as librarians elsewhere (see also IV. Library Personnel/Non-Faculty. Student Employee Profile).

SECTION IV. LIBRARY PERSONNEL/FACULTY AND LIBRARY PERSONNEL/NON-FACULTY

A. *Faculty and Non-Faculty Profile:*

Analyze faculty data, including a comparison of your faculty profile to the faculty profiles in the university. If the data indicate a need for a response by your department, describe your plan of action. Include analysis regarding: Full and part-time faculty, gender and ethnic composition, and student-faculty ratio/class size.

The ecology of the university depends on a deep and abiding understanding that inquiry, investigation, and discovery are the heart of the enterprise, whether in funded research projects or in undergraduate classrooms or graduate apprenticeships. Everyone at a university should be a discoverer, a learner. That shared mission binds together all that happens on a campus. The teaching responsibility of the university is to make all its students participants in the mission. Those students must undergird their engagement in research with the strong "general" education that creates a unity with their peers, their professors, and the rest of society.*

*Reinventing Undergraduate Education: A Blueprint for America's Research Universities. *Boyer Commission on Educating Undergraduates in the Research University (New York: The Commission, 1998).*

The CSUS library plays an integral and vital role in helping our campus accomplish this mission. Understanding the demographics of the library environment in relation to demographics of the CSUS campus and our peer institutions enables us to promote the discovery process and plan for a more inclusive and expansive teaching and learning enterprise. A commitment to diversity encourages a shared vision of knowledge in its many facets.

This analysis attempts to relate CSUS library personnel statistics to the wider communities of our campus, system-wide, and national figures when possible. Due to statistical incongruencies of available dates and populations, the year and source used for analysis in the appendices will appear in parentheses.

1. Ethnic analysis

In each of the categories in which statistics reveal the CSUS campus to reflect a diverse student body, the percentage of library faculty representing the various categories was lower than the percentage of students represented in the category. Although the percentage of white library faculty (79 percent) is only slightly higher than the percentage of white instructional faculty (76 percent), both of these groups were approximately 30 percent higher than the percentage of the total white student population (45 percent). These demographics hinder the library's ability to provide value-enhanced services to a diverse and multicultural campus. It is noteworthy that certain ethnic groups represented among both the instructional faculty and student body — such as American Indians, Black Americans, Filipinos, and Pacific Islanders — were not represented at all among the CSUS library faculty.

2. Gender Analysis

The 3:1 gender ratio of female (75 percent) to male (25 percent) librarians that existed in March 2003 has decreased as the library has since hired several male librarians. These recent hires should bring the library closer to the total student (59 percent female, 41 percent male) and instructional faculty (47 percent female, 53 percent male) ratios.

3. Students to Librarians and Other Professional Staff Analysis

The CSUS librarian to student ratio is roughly 943 to 1. This figure compares similarly with ratios at selected CSU peer institutions (SFSU, 958:1; SJSU, 1120:1; CSULB, 1054:1). Among Association of Research Libraries (ARL), the median librarian to student ratio was much lower (256:1). The librarian to student ratio at UC Davis (529:1), whose total enrollment is comparable to CSUS enrollment, is high for an ARL library, but still much lower than the CSUS ratio. The CSUS library is included in the Association of College and Research Library (ACRL) statistics. It is worth mentioning that among those institutions with "high" enrollments, the ratio of students to professional staff is 446:1, less than half of our ratio of 943:1. This ratio makes one-on-one contact with students — the teaching and learning model governing the library's service philosophy — extremely challenging.

4. Plan of Action

The available statistics indicate that the CSUS library falls short of reaching an optimal service level due to an inadequate student-faculty ratio, and a lack of gender and ethnic parity.

The library should try to remedy these weaknesses. Possible courses of action are:

   a. Advertise for and interview librarians from diverse backgrounds

   b. Secure funds for an endowed librarian position

   c. Ensure that all interviewees are informed of campus-wide diversity and gender parity programs and activities, and introduced to representatives from relevant campus organizations and groups

   d. Mentor CSUS students who are interested in attending library and information science graduate programs

5. **General characteristics of CSUS library faculty**
(March 3, 2003, CSUS Office of Human Resources):
Total 22 Full time, 6 part time
Gender: 21 female, 7 male
Ethnicity: Asian: 3, Hispanic: 2, Other: 1, White: 22
Rank: Librarian: 11, Associate Librarian: 4; Senior Assistant: 8; Assistant: 5
Ratio of students to faculty: 963:1

6. **Comparison of CSUS library faculty to other populations**
   a. **CSUS (CSU Annual Library Statistics, 2001–02)**
     Total enrollment: 28,588
     Librarians and other professional staff: 30.3
     Ratio of students to CSUS librarians and other professional staff: 943:1

   b. **CSU**
     Total enrollment: 409,000
     Librarians and other professional staff: 429
     Ratio of students to CSU librarians and other professional staff: 953:1

     (1) **San Francisco State University**
       Total enrollment: 28,378
       Librarians and other professional staff: 28.8
       Ratio of students to librarians and other professional staff: 985:1

     (2) **San Jose State University**
       Total enrollment: 30,350
       Librarians and other professional staff: 27.1
       Ratio of students to librarians and other professional staff: 1120:1

     (3) **California State University Long Beach**
       Total enrollment: 34,566
       Librarians and other professional staff: 32.8
       Ratio of students to librarians and other professional staff: 1054:1

   c. **University of California, Davis**
     Total enrollment: 29,087
     Librarians and other professional staff: 55
     Ratio of students to librarians and other professional staff: 529:1

   d. **ACRL (ACRL Library Data Tables, 2001)**
     http://www.virginia.edu/surveys/ACRL/2001/sdphdall.pdf
     Total FTE enrollment:
     High: 29,000

Median: 1549

Professional staff

High: 65

Median: 6

Ratio to students to professional staff:

High: 446:1

Median: 258:1

ARL (Association of Research Libraries Statistics, 2001, p 17 & 46), http://www.arl.org/stats/arlstat/index.html Ratio is derived by multiplying the total number of staff per 1000 by the percentage of professional staff, i.e., $13.7 \times 28.08\% = 3.84696$, $1000/3.9 = 256$)

Ratio of students to librarians (median): 256:1

7. Ethnic and Gender Diversity

(CSUS Office of Human Resources, most recent statistics available)

	Instructional faculty	*Library faculty*	*Students*
Female, full time:	322 (42%)	19 (86%)	
Male, full time:	451 (58%)	3 (14%)	
Female, part time:	401 (52%)	2 (33%)	
Male, part time:	364 (48%)	4 (67%)	
Total Female	723 (47%)	21 (75%)	16,867 (59%)
Total Male	815 (53%)	7 (25%)	11,721 (41%)
American Indian, full time:	11 (1%)	0	
American Indian, part time:	8 (1%)	0	
Total	19 (1%)	0	286 (1%)
Asian, full time:	87 (11%)	3 (14%)	
Asian, part time:	48 (6%)	0	
Total	135 (9%)	3 (11%)	4,860 (17%)
Black, full time:	40 (5%)	0	
Black, part time:	26 (3%)	0	
Total	66 (4%)	0	1,715 (6%)
Filipino, full time:	4 (1%)	0	
Filipino, part time:	11 (1%)	0	
Total	51 (1%)	0	N/A
Hispanic, full time:	60 (8%)	2 (7%)	
Hispanic, part time:	46 (6%)	0	
Total	106 (7%)	2 (7%)	3,716 (13%)
Other, full time:	10 (1%)	1 (3%)	
Other, part time:	18 (2%)	0	
Total	28 (2%)	1 (3%)	4,288 (15%)
Pacific Islander, full time:	3 (<1%)	0	
Pacific Islander, part time:	3 (<1%)	0	
Total	6 (<1%)	0	N/A
White, full time:	558 (72%)	16 (73%)	
White, part time:	605 (79%)	6 (100%)	
Total	1,163 (76%)	22 (79%)	12,865 (45%)

B. Assess faculty profile for the ability to offer the curriculum and to support program goals. Describe plans for addressing any identified issues. To what extent are adjunct faculty needed?

The library faculty, in addition to the MLIS degree, has Bachelor's or higher degrees in various disciplines (see Appendix A, Table 2). These academic qualifications, along with past working experience, qualify librarians to be hired as faculty eligible for retention, tenure, and promotion.

Part-time librarians meet the same educational requirements as full-time librarians. Similar to the rest of the campus, the library tends to rely on the help of part time librarians because it does not have a sufficient number of tenure track faculty. The CSUS administration expects that within the next year, part-time instructional faculty will constitute approximately 30 percent of the university's instructional faculty. The number of part-time librarians at CSUS currently constitutes one-third of all librarians. These ratios all might change as a result of expected budget cuts, however.

C. Faculty as Teachers

1. Analyze data available from the College Outcomes Survey (COS) and Program Assessment Questionnaire (PAQ) [Available from the Office of Institutional Research] to identify any issues that need action. Describe plans for addressing issues.

The library is not included in these surveys. While probably most of the questions would not be relevant, a library task force should review the instrument to determine if it would provide appropriate information for informing the university and the library about the library as a program.

2. Describe how the faculty are involved in professional development activities to improve and enhance their teaching effectiveness or professional effectiveness.

Librarians attend numerous conferences, programs, and workshops to improve both their teaching and professional effectiveness by obtaining information about best practices and innovation in their respective fields.

Members of the library faculty belong to a wide range of professional organizations and have long received encouragement and travel support to attend conferences and workshops, both as presenters and attendees. In a field where technology plays such an important role, it is vital to remain current and be involved in the latest advances.

During the past six years librarians have participated in professional workshops and seminars related to library issues in budgeting, cataloging, chemistry research, computing, copyright, distance education, e-research, engineering research, government documents, information literacy/competency, instructional technology, media, multiple literacies, personnel management, periodicals collections, publishing, technical services, telecommunications, and web development.

In addition to national, state and local programs, this past year the library sponsored an enrichment program for library faculty and non-faculty development. This program invited library personnel and outside speakers to share their knowledge and experience.

A detailed summary of CSUS library faculty professional development appears in Appendix B.

3. To what extent are faculty using "best practices" in their roles as teachers? How are faculty offering students a variety of learning experiences to address the diversity of student learning styles?

Recognition of the importance of student learning styles is built into the Library Instruction Program. Instruction is offered in a variety of formats including formal lecture sessions, interactive learning activities, hands-on sessions, and one-on-one research appointments with individual librarians.

The Information Competence Program run by the Library's Instructional Services unit is perhaps the best example of how librarians have implemented professional standards and best practices in teaching. The program is offered as a required part of General Education in Communication Studies. The web-based Information Competence tutorials are closely aligned with the Information Literacy Competency Standards for Higher Education adopted by ACRL in 2000, and incorporate many of the characteristics identified in the ACRL Information Literacy Best Practices Project.

This last document identifies best practice characteristics in the following categories: Mission, Goals and Objective, Planning, Administrative and Institutional Support, Articulation with the Curriculum, Pedagogy, Staffing, Outreach, and Assessment/Evaluation. The CSUS Library Instruction Program and particularly the Information Competence Program have articulated these in a variety of documents and web pages:

The CSUS Library Instruction Master Plan (1988), the *Library Instruction Home Page*, http://library.csus.edu/services/inst/indiv/libinst/libinst.htm, the *Library Instruction Assessment Plan* http://library.csus.edu/services/inst/indiv/libinst/assess.htm (1999), and *Welcome to the Information Competence Assignment* http://library.csus.edu/services/inst/ICCS/infocomp/welcome.htm.

4. Comment on your facultys' innovations in pedagogy and their knowledge of current trends in their academic specialties.

The list of presentations and poster sessions done by our library faculty at ALA, ACRL CARL and LOEX etc. (appearing elsewhere in this document) is indicative of their innovation in instruction. Most librarians subscribe to one or more listservs in their area of specialization and remain current through daily email interactions.

The Online Curriculum Library Services (OCLS) department has worked closely with participants of the Center for Teaching and Learning and the Teaching Using Technology Summer Institute "to provide to 'novice' technology faculty users the services of 'experienced' technology faculty users who have been trained on adult learning strategies...." This provides support to faculty when they choose to incorporate teaching and learning technology tools into their teaching. In addition, OCLS has been working on an innovative project that will allow instructional faculty who already use technology in their teaching to manage their online library resources in particular classes.

5. Describe the department's process for evaluating teaching effectiveness (in the major and in general education offerings). How are data used to enhance or improve teaching?

Library ARPT reviews do not normally include evaluation of librarian teaching effectiveness. As library instruction sessions generally last either 50 or 75 minutes and are usually only done once with each class, the opportunity to observe improvement in student outcomes over the length of a semester is unavailable to librarians.

User satisfaction data from library workshops is voluntarily collected at the end of sessions held in the instruction labs, using the web form found at http://library.csus.edu/scripts/instruction/evalweb1.asp. Compilation of this data reveals that most users agree or strongly agree that the purpose of the session was clear, that they are confident they can use the tools that have been explained, that the librarian was knowledgeable, responsive and enthusiastic, that they presented the material clearly, and that the handouts were helpful. They further agree that the session met or exceeded their expectations and that they covered new and useful material. A summary of the data can be found in Appendix D: *Library Instruction Evaluation Form*. The Library Instruction Committee members who developed this form are currently working on two additional online forms to collect feedback from faculty members who have brought their classes to the library for instruction. They have also recommended that the library:

    a. Create a peer coaching program and train library faculty to work with their colleagues to share teaching methods and strategies and improve their teaching skills.

    b. Establish a formal evaluation of librarians as teachers within the library R.T.P. procedures, including such things as class observation, teaching portfolios and student evaluations. Sources for standards and best practices are listed in Appendix E.

D. Faculty as Scholars

1. Describe the department's specific expectations for scholarly, creative activities.

According to the Library Faculty Guidelines for RTP (Approved April 15, 1999) the library's specific expectations for scholarly and creative activities fall within three categories. The first category is publication. Publication includes authorship of articles, monographs, contributions to edited books, and contributions for scholarly communication. A subset of publications is bibliographies and annotated bibliographies. Bibliographies assist students and patrons in their research endeavors; some of these are quite comprehensive. Bibliographies are considered scholarly activities, but will not be listed in the Appendix. (The creation of information and guides in an online format is becoming a vital means to disseminate information to library users. Guides often take the place of traditional print bibliographies.)

The second category of Scholarly/Creative Activities is presentations. These presentations may be at professional meetings, workshops, or conferences. Presentations may be related to the library profession or to the librarian's area of expertise or subject specialization. Presentations are given the same weight by library faculty as publications.

Finally, the library recognizes professional activities and continuing education as scholarly and creative activities. Active participation in library associations is recognized as a means to further develop and implement "...national policies, procedures, standards, guidelines, and disseminating best practice" (Library Faculty Guidelines for RTP, pg 7).

Continuing education that relates to the librarian's professional activities and best practices is also an important part of scholarly and creative activities. Though not specifically stated within the LARTP Guidelines, grant writing and the receiving of grant awards are included within the sphere of scholarly and creative activities.

2. Describe scholarly and creative activities of faculty in the last six years (vita).

The library faculty is active in scholarly and creative activities. The following is a descriptive list of the scholarly/creative activities undertaken over the last six years. This information was taken from library faculty resumes and curricula vitae.

a. Publication

Contributions to the monographic literature:

(1) **Author, co-author, or editor:** *The Power of Language/El Poder de la Palabra (2001), Annotated Bibliography of the Institute of Physics, Chinese Academia Sinica, 1980–1985, Annotated Bibliography of Physics Research in the Chinese Academia Sinica, 1986–1987.*

(2) **Chapters within the following edited works:** *Libraries without Walls 4: Delivery of Library Services to Distant Users (2002). NACCS Conference Proceedings (Forthcoming). Finding Common Ground: Creating the Library of the Future Without Diminishing the Library of the Past (1998). Strategic Challenge to U.S. Foreign Policy in the Post-Cold War (1998). Immigrant Politics and the Public Library (2001), Latino Library Services (2000), Immigrant Politics and the Public Library (2001).*

(3) **Journal articles in the following publications:** *World Libraries. CCLI Newsletter. Behavior Research Methods, Instruments, & Computers. American Society for Engineering Education Engineering Librarians Division Newsletter. Journal of Chemical Education. Library Acquisitions: Practice and Theory, Computers in Libraries. Journal of Access Services. Technical Services Quarterly. Libraries for the Future. Library Advocate. California Libraries. Information Technology and Libraries. Journal of Library and Information Science. Journal of Information, Communication, and Library Science. The Journal of Interlibrary Loan, Document Delivery & Information Supply. Cataloging and Classification Quarterly. Latino Studies.*

(4) **Book reviews in the following publications:** *Choice. Reference and User Services Quarterly. Government Information Quarterly. E-STREAMS. Journal of Information, Communication and Library Science.*

(5) **Abstracter in the following index:** *Repertoire International de Literature Musicale (RILM).*

b. **Appointments to Editorial Boards or Advisory Committees of the following publications:** Journal of Library & Information Services in Distance Education, Documents to the People, HW Wilson Company Publications, Bi-Resource Guide.

c. **Presentations and Poster Sessions at the following Conferences or Organizations:** Libraries without Walls 4th International Conference, Online Northwest 17th Annual Conference, California Academic & Research Libraries Annual Conference, Mid-Atlantic Archives Conference, National Academy of Science, NASIG, American Library Association Annual Conferences, National Association for Chicana and Chicano Studies Fall Symposium, California Library Association Annual Conference, REFORMA National Library Conference, LOEX of the West, California Clearinghouse on Library Instruction, Innovative Users Group, CFA Equity Conference.

d. **Grants:** Grants and grant writing are an increasingly important source of funding for librarians. The library faculty has received grants from the following sources: CSUS Faculty Professional Development Mini-grant, CSU Information Competence Work Group, CSUS Minor Capital Outlay, Visiting Scholars, Project Activity Grants. In addition, competitive grants funded through the CSUS Friends of the library to support the purchase of or increase access to library materials have been awarded to library faculty.

e. **Continuing Education:** Librarians have actively attended workshops, conferences and meetings on the national, state, and local levels as part of their continuing education and best practice. These conferences represent the gamut of the library profession from general association conferences to specialized conferences related to disciplines or subject areas. This shows the breadth of participation and involvement of our librarians in the field of librarianship.

Continuing education also includes university coursework that supports or compliments the expertise of the librarian. Many librarians' CV's demonstrate continued education in their field of specialization up through the attainment of a Master's degree or a Ph.D. in a discipline.

3. Analyze the extent to which the faculty meet the department's expectations for scholarly/creative activities. Identify issues in need of improvement and describe action plans.

It is clear from a review of librarians' resumes and CV's that the library faculty is active in all areas of scholarly and creative activities. This is especially the case in relation to active membership or leadership in professional library organizations. Determining the extent of the match between departmental guidelines and individual librarians is best assessed on a case-by-case basis in Annual Reviews, Tenure and Promotion Recommendations, or Post-Tenure Review documents.

a. **Recommendations**

While the library faculty is active in all areas of scholarly and creative activities the following area could use improvement.

b. **Grant writing**

In light of ongoing, statewide budget difficulties, a greater effort to secure external sources of funding could help alleviate the burden on new programs and on existing programs that face budget cuts. Furthermore, receiving grants often garners recognition on the nation/state/local level as well as within the university.

c. **Action Plan**

The library administration will encourage librarians to attend grant-writing workshops and assist in the identification of grant opportunities. It is recommended that the Departmental Guidelines for Scholarly and Creative Activity be reviewed as soon as possible. Additional activities, in which librarians commonly participate, such as book reviews, exhibits, poster sessions, performances, web pages and online guides, are not specified in these guidelines, which tend to emphasize scholarly achievements over creative achievements.

E. Faculty Service to the University and Community

1. Describe faculty involvement in service to the university and community in the last six years.

The library faculty are committed to shared governance, both in principle and practice and, therefore, provide extensive service to the university by serving on a wide range of university and library committees. As such, during the past six years librarians have contributed substantially to the university and community. See Appendix F for a list of their participation in university committees.

Library faculty also participate in the governance of the library through committee work. All department heads serve on the Library's Administrative Council, which consults with the library's dean on major policy issues. All librarians belong to the library faculty who consider all professional issues and governance and make recommendations to the dean and associate deans. Two librarians are elected annually to serve as Chair and Vice Chair. In the last three years, librarians have served on twelve faculty search committees, including the library dean's search. There are numerous standing committees that the library administration utilizes for developing policy and decision-making.

Librarians contribute to the community in a variety of ways. See Appendix H for a list of the many community service activities in which librarians are involved.

2. Analyze the extent to which the faculty meet the department's expectations for service. Identify issues in need of improvement and describe action plans.

The library's expectations for service are identified in the LARTP section on "Contributions to the Institution" which include service to the library and service to the university, and "Contributions to the Community," which may include a broad range of professional and community services.

Expectations for the evaluation of service to the institution are based on the appropriateness of the service activity and its relevance to the overall mission of the library or institution. Community service is evaluated in a broader way. As long as library faculty are engaged as professionals and bring credit to the university, their contributions meet the expectations. The library faculty meet expectations for service and hence no action plan is required.

LIBRARY PERSONNEL/NON-FACULTY

A. Non-Faculty Personnel Profile:

Analyze library personnel non-faculty (LPNF) data, including a comparison of your personnel profile to the non-faculty profiles in the university. If the data indicate a need for a response by your department, describe your plan of action. Include analysis regarding: Full and part-time LPNF, gender and ethnic composition, and student-personnel ratio/class size.

Non-faculty personnel comprise a group who is not usually included in self-study reviews. This self-study is based on the premise that, "everyone at a university should be a discoverer, a learner. That shared mission binds together all that happens on a campus."* The omission of a group twice as large as the library faculty, who are essential to the

---

*Op. cit. Boyer.

everyday operations of the library and who provide multi-functional services in every unit is indefensible and fails to portray a complete picture of the library's teaching and learning environment. There are a variety of classifications that exist to describe the different library positions not occupied by librarians (see Section VI. F. 2.); therefore, this committee has chosen to use the term "library personnel/non-faculty" because it is the most inclusive.

The following statistics are based on available data at the time this review was written.

1. **General characteristics of CSUS library personnel/non-faculty**
   (March 3, 2003, CSUS Office of Human Resources):
   Total 49 Full time, 4 part time
   Gender: 33 female, 16 male
   Ethnicity: African-American: 4, Asian: 2, Hispanic: 9, Other: 2, White: 32
   Ratio of students to library personnel/non-faculty: 583:1
2. **Comparison of CSUS library personnel/non-faculty to other populations**
   a. **CSUS (CSU Annual Library Statistics, 2001–02)**
      Total enrollment: 28,588
      Other paid staff: 56.5
      Ratio of students to CSUS other paid staff: 506:1
   b. **CSU**
      Total enrollment: 409,000
      Other paid staff: 739
      Ratio of students to CSU other paid staff: 554:1
      (1) San Francisco State University
          Total enrollment: 28,378
          Other paid staff: 59.6
          Ratio of students to other paid staff: 476:1
      (2) San Jose State University
          Total enrollment: 30,350
          Other paid staff: 48.5
          Ratio of students to other paid staff: 626:1
      (3) California State University Long Beach
          Total enrollment: 34,566
          Other paid staff: 44.0
          Ratio of students to other paid staff: 786:1
   c. **University of California, Davis**
      Total enrollment: 29,087
      Other paid staff: 173
      Ratio of students to other paid staff: 168:1
   d. **ACRL (ACRL Library Data Tables, 2001) http://www.virginia.edu/sur veys/ACRL/2001/sdphdall.pdf**
      Total FTE enrollment:
      High: 29,000
      Median: 1,549

Other paid staff
High: 87
Median: 5
Ratio to students to other paid staff:
High: 333:1
Median: 310:1

e. **ARL (Association of Research Libraries Statistics, 2001, p 17 & 46),** http://www.arl.org/stats/arlstat/index.html Ratio is derived by multiplying the total number of staff per 1000 by the percentage of support staff, i.e., 13.7 × 48.97% = 6.7, 1000/6.7 = 149. Ratio of students to support staff (median): 149:1

3. **Gender Composition**
Full-Time library personnel/non-faculty : 49 = 16 Male/ 33 Female
Part-Time library personnel/non-faculty : 4 = 1 Male/3 Female
Hourly Intermittent (HI): 1 = 1 Female

4. **Ethnic Composition**
Full-Time: 49 = 9 Latino/ 2 Asian/ 4 African American/
2 Other Non-White/ 32 Caucasian
Part-Time: 4 = 1 Other Non-White/ 3 Caucasian
Hourly Intermittent (HI): 1 = 1 Caucasian

5. **Ethnic analysis**
In each of the categories in which statistics reveal the CSUS campus to reflect a diverse student body, the percentage of library faculty representing the various categories was lower than the percentage of students represented in the category. Although the percentage of white library personnel/non-faculty (66 percent) is lower than that of the library faculty (79 percent), it is still approximately 21 percent higher than the percentage of the total white student population (45 percent). As stated previously, these demographics hinder the library's ability to provide value-enhanced services to a diverse and multicultural student body.

6. **Gender Analysis**
The 2:1 gender ratio of female (70 percent) to male (30 percent) library personnel/non-faculty falls between the ratio of library faculty (3:1) and the gender ratio of students (1:1), but comparable statistics for library personnel/non-faculty at other institutions were not available.

7. **Analysis of CSUS Library Personnel/non–Faculty to Other Populations**
The CSUS Library Personnel/non-faculty to student ratio is roughly 506 to 1. This figure compares similarly with ratios at selected CSU peer institutions (SFSU, 476:1; SJSU, 626:1; CSULB, 786:1). Among Association of Research Libraries (ARL), the median support staff to student ratio was much lower (149:1). The other paid staff to student ratio at UC Davis (168:1), whose total enrollment is comparable to CSUS enrollment, is above the median for an ARL library, but still much lower than the CSUS ratio. The CSUS library is included in the Association of College and Research Library (ACRL) statistics. It is worth mentioning that among those institutions with "high" enrollments, the ratio of students to other paid staff is 333:1, nearly half of our ratio of 506:1. This ratio makes

one-on-one contact with students — the teaching learning model governing the library's service philosophy — extremely challenging.

8. Ethnic and Gender Diversity

(CSUS Office of Human Resources, most recent statistics available at time of writing)

Total library personnel/non-faculty:		Total Students
Female, full time:	33 (64%)	
Male, full time:	16 (36%)	
Female, part time:	3 (75%)	
Male, part time:	1 (25%)	
Total Female	36 (70%)	16,867 (59%)
Total Male	17 (30%)	11,721 (41%)
American Indian, full time:	0 (0%)	
American Indian, part time:	0 (0%)	
Total	0 (0%)	286 (1%)
Asian, full time:	2 (4%)	
Asian, part time:	0 (0%)	
Total	2 (4%)	4,860 (17%)
Black, full time:	4 (8%)	
Black, part time:	0 (0%)	
Total	4 (8%)	1,715 (6%)
Filipino, full time:	0 (0%)	
Filipino, part time:	0 (0%)	
Total	0 (0%)	N/A
Hispanic, full time:	9 (18%)	
Hispanic, part time:	0 (0%)	
Total	9 (17%)	3,716 (13%)
Other, full time:	2 (4%)	
Other, part time:	1 (25%)	
Total	3 (6%)	4,288 (15%)
Pacific Islander, full time:	0 (0%)	
Pacific Islander, part time:	0 (0%)	
Total	0 (0%)	N/A
White, full time:	32 (91%)	
White, part time:	3 (75%)	
Total	35 (66%)	12,865 (45%)

B. Assess LPNF profile for the ability to offer the curriculum and to support program goals. Describe plans for addressing any identified issues.

Working independently and collaborating with other library personnel, LPNF play a vital role in the ongoing operations of the university library. They work to create an environment for optimal teaching and learning and provide indispensable services to students and faculty. Some volunteer, beyond their assigned tasks, to perform a variety of instructional activities, such as conducting library tours to help faculty, students, and patrons become cognizant of library services and collections. They contribute to CSUS patrons' ability to engage in life-long learning by providing collection development, instruction, and reference services that strengthen and develop the related tools for intellectual exploration.

C. Library Personnel/non–Faculty as teachers

    1. Analyze data available from the College Outcomes Survey (COS) and Program

Assessment Questionnaire (PAQ) [Available from the Office of Institutional Research] to identify any issues that need action. Describe plans for addressing issues.

The library is not included in these surveys. While probably most of the questions would not be relevant, a library task force should review the instrument to determine if it would provide appropriate information for informing the university and the library about the library as a program.

2. Describe how the library personnel/non-faculty is involved in professional development activities to improve and enhance their teaching effectiveness.

One of the most important elements in teaching is having expert knowledge in the subject area. Professional development opportunities enable staff to take a proactive role that impacts their work environment. With the fast-changing environment of information and technology, there has been a great need for library personnel/non-faculty to engage in professional development opportunities in order to enhance their teaching effectiveness. LPNF attend and participate in formal computer and database training, enrichment sessions, online tutorials, off campus workshops, Faculty and Staff Development workshops and CSU Seminars. Several are enrolled in career development or job-related courses through the campus Fee Waiver Program. Many hold graduate degrees in languages, sciences, arts, business, communication and education. A number teach at the college level.

The Library Staff Training Program is another opportunity for professional development. This program offers the opportunity to cross-train in other library departments for job enrichment and to gain work experience, on-the-job training, and exposure to other areas of the library. This training program also provides greater flexibility in personnel management within the library as temporary needs occur.

3. To what extent is library personnel/non-faculty using "best practices" in their roles as teachers?

The work of LPNF has assumed a much more important role in the CSUS library since the last self-study. Assignments in the areas of the reference and information desk, collections cataloging, acquisitions, document delivery, interlibrary loan, circulation, reserve and technological tasks have all expanded. Consequently, the responsibilities of LPNF in all of these areas have changed and grown, often without recognition in the employee's job description.

The primary role of LPNF as teachers is to instruct and otherwise assist library users in locating and using information resources. This instruction includes but is not limited to library orientations, tours, directional inquiries, bibliographic verification searches, navigation in electronic research databases, and technical assistance with computer hardware and software. As patrons enter the library, LPNF is frequently the initial and occasionally the only source of information for the patron. They provide learning opportunities for the patron in his or her search for better performance and new knowledge and skills.

In addition to these one-on-one teaching activities, LPNF accomplish the library's teaching mission by serving as representatives of the library to various departments on campus when dealing with matters related to university policies and procedures, Faculty and Staff Affairs issues, budget matters, Chancellor's Office correspondence, and on- and off-campus organizations (e.g., Friends of the Library, Japanese American Archival Collection Advisory Board, grants agencies, Innovative Interfaces, library vendors, etc.).

LPNF provides many functions behind the scenes that include ordering, cataloging, receiving, preparing, processing, and record-maintenance of library information resources for patron learning. These tasks have never been reviewed in terms of best practices. However, because these practices are vital for library users to achieve academic success, it is important to develop a process of recognition for these efforts. Results of this process could be included in subsequent self-study reports.

4. How are LPNF offering students a variety of learning experiences to address the diversity of student learning styles?

LPNF interacts with students both as patrons and as employees. Given the diversity of our student population, the LPNF provides instructional services based on individual needs. There are guided tours for visual learners as well as self-guided tours and telephone consultations for audio learners. Some LPNF use expertise in foreign languages to interact with the diverse student population. In addition to professional contributions supporting teaching and learning, LPNF provides students and faculty with one-on-one consultation in accessing library resources.

LPNF maintains a very special role in providing enrichment to library student employees via training, support, and mentoring. LPNF also train library student employees in handling various library services with professional skills related to: Eureka Online Catalog, electronic research databases, microform machines, audio-video equipment, copyright laws, and multimedia technologies.

5. Comment on LPNF's innovations in teaching, learning, and knowledge of current trends in academic specialties.

Because this focus has rarely been turned on LPNF, answering this question comprehensively is not possible at this time. In one unit, however, this information has been captured. Employees in the Systems Office keep abreast of technological updates and advances crucial to the current learning demands. A Systems Liaison Program has been formed so that LPNF can work with the Systems Department to maintain and develop the library's technological environment. This changing environment will add more fully to the learning process. Hopefully this program will also change the image of technology as an obstacle to the success of the patrons' goals.

6. Describe your department's process for evaluating teaching effectiveness. How are data used to enhance or improve the teaching and learning process?

Library Personnel/non-faculty have an annual review for permanent employees. Consideration should be given to include within this review a means of encouraging employees to develop their learning and teaching opportunities.

D. Library Personnel/non-faculty as Scholars

1. Describe the department's specific expectations for scholarly, creative activities.

(See #3 below)

2. Describe scholarly and creative activities of NFLP in the last six years (vita).

Neither one nor two have been considered part of the self-study previously. This information has therefore never been compiled.

3. Analyze the extent to which the LPNF meets the department's expectations

for scholarly/creative activities. Identify issues in need of improvement and describe action plans.

Even though there is no current data to analyze, we would like to provide examples of LPNF scholarly/creative activities, which should illustrate the need to comprehensively collect data in future self-studies.

All Library Personnel/non-faculty hold a Bachelor or Associate Degree in a discipline or in library and information technology. Some also hold a Master's Degree in Library Science or other subjects as well as professional degrees, and provide significant related input within the library organization.

An example of scholarly/creative activities that could be used in this analysis would be the LPNF contributions through the Library Exhibits Program. The program supports the curriculum of the university and enhances the campus and community culturally and intellectually. At the time of this report, an LPNF is chairing the exhibits committee and coordinating the program.

E. Library Personnel/non-faculty Service to the University and Community

1. Describe LPNF involvement in service to the university and community in the last six years.

This question has not been considered part of the self-study review previously. This information has therefore never been compiled. Listed below are examples of staff involvement in services to the university and community:

LPNF served on the U.S. Olympics Track and Field Trials Special Exhibits and Events Committee in 2000. This committee was responsible for planning and implementing a set of special library exhibits and events held in conjunction with the summer 2000 U.S. Olympics Track and Field Trials at CSUS. LPNF is involved in broader library planning functions such as National Library Week, Friends of the CSUS library, Japanese American Archival Committee, and the Faculty Wives and Affiliates. Others contribute their creative talents for library special events. For instance, LPNF expresses artistic abilities encompassing but not limited to poetry readings, story telling, and theatrical and musical interpretations.

2. Analyze the extent to which the library personnel/non-faculty meets the department's expectations for service.

Since no formal expectations have been identified nor data gathered, we are unable to complete this section.

F. Recommendation for Plan of Action concerning Section IV. Library Personnel/non-faculty

Because this section has never existed in this form previously, there is a lack of information needed to respond to the questions. We realize that this Section IV is an attempt to focus on a group that has not been a part of prior self-study reviews.

1. Library Administration should develop policies and procedures to capture this group's achievements and contributions to the learning and teaching process in an ongoing and organized way.

2. This section should be included in future self-study reviews.

3. Ideally, LPNF would be surveyed to discover the scope and extent of their contribution to the learning and teaching environment of the CSUS library.

4. LPNF should be encouraged to think of themselves and their work as an integral part of the teaching and learning process at CSUS.

STUDENT EMPLOYEE PROFILE

The library is the largest employer of students at CSUS. There are currently 126 Student Assistants employed in the library. Due to a lack of statistics we are unable to provide comparative gender and ethnic composition. The role of student assistants is to provide support for library personnel. Due to the relatively high faculty and LPNF to student ratios on campus, however, the role of student assistants has tended to expand as they have been assigned additional tasks and responsibilities.

One possible recommendation is that these tasks and responsibilities be assessed to determine whether student assistants are the appropriate group to perform these services, or whether these services should be assigned to other library employees.

Many students are employed at the library for a substantial portion of their time on campus, enabling library personnel to nurture and mentor many students over time. The interactive learning environment in the library helps shape the future careers of many students and provides mutually beneficial learning and teaching opportunities.

SECTION V. GOVERNANCE PROCESS AT THE PROGRAM, COLLEGE & UNIVERSITY LEVELS

A. Describe faculty/staff involvement in planning, developing, and implementing library policies

1. Indicate the role of the library director and dean in library governance.

The library dean is the chief administrative officer and spokesperson of the university library, and reports to the provost and vice president for Academic Affairs. The dean chairs the Library Executive Group (composed of the dean, two associate deans, and the administrative analyst specialist, i.e., dean's assistant), and the Library Administrative Council (composed of all faculty- and MPP-level department heads), and participates on university committees as a representative of the library.

The library dean oversees library planning and policy development in a collegial environment, and oversees development of annual budget requests and administers the library's budget. The dean also has primary responsibility for external fund development for the library, including gifts, grants and contracts.

The library dean is responsible for personnel matters, including coordinating and supervising the administrative duties of the departments and units, and making independent recommendations on all library appointments, as well as retention, tenure, and promotion requests. The dean also participates in and/or presides over all-employee meetings to solicit and share information about current and future issues affecting the library.

2. Indicate the role of library associate deans in governance.

Library associate deans report to and work in close consultation with the library dean in planning programs and services. They advise and assist the dean in the development and implementation of overall policies affecting all aspects of library operations.

Library associate deans serve on the Executive Group, conduct Library Administrative Council meetings on a rotating basis with the dean, and participate on university committees as representatives of the library. They also are involved in various aspects of human resource administration, strategic and long-range planning, and fiscal administration.

Library associate deans carry out a variety of other assignments and projects at the request of the library dean. They oversee the work of relevant department heads as the department heads attempt to achieve departmental goals.

Library associate deans seek to maintain effective relations with faculty, non-faculty personnel, and student employees both personally and through the quality of library services.

3. Indicate the role of library faculty in library governance.

Library faculty members assist in the recommendation of library policies and procedures through participation in departmental and library-wide meetings. They also participate in library standing committees, ad hoc committees, and other venues that help plan, develop and implement library policies. Library faculty members also serve on the CSUS and CSU Faculty Senates and on university and system-wide committees.

Library faculty members hold monthly meetings presided over by the faculty chair who is elected by the body to serve a one-year term. The chair has the authority to call special meetings of the library faculty any time it is deemed necessary. Library faculty meetings deal with issues such as professional status, management, and matters pertinent to policies, actions, and the well being of the library and library faculty. Library faculty members also provide the dean with proposals and viewpoints for decisions. The library dean and associate deans participate in the library faculty meetings, but do not have voting privileges.

4. Indicate the role of library personnel/non-faculty in library governance.

LPNF serve on both library standing committees and ad hoc committees involving daily operations of the library. They also make recommendations to their department heads with respect to planning, developing, and implementing library policies. The LPNF also serve on university committees.

LPNF have not consistently served on the library administrative council and have felt only a limited capability to influence library governance there. With encouragement from the dean, however, LPNF have recently re-instituted formal LPNF meetings that are somewhat analogous to the faculty meetings. The intent is to provide a forum for discussion of issues that affect LPNF in the library and to facilitate more direct input on LPNF concerns to the dean and associate deans, who are invited to the meetings but do not have voting privileges. Also, an LPNF representative now attends and contributes to the library administrative council, another action encouraged by the dean.

5. Indicate whether the library has a formalized set of rules or procedures for departmental governance (If so, please include such guidelines as an appendix to the self-study)

The library's faculty role in shared governance is under the authority of the CSUS ARTP Policy and the library's ARTP policy and procedures. Most decisions of the faculty as a group and as individuals must follow a "chain of command" through the department heads, the Library Administrative Council, and the associate deans and the dean. The library lacks a formalized set of governance rules or procedures pertaining to Library Personnel/non-faculty and student employees.

B. Describe student involvement in the library governance process

1. Student library users

The involvement of student library users in library governance processes is rather indirect. Although all fees charged by the library are regularly reviewed by the university's Student Fee Advisory Committee — which can result in changes to fees and their use — the library has no formal mechanism for students to participate in library governance. See Section II., Reference Services and Information Access, E. for methods of informal student input into library operations.

2. Library student employees and their role in library governance

Student employees are actively involved in the governance of the library. For example, there are two student representatives on the Library's Student Employee Advisory Committee (SEAC), which recommends policies and procedures for library student employees. The two student representatives are an integral part of the committee. Their perspective is sought, valued, and often becomes the basis for how SEAC proceeds.

Student members of SEAC were involved in developing the revised library student salary pay schedule. And recently the student SEAC members assisted in making recommendations and clarifications for the new edition of the student employee handbook. In addition, student committee members worked to develop a student evaluation form used by supervisors of student employees.

The library encourages participation of all its student employees in library discussions. Student employees in several departments are involved in the development and revision of their departments' policies and procedures manuals. Student employees will also have an active voice in the fiscal planning of the library in light of the budget reductions that have had a direct impact on the library's student employee allocations (see Section VI. F. 3.).

Student employees offer a vital viewpoint on many aspects of their departments and on the library as a whole. Their contributions to the overall success of the library are essential to the library's day-to-day operation, and they are appreciated and valued by everyone in the library.

C. Comment on the relationships of the library with the university

The university library is generally considered to be equivalent to the colleges and participates in the numerous governance activities of CSUS through representatives and committees. The library dean represents the interests of the university library, meeting regularly with campus administration and peers. Information is disseminated at these meetings. Action items are also a product of these meetings.

The library dean meets regularly with the provost/vice president of Academic Affairs, who delegates assignments and receives reports about the library. The library dean also participates in the Deans' Council twice a month, the university's Administrative Council monthly, and meets with college department chairs once a month.

The library dean reports on the above meetings as needed to the Library's Administrative Council. Minutes of the Administrative Council circulate to all employees. Department heads also report on Administrative Council meetings in their own department meetings.

The university provost/vice president of Academic Affairs evaluates the library dean's performance once a year. The dean's performance is also reviewed campus-wide every five years. At the faculty level, a library senator represents the interests of the library faculty at the Faculty Senate. The library senator may report on the Senate meetings through minutes, circulated by email, and is also given the chance to report verbally at library faculty meetings. The library senator is elected by the library faculty to serve a two-year term and can be re-elected twice.

The university library's primary patron base consists of campus students, faculty and staff. Some of our resources and services to the campus community are as follows: use of library materials, both in-house and remote, use of library as a study space, interlibrary loan, circulation, reserves, and multimedia, use of exhibit space, gallery and library exhibits, archives and special collections, tours and instruction, reference and research assistance, and online curriculum library services.

The university library also provides most of these services to the Sacramento and regional community.

Recommendations

1. Revise the mission of the CSUS library.

The current library mission statement does not sponsor the promotion of an active learning environment for students, staff and faculty. The library mission statement should be brought up to date and be more aligned with the university mission.

The current mission statement is as follows: The primary purpose of the CSUS library is to support the quest for knowledge as well as the information needs of the students, faculty, and staff. The library also serves as a major regional information resource center.

A proposed revision of the mission statement is as follows: The mission of the CSUS library is to promote the life of the mind and the vitality of the spirit by fostering critical reflection of self, others, and society, intellectual curiosity, organized and serendipitous discovery, new forms of scholarly communication, instantaneous access to intricate, multidimensional knowledge networks, equal access to information, and respect for diversity in teaching and learning styles. The library's mission is guided by the fundamental values of CSUS, which reflect its identity as a public, regional, comprehensive, and metropolitan university.

2. Examine the library's current governance model and decision-making processes to ensure that the library operates effectively, efficiently, and responsively to change.

3. Find ways to make the governance structure more transparent, flexible, and responsive to the needs of all library employees.

4. Develop a current strategic plan as a follow-up to the recommendations put forth in this self-study. Review and assess the recommendations of the last self-study, as well as the changes that were implemented.

5. Review hierarchical structure in light of alternative structures (See Appendix). Invite speakers whose institutions have implemented flattened governance structures, such as University of Arizona Library Dean Carla Stoffle.

SECTION VI. INSTITUTIONAL SUPPORT/RESOURCES

Please describe adequacy of support, strengths, and concerns about the following resources and services:

A. Library

The library's main academic programs described in Section II are supported by other, facilitating operations throughout the library that are too numerous and diverse to have been fully described in the body of this self-study. These operations, too, contribute directly and importantly to the library's teaching strategies and learning objectives. Furthermore, given the integrated nature of the library's main academic programs, the contribution of each facilitating operation is magnified by its various connections to each of the program-level processes. These operations include library special events, exhibits, faculty liaison activities, shelving, administration, and many others.

The strengths and concerns expressed in the body of the self-study regarding the library's academic programs, therefore, extend as well to the network of facilitating operations in the library itself that support those programs.

B. Computer/Technology

1. Technology/resources for meeting program and faculty needs.

Access to technology and network resources is adequate. Most of the technology and resources needed to meet the library and faculty needs are provided and supported by the Library Information Systems (LIS) Department. The LIS Department has a good working relationship with UCCS. However, we would like to be more involved in the decision making process regarding new campus technologies and become more of a partner in the creation of new information technology services. The campus needs a formal process for providing input into those processes. The library also welcomes all UCCS communications that make us aware of new technologies available to the campus community.

The library would also like to see improved publicity of emerging technologies. The library is undergoing tremendous changes brought about by technology. It would be advantageous to strengthen the relationship the library has with campus computing, which could lead to the creation of new cooperative services and programs. The library needs to stay aware of campus software license agreements and the process for requesting additional software licenses. We would also like to partner with UCCS to identify potential external funding as well as consortial licensing agreements for technology services. Also, the library would like to be included in future BATS funding.

2. Services provided by UMS and UCCS for faculty and students.

The library also has an especially strong relationship with Computing, Communications, and Media Services, which also shares space in the library building, and with whom we collaborate on a variety of regular services and special projects.

UCCS courses are very good overall. UMS equipment is good. Technical support for all media in the Library's Media Center (LMC) is very good. The LMC also has a very good working relationship with UMS.

C. Student Support Services (e.g., Admissions and Records, Advising Center, Learning Skills Center, Union, Multicultural Center, Educational Opportunities Program, Writing Center)

Partnering with other university entities is critical in providing quality services, and the library maintains strong and useful relationships with many other university student support services organizations. For example, the library works cooperatively with One Card, University Support Services, Cashiering, Accounting, UMS, the Bookstore, the Multi-Cultural Center, and others.

Here are some specific examples: The campus OneCard ID allows students to use their PrintSmart accounts for printing in the library and their OneCard for photocopies. Cooperation between the Reserve Book Room and the campus Bookstore permits rush orders of books needed for classes. Disabled Student Services also has a long and close relationship with the library such that both programs work together to provide the best possible services to our disabled users.

The library has been pleased with the quantity and quality of services provided by these and many other campus entities that help us assist students, staff, faculty, and administrators.

D. Faculty Support Services (e.g., Center for Teaching and Learning, Computing, Communications, and Media)

The library also maintains good working relationships with faculty support services. This is demonstrated by the presence of such services in the library building, including the Center for Teaching and Learning, the Office of Community Collaboration, the Women's Resource Center, and the Serna Center.

Instructional Design provided by UMS is very good. Outreach and publicity of services could be improved. Many times library employees may not become aware of all of the services offered by CTL, UCCS and UMS. CTL and the Library's Online Curriculum Library Services (OCLS) have a very strong working relationship and have been involved in numerous cooperative projects.

E. Physical Facilities and Equipment

The upkeep and operation of the library facility is an ongoing project that often calls for major equipment overhauls, frequent construction projects, large electrical upgrades, urgent plumbing and HVAC repairs, and other major alterations and improvements. The library appreciates and benefits from the responsiveness of the University Facilities Management department to unexpected equipment or building emergencies in the library. We also recognize and appreciate their pro-active awareness of the library's near-term and long-range maintenance requirements.

Facilities Management has been especially helpful in several recent major library projects, including their participation in and support of the 2002 architectural feasibility study for renovating the library; special programs and events in the library that have required space reconfigurations; conversion of the Reserve Book Reading Room into a high-tech computer innovation center; and numerous other requests and projects.

Likewise, thorough daily custodial care in the library is extremely important to the library's employees and users. Custodial care, along with other regular operations such as requests for cost estimates, work orders, etc., are generally handled in a timely way, and communication between the Library and Facilities Management is usually clear and productive.

F. Financial Resources (faculty, staff, operating expenses)

1. Enrollment and faculty numbers support of the curriculum

The library's faculty librarians handle the information and research needs of the entire faculty and student enrollment of the university. Unlike some support services on the campus, the library provides significant services directly to the faculty as well as to the students. See sections II, IV, and V for more information about faculty numbers and support of the curriculum.

The number and hours of service of our part-time librarians, who provide many of the same teaching and learning services as the full-time faculty, have been reduced as a result of budget cuts, and additional reductions are likely as deeper budget cuts are announced.

2. Program staff

The library's non-faculty personnel occupy positions in a wide variety of classifications, including library assistants, information technology consultants, administrative support assistants, administrative support coordinator, administrative analysts/specialists, visual resources specialist, analyst/programmer, and graphic designer (some at various levels within those classifications). These highly qualified individuals handle numerous operations crucial to the library's academic programs and to the mission of the university.

Also, the library has customarily employed as many as 120–130 (approximately 45 FTE) students whose work is essential to the smooth operation of the library. The number of student employees is also expected to decrease yearly as a result of anticipated budget cuts. See Sections IV and V for more information about non-faculty personnel and student employees. The library also has 5 managerial (MPP) positions.

3. Total operating expense budget (include statement about processes used for effective use of budget)

In the spring of 2003, the library had a mid-year budget cut of 6.5 percent ($343,273) of its operating budget. The largest single portion of this cut was in the form of a reduction in student employee hours. Because the CSU system considers libraries to be "non-instructional" entities, the library budget was cut an extra 1.0 percent above the reductions to the instructional colleges of 5.5 percent. The library administration believes that it is erroneous to classify libraries as non-instructional, and hopes that this self-study will help demonstrate that libraries are in fact places of instruction where teaching and learning occur regularly.

The library's total budget for 2003–04 is $7,210,930, which is 4.7 percent less than 2002–03. At this writing, there is no certainty that mid-year budget cuts will not be imposed this spring, but it is estimated that cuts in the library's budget for 2004–05 might be 13 percent or more. Furthermore, because the library's materials budget (for books, journals, online resources, etc.) in past years has been a "designated line item," it has been protected from cuts. The library's yearly materials budget has consistently been over $2 million, and is currently the fourth largest in the CSU system. When formulating the 2003–04 budget, however, the CSUS administration was forced by the economic conditions to remove the materials budget from the designated line item category. This means that the materials budget is now subject to any budget cuts that may be imposed.

While this new development gives the library more flexibility to deal with cuts, it greatly increases the total amount of any cuts we sustain.

To better address the 2003 mid-year budget cuts and plan for the budget reductions anticipated for coming years, the library dean formed a "budget task force" composed of the persons who have customarily been at the top of the decision-making process of budget formulation in the library, and who have the broadest budget-related responsibilities across the library. These persons are the dean, the two associate deans, the head of systems (who determines the technology needs throughout the library), the library's administrative analyst/specialist for accounting and budgeting, and the dean's assistant (administrative analyst/specialist). Together, these persons are very aware of the conditions in the areas for which they are responsible, and can make accurate observations and recommendations about the needs for those areas.

In the past, these persons have contributed significantly to finalizing the library's annual expenditure plans, but they customarily acted more or less in isolation, and passed their information to the dean for final decision making. Forming these persons into a task force has generated very insightful discussions and idea sharing to develop new options, clarify alternatives, and reach consensus about the library's expenditure plan. Through regular meetings, the task force is able to monitor and assess the effectiveness of the library's expenditure plan and make minor or major adjustments to the plan as needed.

3

MEANINGFUL LIBRARY ASSESSMENT

After the 2004 Self-Study

The 2004 CSUS self-study was hard work for the library staff, but it was singularly uplifting. We broke new ground in teaching and learning for the library, for CSUS, and for the CSU system. We asserted that we are educators, and chose to use the CSUS self-study guidelines developed for instructional departments as the framework for the library's self-study instead of submitting the customary, loosely structured library program reviews composed merely of tabulations of activity levels that say virtually nothing about the teaching skills of our library staff, and even less about the effect of library activities on the processes of teaching and learning. As mentioned in Chapter 2, we designated three library services as "academic programs" that we believed were comparable to the academic programs in the university's instructional departments. We knew well, of course, that some of the other services provided by the library are equally eligible as academic programs, and those will be reviewed in future self-studies.

The university had joined the Urban University Portfolio Project, mentioned earlier, before our self-study, so the groundwork was already laid for the library's self-evaluation in which we adopted the language of teaching and learning as it is spoken at CSUS, and put us on a fast track to move CSUS from its "culture of learning" to a "culture of assessment." According to Covey (2002), "Creating a culture of assessment is not simply a matter of developing and deploying new measures or acquiring new skills. It means changing the mind set and daily activity of librarians and support staff." The 2004 self-study became the CSUS library's formal entrée into that culture.

I think we made some good advances for the library in our transitional self-study, not the least of which was the adoption of the CSUS language of teaching and learning, which included our use of the same self-study outline used by the instructional faculty. Portions of the self-study outline were extremely problematic for us, however. These were the sections about assessing and measuring the effectiveness of our programs. Although we had plenty of data from many sources regarding library activity levels, including numerous surveys, circulation statistics, information literacy instructional sessions, and the like, we had no way of correlating student library usage to their overall academic performance in their disciplines.

A major finding of our self-study, then, was that the data from the library's instruments could not substantiate any measurable positive or negative effect of the library's academic programs on the overall academic performance of the students who participated in our programs. While instructional departments have ample quantitative data to validate their teaching effectiveness by assessing the learning of their students through their learning objectives, assignments, papers, exams, and presentations, which establish their grade point averages (GPAs) in their courses, the library could *not* put forward any real data that demonstrated the effect of our programs on student learning.

As a result, for the next self-study, in 2010, the staff committed themselves to develop methods that would demonstrate empirically the effect of the library's academic programs on (1) the overall performance of CSUS students, and (2) the goals and effectiveness of the university. After the 2004 self-study, we began working with the CSUS Office of Institutional Research to compare the GPAs of senior students who were frequent library users with the GPAs of students who were infrequent library users. We gathered some initial data from student samples, but they were too small to derive a valid correlation. The results, however, suggested that there was a positive relationship. As an unscientific poll taken at CSUS before I left, the CSUS assessment movement turned out to reinforce the assessment at Hong Kong Baptist University as soon as I arrived.

Assessment and ALA Standards

Of course, ALA does not accredit libraries, but in the 20th century, ALA standards for libraries made it relatively simple to calculate a library's rightful share of its institutional budget: the library director would look up ALA's current percentage of the college or university budget that should be earmarked for libraries in the areas of staffing, collections, degrees offered, student enrollment, and so on, and then go arm-wrestle with the VP.

For example, *Standards for College Libraries* in its 1995 edition included ALA–approved budget formulas for (1) collection size based on student and faculty FTE; undergraduate major or minor fields; master's and doctoral fields; (2) number of librarians based on the number of book volumes, and FTE students; (3) size of buildings according to space for users, books, and staff; seating capacity, and total square footage. My favorite ALA formula, of course, was the library's annual operating budget, which was to be calculated as a percentage of the parent institution's total budget, which "shall be at least six percent of the total institutional expenditure for educational and general purposes" (ALA, *Standards for College Libraries*, 1995).

In those days, and even at present, I would kill for a 6 percent budget. And, as if demanding the icing on the cake from university administrators, ALA added, "The library shall receive its appropriation at the beginning of the budget cycle for the institution." ALA was rather delusional about all this and tried to sound firm and tough by using verbs like *must* and *shall*, but university administrators weren't fooled a bit. They brushed off the *must*s and *shall*s, as they saw fit. Too bad ALA does not accredit libraries, but even if it did, no one would pay attention, at least not without good data. For libraries, accreditation standards or anything like them will simply not work unless more champions like Howard Simmons arise in commissions of higher education associations, or when university administrators learn that librarians are educators, and fine ones at that.

The "standards" appeared to be something close to accreditation criteria, and although no ALA sanctions would be imposed if a library were below any of the standards, self-studies were a little easier to complete when we could refer to these criteria produced and blessed by the ALA. They provided some leverage at least for librarians to have a meaningful dialogue with university administrators. The "standards," of course, were best guesses by the ALA, and in fact were meaningless because they proved little about the quality of collections or services; nor did they relate in any clear way to the missions, objectives, and effectiveness of the parent institutions; nor did the standards establish any clear relationship to teaching, learning, and research in those institutions. In addition, university administrators knew perfectly well that the standards were only recommendations with little solid grounding in the assessment processes of academic institutions, and lacking any sanctioning power by the ALA. So when bad budget times hit, and often even in good budget circumstances, university administrators felt free to cut library funds liberally.

ALA put less and less stock in its own standards. The message to librarians in the field was, "You're on your own; make the best deals you can with your administrators; work out your own self-study assessments with fear and dread." Self-studies, however, were a lot more promising in those halcyon days when we had at least some objective criteria to fall back on. Library administrators at least had some concrete numbers supplied by a major library association acting with a certain measure of clout and standards that might serve as a substitute accreditation tool similar to those of the instructional programs, departments, and schools.

ALA still maintains weak standards for libraries. The 2004 *Standards for Libraries in Higher Education* "apply to all types of libraries in higher education," and claims that the standards "can be used as part of a librarian's analytical structure as appropriate." This sounds flat to me; this sounds like the library is turning inward, not outward. The last thing we need is more isolation. Sure, there is plenty of verbiage about collaboration with faculty, student surveys, establishing library goals "in the context of the institutional goals," benchmarking, input and output measures, and outcomes assessment, but the process is flat, unconnected to the hard-number empirical assessment techniques instructional faculty apply to assess their students, who also happen to be *our* students too.

In the current ALA "standards," there is little constructiveness or daring to motivate librarians to act like university-level educators and create real fusion of teaching and valid assessment among all the players: librarians and other library staff, instructional faculty, students, and university administrators.

When ALA discovered that the VPs did not want to arm-wrestle anymore because institutional budgets were shrinking at a shocking rate while library materials kept getting more and more costly, it realized that ALA was not a library accrediting agency anyway. ALA scrapped the budget percentage ploy and told library directors to work it out with their VPs. Somehow. The budget rug was pulled out from under us. Although ALA was never a library accrediting agency, maybe now is the time for ALA to step up and make some serious changes in the profession.

Meaningful Assessment

Like any other university department, a library is obligated to promote the university's mission to teach students effectively. As stated in Chapter 2, the university chooses its performance measures, and the library then must develop ways to contribute demonstrably to those objectives by quantitatively assessing its contribution, and then increasing it.

I think almost everyone, including academics and administrators, believes intuitively that students will perform better academically if they use the library than if they do not, or its corollary — students who use a library will perform better academically than those who do not. Libraries will certainly enhance a university's effectiveness to the degree that this belief is true. But where is the proof? Customary library assessment practices of simply recording the rising numbers of library "activity levels," such as the number of new books in the collection, book circulations, or reference questions answered fall short of evaluating a library's positive effect on student learning, and do not allow for any meaningful assessment of a library's contribution to the university's effectiveness.

New Meanings, New Measures

Around the turn of the current millennium, ALA undertook several new ways to measure the effectiveness of libraries. Truly dedicated library leaders produced a flurry of new data-gathering "products," including E-metrics, SAILS (Standardized Assessment of Information Literacy), COUNTER, MINES (Measuring the Impact of Networked Electronic Services), E-QUAL, and Digiqual.

I use the word *products* because these new measurements and meanings are based on user surveys, customer satisfaction, and qualitative feedback instead of quantitative outcomes for library users. Kyrillidou (2004) observes, "These [business model] elements are what make the New Measures initiative new.... Ultimately we have experienced what many who are engaged in collaborative work with a strong commitment to ... real progress. We now have new ways for evaluating libraries. These methods definitely have their contextual limitations, but we are farther along compared to where we were ten years ago." Kyrillidou also reports that now "libraries can engage users in extensive dialogue ... to engage people into 'deep listening.'"

Real progress? New Measures? I think not. "Deep listening" sounds like an Al Franken routine on *Saturday Night Live*. I cannot imagine a professor using his/her time to engage in "deep listening" sessions while his/her students attempt to get their grades changed.

Furthermore, sheer collaboration, commitment, and action do not necessarily produce progress. For instance, to me LibQUAL by itself is LibQUACK. It is described, unfortunately, as "the most mature of these models." According to the ARL, "It is a suite of services that libraries use to solicit, track, understand, and act upon users' *opinions of service quality* [emphasis added]. Results have been used to develop a better understanding of perceptions of library service quality, interpret user feedback systematically over time, and identify best practices across institutions" (http://www.arl.org/stats/initiatives/index.shtml).

To be sure, surveys, questionnaires, and focus groups are very common methods used to gather data for library "assessment," which can illuminate for us the students' *perceptions* of their engagement with the library's services and staff. These perceptions can fill in much valuable background information that we need to know about the behavior of students in the library. These student perceptions, however, remain anecdotal and imprecise in any attempt to measure empirically the correlation between students' library involvement and their overall academic performance in their subject fields. We must have empirical, quantitative data that correlate student library usage with student academic performance, linked to their GPAs. Touchy-feely student emotions just won't suffice.

Surveys and Such

Surveys, benchmarking, user groups, and their ilk are always suspect. It's like trying to describe a clothespin inside a burlap bag: You can't be sure what you're holding. Instructional faculty don't evaluate their students based on self-reporting surveys of themselves and their intellectual growth in their courses. Faculty evaluate their students based on the students' "deliverables": papers, exams, presentations, projects, and classroom participation. And this all comes out in the GPA wash. GPAs have no provision for direct student input. Customer satisfaction, or the lack thereof, has nothing to do with GPAs. If we actually believe that students who use the library perform better academically than students who don't, let's measure that instead of deep listening. This chapter shows that we *can* measure that now.

Likewise, comparisons of a library's characteristics through benchmarking with those of its peer institutions can tell us something about the organizations themselves, but say little about product quality. Gathering perennial statistics on the rising numbers of reference questions, book circulations, and gate counts really says nothing about a library's directly positive effect on student learning. And these days, reporting quotients of students' "information literacy" derived from library instruction programs has become popular. But, as mentioned earlier, even though measures of information literacy are quantitative, they generally remain isolated data that are not normally correlated with the students' overall academic success or university effectiveness.

None of these methods can substantiate the effect of a specific library's academic programs on student learning, which raises doubts about the effect library programs have on the mission of their institutions. There must be a direct linkage between student GPAs and their usage of library services and materials. As a classroom instructor, I could fairly evaluate the learning of my students. It was my job to do so. I knew how to assess their assignment results. Grades, of course, can be inaccurate for a variety of reasons, but be that as it may, it is the way academic institutions evaluate the success of their students and their institutional missions. Without GPAs, no other feasible, reasonable measure will do. I learned that truth when I received my high school teaching certificate. If the GPA is the approved rating of students, the library must graft itself into the GPA model.

It should not be difficult. It is not that the GPAs are an absolutely perfect evaluation of student performance, but it's the one system in place almost everywhere. Until a more fair evaluation model appears, librarians must align their evaluations of student learning in libraries by devising mathematical ways to correlate student library usage with their GPAs. It's the only sheet hanging on the clothesline, and it works well enough for libraries to hang along with it.

Libraries must patch into GPAs to validate the true effectiveness of library instruction, and to determine if libraries are to remain relevant in academe. We are divided from university missions because we have no quantitative measure for our effect on direct student performance. Libraries need solid empirical data, or at least inferentially via a reliable correlation factor, that library usage does, after all, contribute positively to student performance and, thereby, to the university's effectiveness. To the degree that libraries cannot do that, I believe they are at risk in these increasingly unfriendly budget times, and with so many commercial competitors in the information marketplace. Why should a university president or provost give me more money for library services if I have no quantitative data to substantiate a meaningful positive impact on students who use the library? We're already at a disadvantage because we "don't teach," supposedly. We must disabuse our colleagues of their error, and GPA is the answer.

Institutional Research

The CSUS self-study showed us that academic libraries must devise meaningful new library assessment methods equivalent to those used by instructional academic departments to measure the real effect of libraries and librarians on student academic performance.

After the self-study was completed, the library and the university's Office of Institutional Research (OIR) began developing ways to measure the academic success of students who use the library's services compared with students who do not. This involved making the library's computers talk to the university's computers so that our data on library usage could be linked to the student performance data on the university's mainframes. This could allow us to derive a correlation between library usage and student performance, which can then tie library programs to the university's effectiveness measures, such as recruitment, retention and regular progress to graduation ("the new 3 Rs"), and grade point averages. We knew that if we could gather the data and calculate a correlation between our students' library usage and their academic success in the university, we could strengthen the correlation by improving library programs and services according to what the data would tell us.

Historical Approaches

After the self-study at CSUS, we began looking at assessment methods that would connect student library usage to overall student academic performance as reflected in their GPAs. I began to feel jealous that only teaching faculty can definitively measure the academic performance of students that I might have helped in my capacity as a librarian and a library administrator. But how would we make that all-important connection between time well spent on library resources and time spent in the classroom?

We found out that correlating GPAs and library usage is nothing new. We began looking for assessment methods that would correlate library instruction with GPAs, and found an important paper by Elizabeth Mezick (2007), a CPA and assistant professor in the Center for Business Research (CBR) at Long Island University. Mezick resurrected several studies, some of which were decades old, but which nevertheless pointed in the direction we were going. Some of these studies were conducted before the advent of the "sophisticated" and very expensive library management systems we now use to churn out all kinds of statistics, but which still don't talk with other data warehouses on campuses that could logically measure the impact of library services beyond the stacks, the reference desks, the information commons, and the information literacy sessions. With today's technology, it would seem to be much easier to match tens of thousands of data to seek a correlation between library usage and student GPAs, but that isn't happening because we don't demand it of our library automation vendors.

These studies, mostly from the 1960s through the 1980s, were conducted largely as manual processes, yet they established correlations between library usage and student retention rates, GPAs, gender, academic year, and academic program. Barkey's 1965 project collected book call slips from closed stacks and arranged the slips by the student ID numbers (evidently privacy issues and practices were more sensible then). The university records department provided a complete list of students, also arranged by their IDs. The library staff counted the number of call slips for each student and marked the total number of books checked out for each student. Barkey stated that his study "seems to indicate that more of the better students use the library and that the lower the grade point average, the fewer library withdrawals," but he added that the correlation between GPAs and books borrowed was not very reliable.

Kramer and Kramer (1968) found a statistically meaningful correlation between book circulation and student retention among a freshman class. True, student retention is not precisely the same as raising academic performance; nevertheless, the same forms of service that increase retention can certainly serve to positively influence overall student academic performance. The problem is in the measuring. Kramer and Kramer found "no significant GPA advantage" among science and engineering students. This is not surprising in that science and engineering students tend to gather their learning in the labs more than in the library. The art majors in the research of Kramer and Kramer, however, measured at 2.37 GPA for library users and 2.10 for students who did not use the library. Agriculture student library users registered 2.13 GPA and non-users measured at 1.70 GPA. Across the arts and agriculture majors, of "the freshmen doing 'A' work, 80 per cent used the library."

Hiscock (1986) found a "positive relationship" between student academic performance and frequent use of library catalogs: "Those who reported frequent usage of library catalogues performed better academically than those who did not report such frequent use of library catalogues."

Knapp (1996) wisely observed that "students attain library competence ... only when they actually use the library and only when their use of it is significantly related to what they consider the real business of college, that is, substantive content of courses" (p. 39). So Knapp's project (1996) involved "exposing" one group of students to carefully devised "library experiences." The study demonstrated that students exposed to library skills programs showed higher GPAs, higher retention, and higher GRE scores when compared to the students that were not given such programs.

Mezick (2007) phrased our position precisely: "Rarely does empirical research connecting student outcomes with campus services and resources mention libraries. Performance indicators are needed that demonstrate the academic library's impact on desired educational outcomes, as well as methods to measure them. Libraries need to be able to demonstrate how expenditures for resources and services result in significant contributions to academic and social environments that positively impact institutional outcomes." Well stated! We must capture our return on investment (ROI).

We also found the encouraging study *School Libraries and Student Achievement in Ontario* (2006), which was a collaboration project of People for Education, the Ontario Library Association, and the Queen's University Faculty of Education. The project tracked "results for school library staffing, hours open, collections, and fundraising." Data were gathered school by school to determine if there were a positive correlation between increased achievement among schoolchildren in grades 3 and 6 "on provincial tests and school library staff and resources." The findings included:

- Grade 3 and 6 students in schools with teacher-librarians are more likely to report that they enjoy reading.
- Schools with trained library staff are more likely to have a higher proportion of grade 6 students who attained a level 3 or higher on reading tests (the level 3 achievement meets the provincial standard).
- Schools without trained library staff tend to have lower achievement on the grades 3 and 6 reading tests (both in terms of average achievement and attaining level 3 or higher).

I certainly believe congruent results can be obtained at the tertiary level, even though many college students have converted their innocence regarding the sheer joy of learning into getting out of school as fast as possible to secure lucrative careers.

And, sadly, some of Knapp's (1996) comments about faculty involved in his project are still up to date: "These library experiences are not really valued by some instructors. We suspect that their students are aware of this and therefore slight the library assignments."

The Review Committee

Our self-study faculty review panel members, on the other hand, were quite complimentary about our efforts and the directions we took in the self-study. We received ten commendations from the panel. Here are some of them:

The library is commended for developing major innovations in the Self-Study Report that focus on the language of teaching and learning; developing new library assessment measures; and including a section addressing LPNF.

The library is commended for offering a good variety of methods for presenting information on library resources to different styles of learners (including guided tours, self-guided tours, and virtual tours).

We commend the Library Instructional Services' effort, requiring extensive time, to develop and implement an Information Competence Program in WebCT.

We commend the library for offering a good variety of discipline-specific methods of assistance to faculty and students through hands-on instruction in labs, drop-in workshops for individuals, subject guides and handouts on the library website.

All library personnel continually provide courteous and professional service to library users. This is especially commendable because of a student-to-staff ratio of 334:1, which is higher than comparable institutions.

The panel also made a number of recommendations, including:

We recommend that the library revise its 1998 mission statement to better reflect the goal of integrating the library more actively into the processes of teaching and learning.

Library administration should work closely with faculty to specify clear guidelines for evaluation of librarians as teachers for the RTP (retention, tenure, and promotion) assessment process.

Increase outreach activities to both students and faculty through additional advertising of library resources and discipline-specific assistance. This should be done at the campus level and department level.

The Review Team recommends an assessment of the Information Competence Program process should be performed in order to determine how effective it is in addressing the IC requirement.

The Library Instruction and Information Use Department should initiate ways to make the campus community more aware of the Information Competence requirement for students. Departments and faculty should be encouraged to integrate IC concepts into key major courses within the discipline.

The library should collaborate with the university to develop a method to officially record that a student has passed the Information Competence requirement.

Face to Face

Despite the commendations and good recommendations, in a discussion with the Library Administration after the review, the panel had difficulty perceiving the processes of collection development as an academic program. The panel made two recommendations regarding the Library Collections and Information Organization section of the self-study:

The Collections Department should build on the mission of the Self-Study by further explaining and justifying the new direction proposed and clarify both the direct and indirect ways in which Collections functions as a teaching and learning segment of the library.

The Collections Department should operationalize the concept of a "meaningful" and "significant" collection, including special collections by developing guidelines for collections.

"Downer"

Here we clearly failed to educate the members of the review panel that collection development is a crucially important process of teaching and learning, as well as an essential library academic program. Instead, we described a number of surveys and statistics. It is quite clear that we did not go far enough in the self-study to convey the crucial points of collection development. We did not explain that the intellectual processes followed by collection development librarians are quite comparable to processes used by instructional faculty when they create learning objectives for their students, develop proposals for new courses and programs, incorporate their research into their teaching, and lead their students through the complexities of their disciplines. One of the purposes of this book is to correct this misassumption among CSUS teaching faculty and university administrators.

Few library programs are more important or specific to student learning and faculty research than collecting learning materials, properly describing them in the catalog, and organizing these resources for easy location on the shelves. A clear, explicit statement to the panel about the role of collection development in teaching and learning, along with discussions, could have avoided the panel's disappointing response to collection development as a library academic program.

Library Collections and Information Organization

Using assessment data, analyze the effectiveness of your program including the ability of students to meet: (1) the department's learning expectations; (2) the university's learning goals; (3) writing and reading standards in the major; (4) computer/information competence standards.

The university routinely surveys students and faculty for various purposes. Occasionally survey questions are included that concern use of the library and its collections. We were able to locate five such surveys that yielded information relevant to the library's collections: the 1999 CSUS Student Needs and Priorities Survey (SNAPS); the National Survey of Student Engagement 2002 (NSSE); CASPER (Computer Assisted Student Phone Entry Registration) Fall 2002 Survey; and the 1999–2000 CSUS Faculty Survey. Also, in 2001–2002, the library did a user survey with the assistance of the Institute for Social Research. Results of those surveys that pertain to library collections are summarized below.

SNAPS 1999

This survey is directed by the chancellor's office every 4 years. Its purpose is to look at many aspects of the student experience at CSU campuses. Students are asked to rate both the importance of a service/characteristic and the quality of that same service/characteristic. When asked to rate the importance of Library Collections, 63 percent of students responded with "very important." When asked to rate the quality of CSUS Library Collections, 66 percent responded "Excellent" or "Good." Students were also asked to rate the difficulty of particular school related activities: 24 percent rated the activity "Locating and retrieving information" as "Very difficult" or "Difficult."

National Survey of Student Engagement 2002

The National Survey of Student Engagement is designed to measure the quality of the connection that students are making with their institutions. Survey questions focus on how students spend their time and the nature of their classroom experiences. There were some questions that have bearing on library collections and services. Among the findings: (1) CSUS freshmen are required to read fewer assigned textbooks or books per year than freshmen in the national comparison group; (2) CSUS freshmen read fewer books on their own per year than do students in the national comparison group, and (3) CSUS seniors are required to read fewer assigned textbooks or books per year than the national comparison group.

Also, CSUS students report spending fewer hours in a typical seven-day week using the campus Library in person or electronically. CSUS freshmen averaged 1.86 hours and seniors averaged 2.19 hours. The CSU system-wide average was 2.05 hours for freshmen and 2.20 hours for seniors.

When asked to rank a list of 22 educational experiences by frequency, the top two activities of CSUS students were: (1) worked on a paper or project that required integrating ideas or information from various sources; and (2) included diverse perspectives (different races, religions, genders, political beliefs, and so on) in class discussions or writing assignments. Both these responses have significance for the use of library collections.

CSUS Faculty Survey 1999–2000

In 1999, a CSUS faculty survey was undertaken to get faculty feedback for strategic planning purposes. A few questions about the library were included. There was a 30 percent response rate. When asked to rate CSUS library holdings relative to their field, our faculty rated us at 2.36, while the average for 64 comparison institutions was 2.55. (Based on a 4-point Likert scale where 1 = poor and 4 = excellent.)

When asked to rate their satisfaction with the library's "ability to meet the research needs of students in their program," the average was 3.16. Closer examination of the responses shows that 29 percent were either dissatisfied or very dissatisfied and 43 percent were either satisfied or very satisfied, while 23 percent were neutral. While the CSUS Office of Institutional Research interpreted this as positive, the library was concerned about the large number of dissatisfied faculty. (Based on a 5-point Likert scale where 1 = very dissatisfied and 5 = very satisfied.)

CASPER

In fall 2002 many of the CASPER survey questions looked at class-related learning experiences. Because the curriculum support role of the library is driven by these experiences, many of the responses are useful to the library. Most interesting was that among lower division students, 73 percent reported that the classes they took last year required writing a paper longer than five pages and 81 percent of their classes required library use. Upper division students reported that 79 percent of their classes required a paper and 75 percent required library use.

In fall 2001 CASPER focused on CSUS learning goals for the baccalaureate. To this end, some questions regarding information competence were included. When asked to what degree CSUS courses are giving students "the skills to locate information using a variety of resources including journals, books and other media," 58 percent of undergraduates indicated "some" and 30 percent indicated "a lot." Among graduate students 52 percent responded "some" and 40 percent "a lot."

Library User Survey 2001–02

In fall 2001, the library conducted a user survey with the assistance of the CSUS Institute for Social Research. Questions were asked about use of library resources and about usefulness of those resources. The mean usefulness ratings ranged from 3.52 for media/microform resources to 4.32 for EUREKA (our online catalog), based on a 5-point Likert scale where 1 = poor and 5 = excellent. Users were also asked about usage of library resources during the preceding 12 months. Users reported having used EUREKA an average of 15.4 times, databases/e-journals/e-books an average of 11.7 times, and print books/journals an average of 11.7 times. Since the library has aggregate circulation data for the book collection and in-house use data for current periodicals, the user data from the survey can be compared to hard data from our integrated library system (see OIR below).

When students were asked about "ever having used a Library resource," print resources received the highest use, with 93.9 percent of faculty/staff having used circulating books and 83.9 percent having used print periodicals. Among students, 82.8 percent reported use of circulating books, and 79.5 percent used print periodicals. This contrasted with e-journals/e-books/database usage reports of 75.9 percent (faculty/staff) and 67.0 percent (students).

One unique feature of the library user survey is the data about ability to locate material on the survey day. The library's collections are meant to be used, so it is extremely important that users be able to locate the material needed. One figure in this section of the survey is particularly significant: 48.8 percent of people using EUREKA reported that the item they sought was not owned by the library. Librarians believe that a large part of reported difficulty in locating library material stems from a lack of knowledge about how to navigate a Library or use call numbers. Problems with signage and shelving may also be a factor. Regardless, this large figure means work needs to be done in this area.

Distance and Distributed Education
Student Survey, Spring 2002

A spring 2002 survey of distance and distributed education (DDE) students also provides relevant data. Students were asked if they thought they had adequate access to the library, bookstore, advising, and student services. For the library, only 65 percent of them agreed or strongly agreed in a fall 2001 survey. When asked this same question in spring 2002, the satisfaction rating with access to the library had risen to 80 percent. Preliminary results provided for the fall 2002 survey indicated a 76 percent satisfaction rating for library access.

DDE faculty focus groups were held as part of the same assessment, with the resulting data presented as lists of comments. The focus groups were very small, and the library was mentioned very few times. Two comments reported problems with the "library tutorial," one reported that the library's e-reserves system was getting better, and one comment in the technology category noted that "the library is getting much better and more electronically friendly."

Summary Comment About Surveys

Overall, most of our users appear to be satisfied with the library holdings. Of the available survey data, there are some areas that need further investigation. The faculty survey ratings are particularly troubling, with 18 percent dissatisfied and 11 percent very dissatisfied with the library's ability to meet the research needs of students in their program. While the majority of faculty (66 percent) were either neutral or satisfied, the library needs to find out what faculty believe is needed in order to improve our performance in this area. Other areas that ought to be pursued include the ability of users to locate needed materials. Is it really true that 48 percent of our users are looking for items we do not own?

Libraries need to remain closely connected to users and their needs in order to keep collections relevant. An outstanding collection results from a mix of factors: funding, staffing, and processes that link us to our users and their needs. Surveys such as those summarized above serve to keep us informed about our users' needs and highlight areas in which more work should be done.

The External Reviewer

Our external reviewer was a library director from another CSU campus. She was also generous in her commendations and observations:

"The approach of the self-study describes the library's activities and services in the language of teaching and learning using the self-study format provided by the dean/director of the library. Seven committees with 32 members (not including ad hoc members) participated in the process. Committee membership included faculty, non-faculty, and some students."

The major goals for the coming program review period are timely, appropriate, and well-stated:

- Integrate the library more fully into the processes of teaching and learning across the university.
- Expand the library's digital initiatives, including activities such as information resource development, online publishing ventures, and creation of new forms of scholarship and scholarly communication.
- Develop methods to prove empirically the effect of the library's academic programs on the goals and effectiveness of the university.

The administration, faculty, and staff of the CSUS library should be commended for the innovative approach to the self-study. Their efforts to describe the library's activities and services in the language of teaching and learning are an important step in moving the library even more directly in support of the university's mission. The detailed recommendations and plans of action incorporated in the report should serve the library well in progressing toward these ambitious goals.

Library instruction (information competence) is the section that fits easily into the questions of the self-study and it is clearly the most impressive. The faculty and staff should be commended for their remarkable progress in this area, especially with such limited staffing. In 2001–2002 alone, the number of students attending instruction increased by over 24 percent.

I want to note two areas of accomplishment. First, requiring tutorials through communications studies courses using WebCT is an outstanding example of integrating existing technology to effectively reach more students. Second, the CSUS Baccalaureate Learning Goals are excellent and begin to define and institutionalize a core set of information competence for all students.

I strongly support the goals outlined in the report for this vitally important area of librarianship and recommend that more resources be devoted to these efforts. The self-study includes a thorough and thoughtful review of staffing. The library faculty and staff should be particularly commended for this analysis. The Library Instruction Committee's recommendation for increasing and evaluating faculty teaching effectiveness should be commended and implemented as soon as possible. This program has the potential to provide a model for other libraries.

The self-study's analysis of the staffing situation is excellent. The library administration's work with non-faculty personnel ("library personnel, non-faculty," LPNF) is especially strong. I strongly support their plan of action for diversity and gender balance. I hope library faculty and staff will implement all the possible courses of action in their report. The library administration should move quickly to develop a strategic plan as mentioned in the report. As with the self-study, large numbers of faculty, staff, and students should be involved. In addition, I encourage the library to consider including significant numbers of faculty and administrators outside the library in the process.

Whither Assessment?

In the self-study, we learned a lot about ourselves, the faculty, and the students. We also saw the acutely inadequate assessment measures of academic libraries. Despite the favorable comments of the panel and the external reviewer, and the wealth of data we assembled and presented in the self-study, we were even less satisfied than before we undertook the self-study. We had plenty of statistics from the normal sources, including numerous surveys, questionnaires, benchmarking, and rising library activity levels, for all three academic programs in the library's self-study.

We learned that these instruments could not substantiate any quantitative measurable positive or negative effect of the library's academic programs on the overall academic performance of the students who participated in those library programs. The data indicated only that we *touch* the students, but do not necessarily *teach* them. We enter into their lives to one degree or another, but we do not know for sure how we affect them. This is an uncertainty principle that librarians cannot afford to continue. Instructional faculty have ample quantitative data to measure student performance in their classrooms, and validate their teaching effectiveness by assessing the learning of their students through multiple assignments and exercises, and then averaging each student's performance via his/her GPA.

Furthermore, the new three Rs are measures that figure into every university's mission and effectiveness as well as in assessment of faculty teaching and learning. The CSUS library, however, like the majority of libraries, could not put forward any data that demonstrated a real effect of our programs on these student learning characteristics. Recalling Covey (2005), "Libraries continue to gather traditional input and output data ... but the more purposeful, effective data these days are outcomes and performance.... Measures of efficiency, effectiveness, quality, usability, and [the] difference the libraries make are much needed — and very persuasive — in an era pressured for accountability."

OIR

As a result, for the next self-study in 2010, we committed ourselves to develop empirical methods that will positively affect the library's academic programs on (1) the overall performance of CSUS students, and (2) the goals and effectiveness of the university. A few months after the 2004 self-study, we began collaborating with the CSUS Office of Institutional Research (OIR) to develop and implement ways of measuring the overall academic success of students who use the library's services compared with students who do not use the library. We did this by comparing the GPAs of senior students who were frequent library users with the GPAs of students who were infrequent library users. We gathered some initial data from student samples, but they were too small to derive a valid correlation. The results, however, suggested that there was a positive relationship.

Unfortunately, as we worked with OIR we encountered resistance. The OIR staff argued that there were too many variables besides library usage that could influence students' academic performance, such as the teaching quality of the instructors, previous learning in high school, related learning in the home, the effectiveness of students' study habits, and countless others. Our position, however, was that students could just as easily get high grades in their instructional departments for any of these same reasons mentioned, yet OIR was in the business of evaluating instructional departments as well as the university's overall effectiveness based largely on the students' GPAs. The library simply wanted to search for any observable correlations between student library usage and student overall academic performance.

Road to Hong Kong

Soon after this project, I accepted the position of university librarian (UL) at Hong Kong Baptist University (HKBU). In my application for the UL position, I explained to the recruitment panel the need for libraries to develop empirical methods to measure more accurately the effect of library usage on student overall academic performance, and I described the CSUS project. On my arrival in Hong Kong, I was charged to restart the project in the HKBU library. I was delighted by the wisdom and interest of the university administration in library effectiveness.

At HKBU, we began where the CSUS project ended. We first compared the levels of library usage among large samples of our students with their GPAs, which we extracted from the Academic Registry's (AR) system. This allowed us to derive correlations between library usage and student performance, if in fact there were any correlation, which may then tie Library programs and services to the university's effectiveness measures, such as student retention, progress to graduation rates, grade point averages, and others.

Calculating a library's real effect on students and on a university's effectiveness in this manner can constitute a major breakthrough in library assessment. It will allow library managers to create a baseline in their universities from which they can work to increase the effectiveness of their library programs. The calculations will also form a more scientific basis, perhaps even a formula, for setting the library's budget, not unlike the old ALA standards, but in this case, the budget development would be based on direct quantitative, real-time calculations. And because this type of assessment is comparable to the assessment methods used by instructional departments, it will bring librarians and faculty closer together in the processes of student learning and evaluation.

We were stoic. We knew that with a correlation, positive or negative, between our students' library usage and their success in the university, we would be able to devise ways to increase the correlation positively by enhancing library programs to improve our contribution to the university's mission, which then must include the disciplinary learning areas of the students. If meaningful, reliable, quantitative correlations can be confirmed in this way, libraries can establish valid forms of assessment that were first used in studies on a limited basis decades ago, but which could now be applied much more easily thanks to the sophisticated technology in academic institutions. Still, it could take years to complete all the studies we have in mind.

Although librarians are educators, it is not necessary for us to give examinations, homework, or research assignments, nor need we necessarily assign grades to the students we teach in our information literacy classes. Let the classroom instructors give grades as they always have. If we librarians are correctly doing our jobs as educators, the results of our work should be reflected one way or another in the grades of the students who receive our instruction. If we cannot link student library usage to overall student academic performance as reflected in their GPAs, librarianship will remain an act of faith and not a science of teaching.

Statisticians at the Gates

With data assistance from the AR, we approached the HKBU's Statistics Research and Consultancy Center (SRCC), and the associate vice president account, and asked them if this project might be valid. We were happy that the center's statisticians were intrigued by the project. The library received a $13,000 grant for the project from the university administration.

A professor and SRCC director had worked with libraries before, and was able to see beyond the ken of the OIR staff at CSUS. In May 2007, the professor was selected as a fellow of the American Statistical Association for his work with probability and statistics, dimension-reduction methods, goodness-of-fit testing, and empirical likelihood, terms that were certainly a new language for this librarian. The professor was very willing to undertake the project, which is a tangible and very focused example of Wiegand's (2005) observation that "we have to look much more at the library in the life of our users (and conversely, nonusers) in order to deepen our understanding of the many roles it plays (or could play) in their everyday lives."

Outcome of Initial Study

Our initial study at HKBU was a first pass to match students' library book circulation data to their cumulative GPAs at graduation for the past four years. This study was implemented to see if students who had borrowed books from the library were among those with high GPAs on a department-by-department level. It was a simple study and, as we expected, there was not a very reliable correlation strong enough to confirm that our library does contribute to student academic success. Still, we were glad the project had begun.

Tracking student library activities, such as books borrowed, reserving and/or using study rooms, attending library information literacy classes, and the like, were simple processes, but an empirical correlation between these cumulative activities and the students' GPAs did not appear strong initially.

Outcome of Second Study

The second pass was a longitudinal study of the past three years to see the variations over time between books borrowed and GPAs at graduation. The intent was to see variations in correlations between the same courses over a three-year period. From there we saw the impact that enhanced library services might have over a period of time to raise the correlations within the disciplines. In short, the effectiveness of faculty instruction varied rather widely from one year to the next, where the library staff could assist the faculty in future courses.

When the professor and SRCC director was awarded a sabbatical at a university outside of Hong Kong, the project sadly languished.

Breakthrough

It came when we discovered that one of our HKBU librarians, Rebekah Wong, a math and statistics major, was very agreeable to join the assessment team. Her special talents were extremely important, but the other side of the coin was her experience as a working librarian and section head. She knew very well how students use the library's resources. She also clarified and corrected some approaches of the SRCC staff assessments. Ms. Wong's article "Uncovering Meaningful Correlation between Student Academic Performance and Library Material Usage," accepted by *College and Research Libraries* on August 4, 2010. Excerpts from the article appear at the end of this chapter.

We also reviewed the very first findings of our CSUS colleagues and found that they were compatible with ours, though small in circulation data. This was after CSUS OIR staff opted out of the project. It was clear that CSUS OIR, like the HKBU SRCC, did not fully understand student library behavior, as tabulated in the assessment data. Wong traced the library processes and procedures that could make the correlations more apparent and measurable empirically. Ms. Wong's breakthrough assessments are portrayed at the end of this chapter.

New Measures Indeed!

We've read about, heard about, and used a lot of "new measures." Most of it is the same data dressed as something "new." Granted they are based mainly on business models of customer satisfaction surveys, but modeling on business success is a step or three away from academe. While such exercises might be of some benefit in library management, they are poor and hollow when applied to the effect that libraries must have on the overall academic performance of students.

As I said earlier, LibQUAL is hard to load, but provides lovely charts and graphs suitable for framing; however, I want to know if there is any meaningful quantitative, empirical proof of positive correlations between students' library usage and their GPAs in my library. In addition to my teaching ethic, I want to have reliable data to convince my vice president that the library does enhance student learning, and that with a larger budget our impact of teaching and learning can increase substantially in the library. Pretty graphs won't do the trick. Only GPAs will tell the true story. The library could enhance learning even more, and increase the university's effectiveness in the bargain, if we can have a few more staff and other resources, mainly funding.

By now we should be certain that the only real way to make our point that librarians are fine teachers, and can do more with added resources while expanding our role in achieving the missions of our institutions, is to supply quantitative proof that librarians and libraries directly contribute to student performance in their departmental classes. We must ante up in the GPA game. GPA is the bottom line. It tells us almost everything about the students *and* the faculty. That is pretty much the entire campus community, except for the groundskeepers, counselors, and the librarians in the spotlight.

Do faculty assess their students' performance based on the students' intuitions and circumspections? If this were the case, there would be little need for faculty, just as there is now little opportunity for librarians to have a measurable input into overall student academic performance, whether the students use the library or not. We can always devise and improve and strengthen our correlations by working and teaching better with the faculty.

It is exasperating to try and manage university operations with such uncertainties and instabilities. It is compounded by the libraries' lack of timely, reliable management information, despite the presence of very expensive integrated library management systems (LMS). I remember taking my first automation class in library school. The teacher was Ken Bierman, at that time the director of automation for the Tucson Public Library. He pointed out that one of the most important features of the LMS was to provide vast quantities of management information, such as the activity levels of terminals at the circ desk, using book circulation and copyright statistics to determine which books might be eligible for removal, and so forth. We also had illuminating discussions examining OCLC, WLN, RLIN, and various online circulation systems being developed at that time, and how they might be converted into online catalogs. It was a dynamic class.

If academic librarians are educators, and I insist that we are, we must devise meaningful new library assessment methods equivalent to those used by instructional academic departments to measure quantitatively the real effect libraries and librarians have on overall student academic performance. Why must we develop these new methods ourselves? In his article, Pace (2004) alluded to Jerry Kline's use of "the same intellectual logic" of the older Innovative systems as a strategy for the Java-based add-on for the Millennium version. Pace wrote, "If the vendor can rebuild using the same business logic, while simultaneously allowing either more interoperability or tighter integration with third party products, then so much the better."

In other words, it is because the vendors have led us by our noses in directions *they* want to go. Vendors are all too happy to focus on new applications and money-making innovations that are convenient for them to devise or upgrade, and which are of at least some interest to their clients. But the vendors do not necessarily, and only infrequently, develop systems that are of major importance to the new functions of libraries, such as genuine academic assessment, information literacy online environments, open access tools, and institutional repositories that talk to each other, and so on (Levin 1992).

The most important library data we can have is a positive, quantifiable correlation between the library usage of our students and their overall academic performance. But if Pace is right, we will have to invent methods to do this ourselves, or go to a third party add-on module. As a library director, my biggest gripe against LMS vendors is that these "management" systems don't talk to the other university data resources on our own campuses. That leaves to the library the work of measuring mathematically the effectiveness of the library's services for students and their academic pursuits.

I guess I'm still the maverick, still the doubter, because when I spoke with Mr. Kline a few years ago about connecting Millennium to the CSUS data warehouse in ways that could retrieve information to verify a correlation between student library usage and their overall academic performance, his response was less than lukewarm. I even e-mailed him in an attempt to keep a dialogue going, and received no response. It was clear to me that the importance of having an LMS that can retrieve information from a university's data warehouse for determining a library's role in student retention, timely graduation, recruitment, and their overall GPAs was lost on this vendor, even though it could be crucial in library assessment, and a great leap forward for their clients.

To manage modern libraries effectively, library administrators must have accurate management data to assess the effectiveness of their operations so they can improve their services and demonstrate their impact on the missions of their institutions. The data we need is comparable to the data that is available to instructional department managers that reflect the academic performance of the students enrolled in their programs. By analyzing these data, university administrators can determine which curricula need improvement, expansion, or reductions. For libraries to obtain this type of information, we must go farther to establish our effectiveness as places and librarians as practitioners of excellent teaching and learning.

Privacy Issues

Contrary to the knee-jerk reaction of many librarians, there is no necessary issue of a breach of confidentiality in obtaining and using library users' private information to manage academic libraries. On the contrary, instructional departments have been doing this forever to evaluate their effectiveness and their contributions to learning and to the effectiveness of their universities. At least annually, academic departments are generally required, via the university institutional research offices, to gather and present this very same type of data to demonstrate the level of effectiveness of their departments. This is how universities know which academic programs are contributing to the effectiveness of the university, and which are not. Those that are not effective must either improve their records of quality teaching and learning, or else risk dissolution.

At CSUS, we decided that all library users — regardless of their academic disciplines and the degree to which they use the library — are "our" students, and this perspective carried over to the HKBU library as well. As such we need to track their overall academic performance to determine if library usage has a positive, negative, or negligible effect on their graduation rates, retention, and grades, and if they graduate in a reasonable time-frame. These, after all, had become the effectiveness measures of the universities in the CSU system and most other academic institutions.

While working our way through the CSUS 2004 Library Self-Study, we decided that if librarians are in fact educators and proclaim ourselves as educators, we need to step up and measure our performance with the same methods used by our colleague educators in the instructional departments.

Young and Blixrud (2003) observe, "In the movement toward learner-centered education, the emphasis on the student and on learning outcomes is ... growing in importance as part of the evaluation of academic programs. Evidence of the contribution of the library to students' learning outcomes is therefore an important aspect of demonstrating the value of the library to academic programs and the institution."

This reasoning is so obvious that there should be no need even to say the words, yet it should be said over and over. But the sad fact is that this idea completely escapes academic administrations and instructional faculty. Even more sadly, it escapes many librarians as well. Young and Blixrud (2003) also say, "In order to assess how library programs and services contribute to student learning outcomes at the student, department, or institutional level, librarians need to inform themselves on how learning outcomes assessment is practiced on their own campus. In addition, the contributions of the library to learning outcomes could be described in a broader context of the students' experiences with the library, not just those limited to the instruction activity."

In actual fact, the answer *is* the GPA. In all simplicity, the bottom-line measure of learning outcomes at the student, department, library, and institutional levels can be summed up in the GPA. It is the prevailing institutional effectiveness measure of most American universities and colleges. If academic libraries cannot demonstrate their direct contributions to those institutional effectiveness measures, it will continue to appear that they make no meaningful contribution at all.

CSUS Library Strategic Plan

Following the external evaluator's comments on the CSUS self-study, we plunged into developing the CSUS library's strategic plan. Committees were developed with as much participation as possible of all library staff classifications. Here is the final document.

Strategic Plan:
A Common Paper from the Library
California State University, Sacramento

Mission for the Planning Period

The library will advance teaching, learning, research, and scholarly communication at the university by providing (1) appropriate information and knowledge networks to which the university community can connect their curricular activities; (2) expert instruction and information services to provide information competency; (3) innovative digital channels for more rapid and cost-effective sharing of new knowledge across the scholarly community; and (4) improved physical and digital environments to facilitate these processes. The library will achieve this mission by integrating more fully its academic programs, enriched and expanded, into the processes of teaching and learning in the university.*

Our Core Values

1. The library's critical role in teaching and learning at the university.
2. Open access to scholarship and creative work in all their forms.
3. The inventiveness and professional excellence of the library's personnel.

The Library's Strategic Plan was specifically designed to contribute to Sacramento State's measures of effectiveness, and to articulate with the President's Sacramento State Destination 2010 initiative, the Sacramento State Academic Affairs Strategic Plan (December 2005), and the "Advancing Together" Strategic Plan developed by the CSU Council of Library Directors (September 2005). Strategic plans from several university libraries provided additional insights and organizational structures used in this plan.

4. Shared decision making through information dissemination and inclusive leadership in order to benefit from wide involvement, dialogue, and individual commitment to raise the effectiveness of library operations.

5. The highest esteem for our users.

6. Commitment to diversity and open communication as key elements in the intellectual and interpersonal development of library employees, members of the university, and extended communities.

Preamble

The library employees brought this Plan into being through the 2004 Self-Study, the Program Review, and numerous all-employee meetings. The library employees, therefore, have the right to implement the plan by working through the employee groups — Faculty, Staff, Administrative Council — and the library's standing committees, in consultation with Library Administration.

Strategic Direction 1: Enrich the Library's Academic Programs and Integrate Them More Fully into the Processes of Teaching and Learning at the University

Initiative 1: Achieve budgetary evenness, resiliency, and stability through (1) internal budget restructuring to achieve operational efficiencies and economies; (2) restoration of funds cut during the past three years; (3) larger baseline allocations, including inflation offsets; (4) aggressive fundraising and endowment building; and (5) judicious expenditure planning.

Initiative 2: Increase the reach of library instruction into university departments, programs, and initiatives through (1) expanded information competency curricula (classroom and online); (2) broader and deeper collection development to reach the university's baccalaureate goals, articulate with re-benched master's-level programs, and support the newly announced doctoral programs; (3) dynamic access to all materials; and (4) vibrant reference/research consultations.

Initiative 3: Aim our efforts at raising the university's student retention, enrollment, and timely graduation rates to increase the library's impact on Sacramento State's measures of effectiveness.

Initiative 4: Strive for saturation awareness across the university of the library's services and resources that amplify teaching, learning, and research. Fashion new intersect points between the library and other university entities; e.g., instructional departments, G.E., student groups, honors program, freshman seminars, academic advising, writing across the curriculum, etc.

Initiative 5: Devise and implement quantitative assessment methods that measure the effect of the library's academic programs on student performance, and which will more conclusively substantiate the library's contribution to the university's effectiveness measures.

Initiative 6: Encourage and provide opportunities for professional growth of library personnel. Upgrade professional skills and expand our understanding of the ways of teaching, learning, and research.

Initiative 7: Grow a robust e-scholarship package, including e-repositories, electronic theses and dissertations (ETDs) collections, the digital academic press, Moodle upgrades, and other technology solutions for teaching, learning, and research/scholarship.

Strategic Direction 2: Reconfigure the Library's Infrastructures

Initiative 8: Reconfigure, renovate, and expand the library's physical space, and make it more attractive, comfortable, and user friendly, e.g., increase group and collaborative settings; implement effective way-finding systems; enliven the library's breezeway. Make the library the academic center and cultural heart of the university in the spirit of the CSUS President's Destination 2010 expansion project.

Initiative 9: Build a stable, agile technology foundation in the library with stronger funding, additional staffing, advanced training, and leading-edge facilities.

Initiative 10: Establish and maintain a summit-level network and digital environment with excellent vendor-supplied digital collections and original e-resources created through active R&D. Maximize functionality and interoperability of the library's various systems, e.g., Eureka, portals, Metalib, Innovative, CMS, etc.

Strategic Direction 3: Advance the Library's Engagement with Its Communities

Initiative 11: Elevate the visibility of the library's integral part in teaching, learning, and research, and of its contributions to the university's effectiveness. Support and present wider varieties of events and activities to draw our university constituents to the library and engage their information competency.

Initiative 12: Collaborate with community college, public, and school libraries, and with cultural, historical, and other civic entities to draw support for the library from their memberships while raising the university's student enrollments.

Initiative 13: Host broadly ranging cultural events for the public that will help make the library a destination venue at Sacramento's destination university.

Initiative 14: Attract new memberships and other resources for the Friends of the Library. Increase our attentiveness to alumni, emeriti, and other university-related groups as well as to community groups of various kinds. Cultivate community groups that have interests in common with the library.

Initiative 15: Nurture new sources of revenue in the form of individual and corporate donations as well as government, private, and institutional grants.

Initiative 16: Publicize the library's accomplishments and its value to the community through media exposure, including online newsletters and bulletins, to broad and appropriate audiences. Use the library's website to raise interest in the library's events, accomplishments, and services.

Strategic Direction 4: Retune the Library's Methods of Governance and Planning

Initiative 17: Reorganize and empower the library's standing committees to (1) assume major responsibility for implementing the Strategic Plan's four Directions; (2) create achievable goals and concrete objectives for each of the initiatives; and (3) help steer the Plan as library conditions change, allowing the Plan to be a lasting and evolving document for library decision making, budgeting, growth, and assessment.

Initiative 18: Broaden and deepen the synergies between library departments, committees, classifications, and administration. Strengthen the sense of common purpose across all library units to engender an even more dynamic, participative, and harmonious organizational culture.

Initiative 19: Review, update where necessary, and regularly apply the provisions of tenure and promotion, and reclassification procedures to expand the competencies of, and elicit the best performance from, a corps of vetted information professionals in the library.

Initiative 20: Organize committed faculty, student, and focus groups who will advise and advocate for the library while enlarging the on-campus cadre of informed library constituents.

May 8, 2006

Misguided Assessment

When *American Libraries* labeled me a "maverick," I think it was intended to be a compliment, and I took it as such. I heard a plaintive echo of this from Pace (2004) in his evaluation of the current degraded state of LMS vendors. He said, "Librarians are dismantling systems, and creating new modules, out of frustration with the inflexible and nonextensible technology of their proprietary systems." He added, "Most of the touted interoperability is between the vendor's own modules (sometimes) or between a library's homegrown solutions and its own ILS (sometimes). Today, interoperability in library automation is more myth than reality." This was virtually the same argument I made in the conference and my report to *American Libraries* symposium in 1987.

I would never want to be a university president or vice president, but if I were to have that responsibility, as a librarian I would seriously wonder about the library's effectiveness and the drag it might have on the university's budget and mission, not because I distrust librarians, but because we need to perfect methods to measure empirically and accurately the contribution libraries actually make to teaching, learning, and research.

At the Top

It is exasperating to try and manage university operations with such uncertainties and instabilities. It is compounded by the libraries' lack of timely, reliable management information, despite the presence of expensive integrated LMS money suckers. Beyond these management blinds, however, not much real change has occurred in the scope of library "management" information systems. The current state of university library assessment in general is more "quackademic" than academic, and LMS products have changed very little in giving us the management data we really need to demonstrate our impact on student learning and achieve our institutional objectives.

For a few decades now, librarians have purchased expensive LMS's, but we have never had the clarity of thought to demand of our vendors that their magic machines integrate with the systems of our parent institutions. These parent institution systems hold information that could be very valuable in helping libraries assess their effectiveness and their contributions to the parent institution's effectiveness as well. This is especially true for academic libraries because those systems hold considerable information about our users — students and faculty. For instance, student identification and authorization records are transferred between libraries and registrar's offices on a daily basis to facilitate and confirm the registering of new users and the purging of old records. But academic libraries have not nearly utilized the administrative systems of their institutions to do sampling, longitudinal studies, cohort comparisons, and other analyses to measure the overall academic performance of students who use the library.

Thus I have come to the conclusion that the only way to assess a library's effectiveness in helping its university better achieve its mission, is a newfangled approach to match student records in the library and in the registrar's office.

Excerpts from the HKBU Library Assessment Article

Experimental Design

An essential prerequisite for this study was the approval of the HKBU's administration to exchange information between the library's computerized systems that track student library usage and the systems of the Academic Registry (AR) that contain student academic data. The university librarian conducted meetings with the Academic Vice-President, Academic Registrar, Vice President (Administration), and Director of General Administration for this purpose. After getting the university's support, in November 2009, the university librarian and the author started to meet with the academic registrar and his colleagues to discuss the details of the cooperation. In order to protect the privacy of the graduates, library colleagues were not allowed to know the GPA data with the student's identification, which is the student number in this case. Eventually, we agreed to adopt the procedures below for data exchange. For each sample group (we will define "sample group" later),

1. The library prepared an Excel table with student numbers, student names, graduation years, program of study, and library usage data, and sent it to the AR;
2. AR prepared a list of missing student numbers to the library if any (we found the library's system had some slight errors in the data of graduation year);
3. The library added the information of the missing graduates in the file and re-sent it to AR; and
4. AR replaced the columns of student numbers and student names with corresponding GPA data and shuffled the order of rows before sending it to the library.

Samples and Populations

The subjects of this study were all HKBU students who graduated within the latest three years (from 2007 to 2009) with cumulative GPA given. A total of 8,701 students were identified and analyzed. There were two independent variables selected in this analysis:

1. Graduation GPA of these students (GPA), ranging from 1.82 to 4.00.

2. The total number of times these students checked out books and AV materials during their study at HKBU, not taking the number of renewals into account (CHKOUT). This data ranges from 0 to 1,054.

Cases (pairs of data) were first divided into 53 sample groups, according to their study major (for example, Translation, Biology, etc.) and level of study (undergraduate or postgraduate). Please refer to Table 1. This arrangement was based on the belief that different subject disciplines had different criteria or internal guidelines to assign GPA values, so cases across disciplines were not comparable. Moreover, students' information behaviors are strongly associated with their subject interests and academic level.

Statistical Methods Used

For each sample group, we used the well-known Pearson's Correlation to determine the degree of linear dependence between the two variables (GPA and CHKOUT). The most popular and classic interpretation of the correlation coefficients (r) in behavioral sciences was established by Cohen first in 1983. Please see Table 2 for his approach. We adopted this approach in the study. In fact in behavioral sciences, an r value of 0.8 is already very high and infrequently occurs. Correlation coefficients (r) are also not based on a linear scale. For example, r = 0.6 is not twice as strong as r = 0.3.

A two-tailed significance test was then carried out on the sample correlation coefficient (r) to examine if we could provide valid inferences from the sample to the corresponding population. As the common practice, our null hypothesis was that the two variables in question have a zero correlation in the population (H_0:ρ = 0), where (represents the correlation coefficient of the population. We set the significance criterion (α) as 0.05, which is the classic and widely used standard in behavioral sciences. By using this value, there is a 95 percent chance that our statistical findings are real and not due to chance.

Findings

Among the 48 valid sample groups, 65 percent were statistically proven to have a positive relationship between GPA and CHKOUT in the corresponding population (see Chart 2). These sample groups are listed in Table 3. No populations are found to have a negative correlation between the two variables. The remaining 35 percent have no clear relationship.

Another New Assessment Wrinkle

Mark Maves (2005) found that in well-designed newly constructed libraries, circulation statistics are being replaced by student attendance counts as the measure most demonstrative of library success (qtd. in Carlson 2005). These swelling numbers of students entering the library are certainly not lost on university administrators. I can add that the CSUS library's annual student entries were close to two million. With that volume of traffic into the library, the ideal place for a coffee shop and an information commons was right inside the library's front doors. Maves adds that the library is considered "not so much as a library, but as the academic counterpart to the student center."

More importantly, this number of students entering the library forecasts the enormous interactions of the students with the library staff, collections, information literacy sessions, exhibits, and other activities. We desperately need to know (1) What the students are doing in the libraries, and (2) what effect of this massive number of students has on student learning in their chosen fields. In other words, for all their frequent usage of library services, are they becoming more and more learned?

A new pass of the HKBU library assessment project was published in July 2011, correlating the overall academic performance of students who have taken information literacy classes taught by the librarians. We hope the outcome will be promising.

4

A LIBRARIAN'S EDUCATION

Library Schooling

In 2005, Mayer and Terrill conducted a survey of librarians' attitudes toward advanced subject degrees. The survey was not necessarily intended to question ALA's position that the MLS is the "appropriate" terminal degree for librarians, including academic librarians, but I think the survey responses are a clear indication that ALA should be questioned on the issue of additional advanced subject degrees.

According to Mayer and Terrill, papers published on the issue of advanced subject degrees in the 1980s and early 1990s reported that such degrees played a role in career advancement and enhanced job performance and "campus credibility" for at least some librarians with these degrees. Marcum (1990) said an advanced degree is "critical if the librarian expects to partner in the scholarly process."

Among Mayer's and Terrill's own respondents, some of the benefits mentioned regarding advanced subject degrees were "credibility," "credibility on campus and with other academic librarians," " respect," "status among peers and other faculty," "personal fulfillment." In addition, these were seen as "vital to the development of research skills not taught in library school." Mayer and Terrill state, "A large number of respondents indicated that the MLS *does not meet* the educational goals of academic librarians, especially in terms of teaching research skills."

Mayer and Terrill themselves observed that their own advanced subject degrees were "quite different from their library school experiences, and ultimately, of great value to the practice of librarianship." I know the feeling. My own career as a university student might appear untidy or serendipitous. My humble objective was to learn as much as I could about the operations of culture. With two BAs, in humanities and English, I went further and earned an M.A. in interdisciplinary humanities. Then, while I was working as a library assistant, I chose librarianship as a career and obtained an MLS. I could have stopped then with the advanced subject degree in humanities. Not satisfied with the two master's degrees, however, I obtained a Ph.D. in cultural anthropology. I'm very glad I did. The social sciences doctorate gave me a much wider perspective and a deeper scientific understanding of culture than I had gained solely from the humanities. It made me a better classroom teacher and librarian. Furthermore, as a university library director, the subject Ph.D. in anthropology makes an unexpected but generally favorable impression on faculty and administrative colleagues, who otherwise would look askance if my Ph.D.

were in librarianship. Librarianship is a career a bit thin in the view of faculty. This chapter will explain the reason for this.

I don't recommend that anyone follow my meandering collegiate career. On the contrary, from my perspective with two advanced subject degrees, in addition to the MLS, I believe a second advanced degree is essential for MLS librarians, and that second degree should be a doctorate. Even though second M.A. degrees have been preferred in library recruitment searches for many years, this is still not sufficient. For librarians, especially academic librarians, a second subject master's degree will just not do. A Ph.D. is practically required to play in the academic games, and it will take only somewhat longer to complete than a second master's.

Mayer and Terrill conclude their paper with, "Some librarians see the Ph.D. in library science as a better 'next step' than a subject degree." From my perspective, however, ALA is decades away, and probably much, much longer, from formulating anything as rigorously structured and scholarly as a library-based, accredited doctoral program, or even accrediting some of the independent Ph.D. library programs that have proliferated in the last couple of decades. After all, ALA policy 54.2 is still on the books: "The master's degree from a program accredited by the American Library Association (or from a master's level program in library and information studies accredited or recognized by the appropriate national body of another country) is the appropriate professional degree for librarians."

This is absurd. The Bureau of Labor Statistics (2010–11) plainly states, "The MLS degree provides general preparation for library work, but some individuals specialize in a particular area, such as reference, technical services, or children's services. A Ph.D. in library and information science is advantageous for a college teaching position or a top administrative job in a college or university library or large public library system." The ALA should take a lesson from the bureau, which appears to be more up to date.

It is shameful and most unfortunate that ALA has not made sufficient and determined progress, nor given adequate thought to seriously upgrading library education, despite the Ph.D. clamor, and has instead spent so many decades insisting that the MLS — a professional and not a scholarly degree — is the right terminal degree for librarians. As educators, we must obtain the same level of academic credentials held by instructional faculty. Crowley and Ginsberg (2003) observe that the ALA–accredited master's degree "has been retained as a criterion for hiring librarians even after the rest of the academic community ... adopted the *standard* for employing faculty [i.e., the Ph.D.]." They add, "In the higher-education component of the globalized economy ... long-term survival for many academic librarians may involve adopting faculty requirements ... and enhancing their perceived value through earning doctorates and teaching information analysis and use in real and virtual classrooms to tuition-paying students."

To counter ALA's unwillingness or inability to develop a strong Ph.D.-level librarianship program, a growing number of universities are filling the Ph.D. void in librarianship by partnering or merging with existing doctoral programs, most of which are based on high-level information technologies. These inventive doctoral programs are often run under the aegis of another school, or a cognate faculty or interdisciplinary department that is fully accredited, such as an information science department, a school of communication, an information technology program, or maybe even a business school.

To name just a few, Drexel offers a Ph.D. through the College of Information Science and Technology. The Ph.D. at Emporia State is offered through the School of Library and Information Management. Rutgers' Ph.D. resides in the Department of Library and Information Science. At Simmons College, the doctor of arts in library management is offered in the Graduate School of Library and Information Science. The School of Information Studies at Syracuse University tends the Ph.D. in information transfer.

I first learned of such a degree program in the early 1990s at the University of Hawaii library school. My provost at the time, John Morton, enrolled in the two-year program for a special reason. He didn't necessarily want nor need the Ph.D. for his post. He was expert in his position, and enjoyed it. Nevertheless, he did not want the lack of a Ph.D. to prevent him from applying for potential future promotions or other benefits that would require a doctorate. He also was a great supporter of libraries, and was head and shoulders above the IT people running the systems on all ten UH campuses. He once told me, with real meaning, that he would like to change jobs with me. With his earned doctorate in information management, including library studies, he gained the best of both his worlds, and is now a vice president over the University of Hawaii Community Colleges.

Jackson's heavy lifting virtually established the UH interdisciplinary Ph.D. program in communication and information sciences. He became the inaugural chairman of the program in 1985. At first I was surprised when he said he was pleased that ALA chose *not* to get involved with Ph.D. degrees because it makes life easier to have these interdisciplinary doctoral programs operating and growing without getting bogged down in ALA politics at that level. He told me, "I do not think the doctorate is necessary for every library position, even in academic libraries. However, the doctorate could be of value in many academic library positions." I agree with his perspective, but I also think ALA is turning a blind eye to library doctorates because it doesn't want the burden of coping with them. I believe ALA will become obsolete sooner than we think. I hope another more sensible, insightful, and dynamic entity will emerge.

Sweet Home Tucson

My own graduate school of librarianship at the University of Arizona in Tucson was renamed the School of Information Resources & Library Science (SIRLS), and offers a Ph.D. in library science. SIRLS has had a great deal of good press. In 2003, a dynamic, comprehensive business plan that provides considerable self-sufficiency for SIRLS persuaded the university president to remove SIRLS from a list of 16 programs targeted for elimination. Also in 2003, SIRLS secured $50,000 for scholarships, a contribution for a new faculty member, and a $1.5 million gift to create three endowed professorships. SIRLS also offers a Ph.D. minor in library and information resources that requires 12 units and a written and oral exam. Creative, yes, but from my perspective, a 12-credit Ph.D. "minor" is pretty thin for a doctoral designation.

ALA Hides Out

Quite fortunately, library Ph.D. look-alike programs, though they may not be ALA-accredited, have become more numerous. The doctorates granted in these programs are as genuine as any doctoral degrees offered in other disciplines because they are vested by their respective universities, not by ALA. There are more than 20 such "designer" Ph.D. programs in the U.S. and Canada, and these programs demonstrate that ALA is frozen in the ice on this and other related crucial issues, such as faculty status, tenure, promotion, and university committee assignments, with no apparent leverage regarding Ph.D. degrees.

ALA could have played a major role in this transformation, and been as creative and forward-looking as these academic institutions themselves, and could have worked closer together with these and other universities to bridge the gap between the MLS and the Ph.D. Instead, ALA remained aloof, or just winked, and let these creative enhancements take place — not daring to lift so much as a finger or an eyelid to move the revolution in American librarianship forward, and with no huge costs to ALA, of course.

Librarianship is much better off because of the large number of library schools that have found "safe havens" for Ph.D. degrees. Despite that fact, however, libraries themselves on almost all university campuses may not have a place to lay their heads for quite some time. Establishing a market for Ph.D. librarians will not automatically raise the stature of practicing librarians who are making supreme efforts to perfect their teaching; earning faculty status while convincing faculty and administrators that librarians are fine educators; implementing genuine empirical library assessment methods; and finding the time, money, and opportunity to earn doctoral degrees from the new abundance of library Ph.D. programs.

The proliferation of these library doctoral programs in this century will require much more rigorous curricula that includes theories of curriculum development; pedagogical design; testing and assessment; statistics; managing curriculum change; outcomes-based learning; personal teaching methods; student learning styles; and research, writing, and publication. Beyond the Ph.D. program itself, other new skills that will be needed include better library management and supervision techniques, and indoctrination into tenure, promotion, faculty senate chores, and other faculty and administrative responsibilities.

Also, the establishment of "franchise" Ph.D. programs will certainly raise expectations of new library school recruits, while large numbers of current MLS librarians may leave their careers because they may not be willing to go farther into education. This will have an even larger negative impact on dwindling recruitment streams of librarians. When the Ph.D. librarians come to work from their information- and management-rich programs, they will feel committed to take over their libraries and apply what they learned in their doctoral programs very soon after their arrival. Such a domino effect occurred in the 1980s when many "bibliophile" librarians resigned or retired in the face of escalating library automation and yielded their positions to the new, IT-savvy digital librarians coming from the MLS programs. Many current MLS librarians may unfortunately move out as the Ph.D. becomes increasingly the degree of choice in librarian recruitments.

CLIRing House

There seem to be two shortages in the librarianship recruitment stream: (1) too few librarians with necessary advanced subject degrees, and (2) too few persons entering the general recruitment stream to replace the librarians who are retiring. In 2003, a debate about the first shortage began in the United States when the Council on Library and Information Resources (CLIR) began offering library training fellowships to non-librarians with Ph.D.'s in the humanities to fill the shortage of MLS subject specialists in American academic libraries. The CLIR program provides the fellows with a short-course approach to library methods while giving them on-the-job training in university libraries around the country. This is intended to turn these non-librarians into "information professionals and scholars" without ever completing library school.

Crowley (2004) labels this project "shortsighted and self-abasing" and warns that "these apprenticeships are likely to undermine further the academic librarian's already unstable place within higher education." Perhaps more likely, he argues, the fellowships could "create an alternative, even superior, class of librarians who will be superbly positioned by university standards and custom to challenge more conventionally educated colleagues for dominance in the contemporary academic library." Crowley knows well that the culture of academe tends to leave librarians out of the central functions of higher education, and he advises library leaders to "enhance effective service by embedding librarians in the center of the academic enterprise." In short, librarians and faculty are divided from each other, and CLIR's program could even incite new divisions among librarians in the same libraries. As there is already a class division between MLS librarians and library "support staff," another tier of library specialists would be too much to live with.

Crowley is saying that a large part of our strategy as educators is to integrate libraries and librarians more fully into the processes of teaching, learning, and research in our universities and colleges. That has been my objective from my early days as a library director. CLIR's program can only provoke a deeper division between librarians. Like Crowley, I reject CLIR's idea of short-course library training for non-librarians, despite their subject doctorates. As the CLIR program stands, it demeans librarianship training even lower than Gilman's observation (2003) that library education includes "less-than-rigorous content" (see Oder). In reality, the CLIR program is selling out MLS–bearing librarians, who should rightly be the first recipients of any resources made available for the purpose of increasing the number of librarians with Ph.D.'s.

In other words, the CLIR fellowships should be offered to librarians who already have MLS degrees so they can earn their doctorates. The results may be the same in the long run, but doctoral fellowships for MLS librarians would give the advantage to many persons who have already committed themselves to careers in libraries. They should have first crack at the CLIR fellowships. To do anything else is a slap in the face from ALA. It should be no wonder that the library recruitment stream is dwindling while senior librarians are retiring posthaste.

Brunner (2009), an advocate of CLIR fellowships, says the fellows are engaged at "two ends of the spectrum," in reference work, book selection, teaching information literacy, and other standard operations of academic librarians, while other fellows create digital resources, write grants, develop OA journals, share policies, provide copyright assistance for faculty, and work in academic departments and centers. Good for them, but this only begs the issue of MLS librarians who would very much like to have a leg up on a librarian Ph.D. fellowship. Brunner adds that "roles in academic libraries are becoming less clear, the deeper we go into the digital turn ... or however you want to characterize the present paradigm shift." In other words, from my perspective on CLIR fellowships, libraries and librarians will become even more divided. In the abstract of "Ph.D. Holders in the Academic Library," Brunner observed, "Overall this report shows that there is much that has worked well in the CLIR program for all involved. There is also much that could be improved, but in spite of this needed change, the CLIR Post-doctoral Fellowship Program embodies the transition that academic libraries, as a whole, are undergoing. Consequently, the academic library profession would do well to learn from the CLIR Program experience and explore opportunities to create similar programs to meet other staffing and recruitment needs within the profession." With that I think I can concur. We'll see.

While it is true that many MLS librarians have no interest in earning Ph.D.'s, I am certain that others undoubtedly would jump at the chance to undertake a Ph.D., especially if scholarships or fellowships were available, whether they involve a subject- or a library-related degree.

Still, I say shame on CLIR for not making Ph.D. scholarships or fellowships more available to MLS librarians, and shame on ALA for failing to mandate doctorates as the terminal degree for academic librarians, and for not asserting unequivocally the teaching role of librarians. These three failures — (1) mid-level terminal degrees without a means for practicing librarians to pursue doctoral-level education while on the job, (2) inadequate preparation in pedagogical methods, and (3) not asserting unequivocally the teaching role of librarians — have promulgated the schism and the dual standards between teaching faculty and librarians. A second master's degree in a subject area is not a bad idea, but it simply won't do for dispelling the notion in higher education that librarians are not competent as academics. To become the equals of instructional faculty, librarians must attain the highest levels of intellectual accomplishment and refine the teaching methods they use in their libraries, perhaps in some of the ways suggested in this book.

I was very fortunate to receive a $2,000 fellowship from my anthropology department at the midpoint of my doctoral program, and it helped me greatly. But my real godsend was the standing offer of the City of Phoenix Personnel Department to provide full-tuition reimbursements to city employees for completed educational courses related to their work. At that time I was working in the Business and Social Sciences Department of the central branch of Phoenix Public Library, and this program financed my MLS and also my Ph.D. As of this writing, the Phoenix tuition reimbursement program is still on the books. I know how important that program was for my advanced degrees, so I know how grateful many MLS librarians would be if CLIR/ALA could provide them with fellowships or scholarships to obtain Ph.D.'s.

My Ph.D. made all the difference in my career. It came in very handy in my eye-to-eye dealings with faculty and administrators; it strengthened my case for promotions, even while I was in my Ph.D. program; provided me with self-assurance in my dual career as a library director and a teaching faculty member. Earning the Ph.D. was a grind, and I almost burned out. But now I'm quite glad I have it. It gives entrée to many venues I would not otherwise enjoy. Moreover, it made me a better teacher in my library responsibilities, and also to the students I taught in my classrooms.

The debate raised by CLIR over doctorates in librarianship is not a new one, but it shows again that our own professional association has extended and exacerbated the severe division between instructional faculty and librarians, and that the leaders of our profession, including many of those in the graduate library schools, are side-stepping the obvious solutions: MLS graduates should either earn subject doctorates or at the very least pursue doctorates in library science programs through other appropriate "merger" programs after the MLS.

Do You Know the Way to San Jose?

In 2005, another short-course recruitment program was announced at San Jose State University (SJSU): the Executive MLIS at the SJSU library school (Lane 2005). EMLIS is something like a partner to CLIR's approach to recruitment. The targets for this program, however, are not necessarily Ph.D. holders: the SJSU target recruits are "experienced managers and supervisors looking for increased responsibilities and leadership opportunities in libraries." EMLIS is also open to library staff in a variety of circumstances and classifications "for whom the lack of an MLS is a glass ceiling and glass wall." The program's prospectus states, "Many library leaders in the nation, and beyond, do not hold the MLIS degree, yet are successful librarians and leaders in their various professional and geographic communities. The librarians choose not to pursue the MLIS in its present form for a variety of reasons: full-time residency requirements; perceived relevance; lock-step curriculum sequencing regardless of background; heterogeneous student composition regardless of experience; course content; course scheduling, etc."

To make it easier and quicker to get through graduate library school, EMLIS requires once a year three-week residencies. Only persons with the described qualifications are admitted (http://slisweb.sjsu.edu/classes/exec.htm). This sounds like another program that is even thinner to begin with than the standard ALA MLS curriculum, which Gilman has already aptly described as less than rigorous.

How will the EMLIS program and its graduates stack up to librarians who have completed the normal ALA–accredited MLS? I don't think the MLS librarians will feel particularly chipper about this program. Furthermore, can these "library leaders in the nation, and beyond" pass the normal recruitment requirements for librarians if they are asked to present their transcripts showing in-class credit hours that may be below those of the normal ALA–accredited mandatory contact hours?

What are we really giving to these "experienced" recruits? Sheepskins? Is this a way to bring funds into the SJSU library school? Will this project expand the awareness of their employers that librarians are educators, especially educators of academic quality? Will EMLIS raise or lower the esteem that academic faculty might have for part-time librarian recruits? Will other librarians already on the job embrace these new recruits? I hope so, but I have doubts. Finally, if EMLIS recruits, who are already "experienced managers and supervisors looking for increased responsibilities and leadership opportunities," can suddenly become much more successful with a brief MLS course, what does that say to MLS librarians who want access to their own higher professional development opportunities and learning, be it a second master's or a Ph.D.?

UCB

The University of Colorado at Boulder (UCB) has its own attractive Provost's Fellowship program for individuals already holding a subject master's degree (Knowlton and Imamoto 2006). The provost offers up to five participants the opportunity to combine their graduate degrees with a master's degree in librarianship. The offer states, "The need for academic librarians with subject, language and technical specialties is increasing dramatically as the volume of information available continues to grow, and access to quality information becomes more difficult." Each fellow receives $2,500 "to offset 150 hours" of the program and provides a library faculty mentor. Compared with the CLIR and the SJSU programs, the UCB program is a breath of fresh air because it welcomes students with master's as well as Ph.D. degrees.

Yet despite the opportunities of the UCB fellowship program, it does not reach to the roots of the problems for librarians and academic libraries. The divisions in academic librarianship may still be untouched by the UCB program. Knowlton and Imamoto observe that the CLIR program may well "sidestep" and "devalue" the MLS. I certainly concur. On the other hand, the Boulder program welcomes master's and Ph.D. students to apply for the fellowships. In the initial 2005 recruitment, 13 candidates were master's students and six were Ph.D. candidates. None of the Ph.D. applicants were accepted because they mainly wanted to use the fellowships "as a means of improving themselves as teaching faculty or researchers" (Knowlton and Imamoto 2006). That is, a career in librarianship was not their primary goal. This, of course, was *not* to the liking of the provost! The gang of six blew their chances.

After completing the program, the accepted fellows expressed their satisfaction with the program itself and with the wide diversity of work in academic libraries. One of the brighter candidates observed, "An academic library is a rather upbeat place to work." Unfortunately, that cannot be said for all academic libraries, as will be discussed in Chapter 8 of this book on library management.

Of all these current options, I like John Morton's motivations the best. He received his Ph.D., and shortly thereafter became a vice president of the University of Hawaii. Everything fell into place for him. He knew very well from the beginning what his career was all about, and he took the right steps at the right time. I admire him greatly. The Ph.D. gambit worked for John Morton, and the Phoenix tuition reimbursement program worked for me. I advise MLS librarians to address their scholarly pursuits carefully and seriously in order to raise their contribution to teaching, learning, and research at their institutions. They should do this through further education by earning second master's degrees, and especially Ph.D.'s.

Presidents, ALA

In her President's Message, Leslie Burger (2007) made encouraging comments about changing library education. She recognized the pressing "need for strong, competitive library programs that focus on both the history and foundation of our profession as well as the future and possibilities of libraries in our changing society." She then said there are several ways to effect this change. One that I like is to think "honestly about the level of education required to work in 21st-century libraries and the type of continuing education needed to ensure that our workforce remains fresh and highly skilled." My interpretation of her ambitions may be wrong, but I hope there may be room in them to effect new and much needed stipulations about library education for academic librarians, particularly for advanced subject degrees, especially doctorates. I agree with Burger when she says, "It's time for the discussion to stop and for transformation to take place." I hope some of this rubs off on subsequent yearly ALA presidents.

In any case, Ms. Burger is long gone from her one-year ALA presidency, as are all the rest of the ALA presidents with their catchy slogans, such as "Kids Who Read Succeed," and others as catchy and equally absurd because no program or ALA slogan can endure more than one paltry year. It's an ALA popularity contest. Instead, ALA is stiff and needs nothing less than to revivify itself and librarianship as well. In academe, the troubling objective is to bring academic librarians together with their faculty, students, and administrators to end the divisions between librarians and the other residents in their universities. Again, unbolt the silos and move forward!

Subsequent ALA figurehead prexies have been much less comprehensive about getting down to the bedrock of the library profession; however, I like one of Ms. Roy's platform issues from 2007–08: "supporting library and information science education through *practice*, and including all peoples in the circle of literacy" (ALA, www.ala.org/). This is almost good, if we can interpret her all-inclusive "circle of literacy" as meaning to heal the many enormous divisions librarians face between themselves, their libraries, faculty, students, academic administrators, and library practitioners who have only a mid-level educational target, and who really need to stretch for higher education.

It remains that the real need for further librarian impact can be achieved only through education and more education. It is self-evident. Wringing out education through practice is not nearly enough. This plank in Ms. Roy's literacy circle focuses on fringe issues while the core of librarianship is disintegrating. We need all librarians to be the best teachers they can aspire to be. The 2007–08 platform lacked a hardball approach to education that reaches through the MLS and continues on to higher subject degrees, or better a Ph.D., and broader disciplinary learning.

The 2008–09 ALA presidential incumbent, Mr. Jim Rettig, starts out well. I was struck when I saw that he invoked the term *connections* no less than five times on his website. For a happy moment, I thought that I might be able to discontinue this book about divided libraries. Mr. Rettig went even farther in my direction when he aimed his "connections" at libraries, service communities, and prospective library staff. I even gave thought, at least for a moment, to his mention of benefits available from ALA. That's when I started to doubt him. After about three or four "connections," I fell through huge cracks I still see in librarianship, which he seems unable to perceive. In short, I threw his "connections" at the wall, but they didn't stick. Where was the meaning, and what were the strategies to rivet together the needed connections, especially to raise librarian education? Connection, connection, yes, yes, but where is the centrality that will make LIS — at master and doctoral levels — finally connect to our professional core: teaching and teaching very well because of advanced degrees and continuous learning. This can only occur when we all strive to learn more about our mission as educators.

If Mr. Rettig means that libraries are "integrated ecosystems," I must disagree in light of the rigid classifications among our own staff. If he means libraries are ecosystems integrated *with* the communities we serve, that is, the campuses, students, faculty, and administrators, I most strongly disagree. Librarians do not as yet have the stature of instructional faculty, researchers, and most administrators. Too bad.

Continuing with CLIR, I find it somewhat telling that CLIR fellows "work on projects that exploit current information technology to forge, renovate, and strengthen *connections* [that magic word again] between academic library collections and their users" http://www. clir.org/fellowships/postdoc/postdoc.html. Is that all? Collections only? What about the rest of librarianship? The face-to-face teaching and learning components? CLIR wants to strengthen connections, but the connections don't appear to be in focus. For instance, I don't understand why only humanists are CLIR eligibles. It would seem that exploiting library information technology would be in good hands with Ph.D. information scientists. They can invent new magic buses for us and our users. The CLIR program lives to "prepare a new generation of librarians and scholars for work at the intersections of scholarship, excellent teaching, and librarianship in the emerging research environment." OK, maybe, but I'm not holding my breath.

This is not a new "generation," I suspect, but rather a new breed of "librarians" who will be detached from the strictly MLS path, less than rigorous though it may be, and look for higher peaks to climb. In a number of ways, we are denigrating the MLS, while at the time, those who remain at this level may be stuck forever. How much interest from faculty, then, might the CLIR scholars engender who skip a grade in those lower ranks? As Crowley clearly foresaw (2004), the CLIR fellows and other add-on schemes forged their own circles of colleagues and took librarianship in new, unpredictable directions. To me also it is worrisome.

Faculty Status

Even beyond terminal degrees, librarians must seek faculty status at their institutions equal to that of instructional faculty, actively pursue promotion and tenure, and engage in research and publication in library journals or those of their subject specialties. Holders of doctorates are expected by their doctoral committees to produce new knowledge for the rest of their careers, if not the rest of their lives, for the good of society. This expectation comes with the degree and is part of faculty and tenure processes. And much more so than the instructional faculty, we must emphasize our role as educators, and reject the trite notion that librarians are merely "the stewards of knowledge." As I stated earlier, librarians are not "stewards" of knowledge. We are educators.

Perceptions of Librarianship

At the present time, librarians are desperately trying to maintain a strong claim on their academic presence and importance. Our lack of commonly recognized academic terminal degrees, our failure to acknowledge and promote our teaching skills, and our comparative reluctance to conduct and publish research all detract from our efforts to be viewed as legitimate peers of instructional academic faculty. It's like being underdressed at the opera, and the situation won't change until the library profession lives up to the same high levels of performance as those practiced by faculty and researchers.

CLIR stated that its fellowship program is "designed to challenge [the fellows] to think broadly about the changes under way in research methodologies, the creation of new scholarly resources, and the demands these changes place on critical academic institutions such as universities, libraries, and archives. CLIR believes that the deep subject knowledge Ph.D.'s offer, combined with their experiences in the classroom and with research trends, can be invaluable to the development of pedagogically-sound scholarly resources." Of course! But CLIR pits "the traditional work [*sic*] performed by librarians" against the learning of advanced scholar-professionals "whose abilities span the areas of subject specialization, pedagogy, technology, and new media research." Talk about a put-down of librarians at the expense of ALA through CLIR!

If these expectations of advanced education, excellence in teaching, and ongoing scholarship had been the tuition of librarians a few generations ago, our profession would not now be wondering where it fits in academe. If CLIR, ALA, and all their associated committees, work groups, and roundtables are not willing or able to raise librarianship to the level of a full academic discipline by focusing on teaching excellence, doctoral-level academic preparation, scholarship and research, and full faculty status for all MLS degree holders, as well as CLIR Ph.D. librarians who are just short of getting away with robbery, the future of the profession looks bleak.

Step by Step Upward

There may be hope, however, if even a few of the matters contained in the 2010 Top Ten Trends in Academic Libraries come to fruition, but we must take a firmer hold on our strengths and missions. I won't ever forget the poignant disappearance of the bibliophile librarians in the 1980s and the falling domino effect. They were service-oriented and provided good reading and learning opportunities for their users, but many of the bibliophiles could not easily make the transition into computerized operations, and they became fewer and fewer in librarianship. They were not what I call "machine people," that is, persons who know how to tinker with things like toasters, lamp switches, electric motors, tools, leaky faucets, or even musical instruments, which are a type of machine. Persons with these inclinations seem to have a disposition toward machine logic. In my experience, machine people adapt to computers much more readily than do non-machine people, and can more easily learn the logic and exploit the potential of digital technology.

At the library administrative levels, the 2010 top ten trends tell us, "Widespread retirements will result in a leadership gap and loss of institutional memory." Is it in part that current library leaders are not as gratified by their librarianship careers as they had hoped to be, nor did they achieve their mission?

A few years later, however, a new breed of librarian began to emerge from the library schools. They were not only skilled in the technology, but they could creatively exploit and adapt the strengths of the new systems. With these individuals, librarianship turned an important corner that raised the stature and effectiveness of the profession and also raised the levels of teaching and learning in libraries in digital spaces.

For example, in 1995, at the University of Hawaii Kapiolani campus, the library began a concerted digital publishing program that created repositories of curricular materials in collaboration with the East-West Center (a U.S. federal government think tank); the Pacific Studies Center; the Hamilton Library Business and Science Department; the Center for Chinese Studies; the Kapiolani radiology department; and the department of tropical agriculture, along with a number of digital projects for community groups. I was the director of the Kapiolani Library at that time, and after we had gained experience in creating scholarly online resources and digital repositories, we laid plans for what was later termed a digital academic press (DAP), and identified several collections of materials in the UH system and the larger community that were appropriate for scholarly publication. Because of the rapidly deteriorating economic conditions in Hawaii, however, the Kapiolani DAP never quite materialized (see Chapter 6). Certain collections were digitized, however, and linked to the library's website as stand-alone online resources.

In the last several years, I think I have seen the beginning of another transformation of librarianship in the young professionals who are coming out of the library schools and beginning their careers. In addition to excellent digital understanding, many of these young people are more interested than their predecessors in research and publication; more determined to provide service to users in the form of excellent teaching and learning strategies; more intent on deep involvement in the governing of their institutions; more eager for a voice in the workings of the faculty; and more inclined to advance their own academic preparations beyond the master's level. These are they who will seek Ph.D. degrees wherever they may find them. How much better it would be to provide fellowships to these intelligent and devoted graduate librarians as motivation to earn the doctorates CLIR should be seeking.

This attitudinal shift in the rising library professionals bodes well. With a clear and concerted vision of the teaching role of librarians among the leaders and organizations of the library profession and the courage to make the needed changes in library education, the future of libraries may be brighter than we/I think, perhaps.

Academic Status

The image of librarians as dilettante educators that has been assigned to us won't change until we pay our academic dues. If librarians are college- and university-level educators, and if we intend to play that role fully, it is plain to see that we need to seek the same level of preparation as instructional faculty, with doctoral-level terminal degrees in some valid field of information management, education, or a discipline relevant to the librarian's professional interests and the institutional curricula. We must also aspire to faculty status, sabbaticals, and grants. Bell and Shank (2004) state, "While the evolution of information literacy is a positive sign, the academic librarian is still tangential to what happens in or beyond the classroom. Strategies, techniques, and skills are needed that will allow all academic librarians, from every sector of the organization, to advance proactively their integration into the teaching and learning process." They add that academic librarians lack an "understanding of pedagogy and adoption of instructional design theory and practice."

These skill sets have long been integral to the teaching and learning process. Still, many members of our profession are woefully deficient in their knowledge of how learning takes place, how structures for effective learning are designed, and how learning outcomes are assessed. According to Avery and Ketches (1996), library instruction is not taught formally in many LIS programs. Let's hope times will change for the better and soon.

Academic faculty tend to be pretentious and skeptical by training and in some cases, I think, by nature. It is frequently said that doctoral degrees are mainly for those who wish to be college and university teachers. Ph.D.'s, faculty status, promotion, and tenure are said to be hard for librarians. Of course! These chores are hard for everyone! Such is academe. These processes are good for librarians and the profession. We need to do it because we are bona fide educators and we must keep pace with our faculty peers. It will make us better educators and better librarians and better people. Transmute pain into gain. We need to have the same grounding as the faculty, and that includes doctorates. We have not all yet paid our dues, and I'm *not* referring to ALA dues.

Dues Indeed

It has been my observation in most places where I have worked in academe that librarians are considered by some, if not most, instructional faculty to be more than a few steps behind them, and barefoot. Oh, we get our share of respect and compliments, but we get little credibility. At this time, librarians are desperately trying to maintain a strong claim on their academic presence and importance, partnering with faculty to demonstrate our value to them, and assuming more and more specialized responsibilities and tasks while delegating much of our traditional work to non–MLS staff, who must rise to the call of leadership at all levels. It does not help us to be lacking in recognized academic terminal degrees and skills needed in teaching, research, and publication.

It's too bad ALA refused to see the obvious and failed to require CLIR to make their fellowships available first to MLS librarians. While libraries are increasingly hiring IT and disciplinary specialists to complement the traditional work performed by librarians, they are also becoming aware of the need to hire librarian-scholars who will pursue innovative career paths in universities, libraries, archives, and special collections, and play crucial roles in shaping the future of scholarly resource management and use across academe. Also, CLIR fellowships should be offered first to MLS librarians to provide them with hands-on experience and theoretical foundations in the traditional and emerging approaches to scholarship creation and application. In other words, librarians are likely combatants who will lead with the faculties into a worldwide OA confrontation. Without the corps of librarians, OA will stumble along and eventually dissipate. We're already on that course.

Faculty Status, Promotion, and Tenure

Having observed that the globalized economy threatens the survival of librarianship as we now know it, Crowley and Ginsberg (2003) lean toward adopting faculty requirements, earning doctorates, and teaching information analysis to save our profession. Indeed, I found that working in a library for tenure and promotion and receiving them, and trudging the long row from assistant to full professor, brought about a great deal of learning and discipline in me. While I was working on my Ph.D., progressing toward tenure was a savory experience. Progressing in a Ph.D. program fits well with promotion toward tenure. I also came to appreciate the bond that forms between faculty and administration while conducting my Ph.D. research. Even if a librarian declines to pursue a doctoral degree, taking the promotion and tenure track, if it is offered, is well worth the effort. These experiences become part of a librarian's professional expertise, and leads a step farther toward mastery of one's field and receiving recognition from instructional faculty and administrators. Furthermore, a tenure-track librarian, with or without a Ph.D. in hand, can be a fine mentor for junior librarians.

Miller and Benefiel (1998) conclude that "achieving tenure is difficult under the best of circumstances." Furthermore, "feelings of isolation" also contribute to the hesitancy of applying for promotion and tenure. To help allay the isolation factor, the authors endorse a group approach to provide mutual encouragement to librarians going forward with promotion and tenure. The authors note that of the three major criteria — professional performance, service to the profession, and research and publication — the last is the "most daunting."

My view? Sure, going for promotion and tenure is a reach, but it isn't actually hell. Librarians are smart, they read, they have a good grasp of current subject domains, and most of them are certainly articulate, intellectual, and capable of receiving promotion and tenure. These qualities can greatly reduce the "daunting" fear factor of the tenure track.

Meyer's study (1999) argued that "the number of librarians and whether they are eligible for tenure affects the quality of instruction as measured by graduation rate, graduate school attendance, and cognitive development," and that "faculty stature ... for librarians has a positive impact on the success of institutions concentrating on teaching." He observes, "Finding material relevant to their assignments depends on the extent of their bibliographic skills [which] are positively affected by the number of opportunities they have to receive bibliographic instruction, which is dependent on the number of librarians assigned to classroom bibliographic instruction and one-on-one tutorials at the reference desk."

Drawing on Slattery (1994), Welch and Mozenter (2006) explain, "To its proponents, faculty status is an appropriate complement to our sense of professional identity. It is the passport to greater campus involvement and to enhanced self-esteem and prestige, and is the instrument that allows us to more accurately gauge the quality and variety of services required of us."

In their summary, Welch and Mozenter combined Slattery's views and a "selective" survey to identify the three main benefits for seeking tenure: "full participation in university governance, enhancing the library's role in academe; academic freedom; and full opportunity for professional growth." They emphasize that "only tenure ensures all three conditions."

Tenure is an achievement, a motivation, a pathway to further learning and higher education. Extending tenure is the most prestigious and binding commitment a university can offer faculty. With tenure, the university extends a form of employment to deserving faculty that carries a type of permanence that is virtually unique to academe. Before offering this level of permanence, the university must be more than reasonably convinced that the faculty member will continue to perform at least at the same level of productivity, integrity, and scholarship displayed during the probationary period.

That's the reason probation for university faculty lasts so long. It gives the faculty member ample opportunity to develop into the kind of asset the university truly needs while giving the university enough time to become assured that the faculty member will most likely continue to perform at a very high level throughout his/her tenure. "Most likely," that is. A certain number of tenured faculty start vegetating when they receive tenure, but that is an individual decision. It is not pandemic by any means. It all depends on the integrity of the individual tenured faculty member. In my perception, this existence is the pinnacle of learning and teaching in their purest forms.

Ph.D.: The Razor's Edge

Not only are Ph.D. degrees coin of the realm in academe, some persons who have them are clearly ambitious and self-serving, even egotistical. Quite frankly, some use their doctorates to justify their own obnoxiousness. I know this because I have one, and I am not afraid to play that face card to make the point. But this is hardly an explanation of why certain people seek doctoral degrees; it is the difference between the major and minor leagues, lightweights and heavyweights, and we're hitting below our weight. Here's the razor's edge: having a doctoral degree does not mean that all Ph.D.'s are good teachers. The Ph.D. is a credential that, rightly or wrongly, puts the academic in "the third heaven" (II Corinthians 12:2).

Obtaining a doctoral degree, especially while working in a library, is like a weightlifter performing an intellectual feat on a high wire while running a gauntlet. Even after receiving a Ph.D., the degree does not by itself guarantee tenure by any means, nor does it necessarily ingratiate the MLS ranks. In fact, it could be detrimental if librarians with Ph.D.'s lord their good fortune over MLS holders — ask Crowley and Ginsberg. Promotion for tenure is the gauntlet.

Because of the professionalism and advances of technology and new library intentions, librarians are in a position to change education and better life worldwide. We can muster an amazing potential. For instance, consider Bonnie Maidak, an MLS librarian with a Ph.D. in human genetics, who made a spectacular contribution not only to librarianship but to humanity itself through the Human Genome Project at Johns Hopkins. She made perfectly sure "that what goes into the database is in the right location and that it doesn't conflict with some other set of data" (Levin). ALA should take her as an example of the need for librarianship to reach the pinnacles of academic stature, and also that our librarians can certainly go for the Ph.D. It will mature librarianship. Chapter 7 contains more about this type of "ultimate" librarianship.

With our "less than rigorous" master's curriculum, the image of librarians that has been assigned to us is one of instructor-level educators with little research experience, and this won't change until we take the brave steps. One day when I was an undergraduate, I was waiting in a doctor's office for the nurse to call my name. I casually began reading a keynote conference article in a journal of pharmacy. The paper was impassioned, and was intended to rouse the audience of pharmacists to aspire to greater heights of medical service and exactness with the growing numbers of pharmaceutical products and techniques being developed. In the last line of the paper, the author stated that the mighty goal of the conference attendees should be to raise the pharmacy profession "higher in the healthcare galaxy."

The overstatement amused me. Back then my estimation of pharmacists was not nearly as high as that of physicians. Then, when I had been a librarian for a number of years, I found that university academics have much that same type of perception toward academic librarians. I must say that my estimation of physicians over the years has suffered as well, and now I see that the pharmacist was trying to raise the level of his profession, too. Good luck.

Repeating from Chapter 1, to work well with faculty, we need to know what they do and how they got where they are. We cannot know the highs and lows of a Ph.D. program, along with faculty status, promotion and tenure, research and publishing, and sabbaticals, unless we go after it for ourselves. ALA should reinvent itself into something more worthwhile to move librarians and their cause strictly forward.

5

THE REFORMATION OF
SCHOLARLY COMMUNICATION

Extortion at the Top of the World

A librarian I work with in Hong Kong took a trip to Tibet. It was a strenuous exploit for several reasons — the altitude, the distance, and the difference in food, among others. She described the uniqueness of the locale, the variety of peoples who were there, the smells, the tastes, the over-charging, the hassles, and the spectacular visual rewards.

She told me, however, about a certain human behavioral oddity that particularly annoyed her. She was preparing to take a photograph of a scenic view, but she sensed that someone was standing close beside her. Engrossed in composing the photo, she did not look to see who the person was.

Just as she pressed the shutter button, one of the locals in full ethnic attire jumped quickly into the photo plane, and inserted himself into the picture. He then demanded money from the librarian for taking his picture. She felt obliged to pay, but didn't like it.

Maybe I'm being overly didactic, but as soon as she told me the story, I thought it was strikingly analogous to the ruthless commercial publishers of scholarly communication who, for gain, unscrupulously insert themselves into researchers' attempts to disseminate or access vital information by charging exorbitantly for the information that researchers need.

It may well be that from the day writing was invented, there has been a love-hate relationship between publishers and librarians (excluding my own publisher, of course). Librarians, like Hypatia, wanted to share books magnanimously with their readers, while the publishers were in cahoots with the information industry. This trite little bookman's homily has burgeoned into a fractious cutthroat dilemma: Who gets access to knowledge and learning, and who does not?

Troglodyte History

In the late 1970s and into the 1980s, libraries were concentrating on automating their catalogs, then undertaking giant and very costly and usually wrong-headed retrospective book conversion projects. At the same time, however, commercial publishers were eagerly striving to put information directly into the hands of readers, which librarians should have been directing while the canny publishers were ready to put plenty of money into their own pockets. The publisher's first phase of this venture was to invent and profit from the new medium of CD-ROM to replace printed periodical indexes, but the vendors did not bother to ask librarians what impact this technology might have on libraries and library users. Since that very day, and up to the present hour, library automation vendors usually take their own road and develop products they assume would be glamorous to librarians. Yet they never addressed our needs as librarians (see Pace 2004).

Personal computers were proliferating, creating a market that would thrive on digital storage and retrieval processes, and the CD-ROM storage medium was hailed as a technological breakthrough. It allowed the standard searches of author, title, and subject, but also keyword searching, and the like. A library user could suddenly search through many years of a periodical index in an instant, compared to the toil involved in searching through multiple volumes of tiny-print paper indexes. Compared to fumbling with the paper cumulative volumes and their trailing supplements, using disks was a snap.

The publishers and the vendors of CD-ROM components would of course sell their subscriptions and products to anyone, but this technology was geared to the stand-alone personal computer and the individual researcher. CD-ROM was ill-suited for the simultaneous multiple user conditions libraries required. In this regard, even a card catalog was much more accommodating to simultaneous multiple users than the CD-ROM systems could ever be, even when daisy-chained to each other and cabled to CD-ROM "towers." But librarians felt compelled to provide the new medium or else betray their users, and we found ourselves caught in the escalating and very costly dead-end phases of CD technology that required us to buy more and more public PCs dedicated to CD-ROM networks, towers, and backfiles.

Borrowing terms from Lafferty and Edwards (2004), CD-ROM was a type of "disruptive library technology." It was clearly not sustainable, its functionality was limited, although superior in many ways to paper indexes, and it had a deleterious effect on successful, "mainstream" information providers, that is, libraries. The online full-text industry that succeeded CD-ROM technology has had an even more disruptive impact on libraries by dividing us even more from the processes of scholarly communication in the rampant technology sector. To make a long, sad story sadder, after a few decades the information industry simply wrested control of scholarly communication from libraries. The current conditions of scholarly publishing cannot be sustained.

Some of us in the library profession realized that CD-ROM was only an off-line transitional technology, simply an expensive phase on the way to a fully online, real-time, multi-user platform to access indexes and eventually to full-text online, the sheer contemplation of which seemed likely to be library paradise. This contemplation also was misplaced, however, as this essay is intended to demonstrate, because ever since that contemplation, our profession has become increasingly divided by greedy publishers from full-text online scholarly communication.

Although appearing later than the truly online research databases of the time, such as Dialog and BRS, the CD-ROM boom was actually the beginning of the IT industry. CD-ROM, linked to PCs, jump-started information technology because Dialog and the other early online databases, although hints of things to come, were complicated to use, costly, and very time-consuming even for the relatively few numbers of librarians and others who were trained to construct the arcane search strategies those databases then required. These were *not* free-language platforms.

I remember clearly the days when librarians set appointments with users, in the same manner physicians, attorneys, and analysts dealt with their clients. A number of librarians were selectively trained in their libraries to query Dialog or BRS on behalf of their users. In these appointments, the librarians fully interrogated the users about their symptoms — that is search objectives — then scheduled another appointment to apply the treatment — that is, run the actual searches. Between appointments the librarians carefully constructed a series of Boolean search arguments with the nestings and truncations that were most likely to summon a list of citations that would cure the users' ignorance. For the librarians, it was tedious but invigorating — the ultimate professionalism: diagnosis, prognosis, cure, or so we had hoped.

For the users, it must have seemed like an intervention from the Oracle of Delphi or the Wizard of Oz. Yet these cumbersome databases showed us the real future of IT, librarianship, and, I continue to argue, scholarly communication. At present, scholarly communication is in the hands of commercial publishers who know better than anyone else that knowledge is power, or in other words, the key to colossal wealth. Unless the library profession can break the hold that publishers exert on scholarly communication, academic processes, along with libraries and even universities, are in extreme jeopardy.

Scholarship in Peril

In 1994 on the Kapiolani Campus of the University of Hawaii, our staff developed several online resources in Asian-Pacific studies when *open access* and *institutional repositories* were uncommon terms. On this leading edge, I gave three invited presentations on our resources in Hong Kong and Beijing, 1995, 1996, and 2000. (More about this in Chapter 7.)

From humble beginnings like those at Kapiolani, all around us now the world's finest universities are adopting OA to assure broader and affordable effective scholarly communication. On February 12, 2008, Harvard's arts and sciences faculty voted to permit Harvard to distribute its scholarship online, "instead of signing exclusive agreements with scholarly journals that often have tiny readerships and high subscription costs" http://www.thecrimson.com/article.aspx?ref=521861 (*Harvard Crimson Online*). The decision at Harvard is a strong endorsement for OA. Harvard English professor Stephen Greenblatt, himself an editor of a scholarly journal, said, "This is one of the only ways we can break the backs of the monopolists who are currently seriously damaging our fields." Robert Darnton, Harvard's library director, said, "This is a way of sharing the intellectual wealth of Harvard, which is for the public good.... We think it can make a very important difference ... in scholarly communication."

Stuart Shieber, the Harvard professor of computer science who proposed the policy, said the decision "should be a very powerful message to the academic community that we *want* and *should have* more control over how our work is used and disseminated" (Guterman 2005, emphasis added).

On the same track, a 2008 resolution from the Cornell Faculty Senate stated, "Recognizing that the increasing control by large commercial publishers over the publication and distribution of faculty's scholarship and research threatens to undermine core academic values promoting broad and rapid dissemination of new knowledge and unrestricted access to the results of scholarship and research ... the University Faculty Senate *encourages the library and the faculty vigorously* to explore and support alternatives to commercial venues for scholarly communication" (emphasis added).

In an MIT faculty meeting on March 18, 2009, the faculty voted unanimously to move their scholarly articles to OA to be loaded into a DSpace repository. Approval was practically immediate across the university. Their intention was "to make their scholarly articles available to the public for free and open access on the Web," which prompted Bish Sunyal, chair of the MIT Faculty and Ford International Professor of Urban Development and Planning, to say, "The vote is a signal to the world that we speak in a unified voice; that what we value is the free flow of ideas."

MIT faculty were the first to use and share their scholarly articles for any purpose other than making a profit, and while Harvard and Stanford universities had earlier implemented OA in some of their schools, MIT was the first to implement OA university-wide as a result of a faculty vote.

Hal Abelson, Class of 1922 professor of Electrical Engineering and Computer Science and chair of the Ad-Hoc Faculty Committee on Open Access Publishing, stated, "Scholarly publishing has so far been based purely on contracts between publishers and individual faculty authors." Abelson also observed, "In that system, faculty members and their institutions were powerless. This resolution changes that by creating a role in the publishing process for the faculty as a whole, not just as isolated individuals."

MIT Director of Libraries Ann Wolpert worked closely with Abelson and others to move the resolution forward. She said, "Through this action, MIT faculty have shown great leadership in the promotion of free and open scholarly communication. In the quest for higher profits, publishers have lost sight of the values of the academy. This will allow authors to advance research and education by making their research available to the world" (Richard 2005).

UC, Harvard, Cornell, MIT, and many others deserve thanks from universities around the planet for opposing the price gouging that has a stranglehold on scholarship and higher education itself, and for devising clear strategies and tools to rectify the problems at hand.

Even government agencies now see a need for free access to new research funded by taxpayers. On December 26, 2007 (my birthday, no less), President Bush signed the Consolidated Appropriations Act of 2007 (H.R. 2764), which requires the National Institutes of Health to "provide the public with open online access to findings from its funded research." This is the first time the U.S. government has mandated public access to research funded by a federal agency. More public open access will come, not only from the U.S. government, but also from other government entities.

Harold Varmus, Nobel Prize winner and president of the Memorial Sloan-Kettering

Cancer Center, said, "Facilitated access to new knowledge is key to the rapid advancement of science.... The tremendous benefits of broad, unfettered access to information are already clear from the Human Genome Project, which has made its DNA sequences immediately and freely available to all, via the Internet. Providing widespread access ... to the full text of research articles supported by funds from all institutes at the NIH will increase those benefits dramatically."

David Shulenburger, vice president of the National Association of State Universities and Land-Grant Colleges (U.S.), said, "Public access to publicly funded research contributes directly to the mission of higher education. Improved access will enable universities to maximize their own investment in research, and widen the potential for discovery as the results are more readily available for others to build upon."

In 2005, the Columbia University Senate unanimously endorsed a similar resolution on OA at its meeting on April (Columbia University Libraries News & Information). The resolution was introduced by the Senate's Committee on Libraries and Academic Computing.

James Neal, Columbia's vice president for Information Services and University Librarian at the time, applauded "this bold support by the Columbia community for open access to scholarly work and this endorsement of the university's advocacy for reducing economic, legal, and technological barriers." Portions of the Columbia resolution follow:

> *Whereas* the principle of open access to the fruits of scholarly research is increasingly being adopted and pursued by universities and in the scholarly community at large, and
>
> *Whereas* Columbia University continues to be in the forefront of open-access endeavors, through its advocacy activities and its digital library programs, and
>
> *Whereas* technological, legal and economic barriers continue to be erected to obstruct or limit open access, and
>
> *Whereas* the availability of the fruits of scholarly endeavor ought to reflect the conditions of cooperative endeavor and common resources under which scholarly work is produced,
>
> *Therefore be it resolved*
>
> *That* the Senate urge the university to advance new models for scholarly publishing that will promote open access, helping to reshape the marketplace in which scholarly ideas circulate, in a way that is consistent with standards of peer review and scholarly excellence;
>
> *That* the Senate urge the university to monitor and resist efforts to impose digital rights management regimes and technologies that obstruct or limit open access, except as necessary to secure rights of privacy;
>
> *That* the Senate urge the scholars of Columbia University to play a part in these open-access endeavors in their various capacities as authors, readers, editors, referees, and members of scientific boards and learned associations, etc., (a) by encouraging and collaborating with publishers' efforts to advance open access, (b) by retaining intellectual property rights in their own work where this will help it become more widely available, and (c) by remaining alert to efforts by publishers to impose barriers on access to the fruits of scholarly research.

Another War

For a very long time now, economic warfare has gripped the processes of scholarly communication worldwide. Major universities are outraged by the cost of scholarly publications controlled by commercial publishers. Premier research libraries cannot afford to subscribe to the scholarly journals they need in order to support their continued research in the academic disciplines of their universities. At the same time, library automation developers have created digital publication and electronic repository modules to help libraries move straightaway into an electronic publication environment. How prepared is our profession to seize this opportunity?

Around the world, much more original digital information is becoming available, and not only through the offices of commercial publishers. Many more libraries are becoming information producers, new technologies for sharing scholarly information have proliferated, and huge text digitization initiatives are well underway. Clearly, a reformation of scholarly communication is mounting.

True to their word, the libraries of the University of California (UC, not to be confused with CSU) made very clear their commitment about "reshaping scholarly communication [to] understand the challenges, the crises they have produced, and opportunities to address them." UC's bottom line, though, is this: "Current scholarly publishing models are not economically sustainable. UC libraries encourage faculty publishing innovations, support 'transformative business models' for scholarly publishing 'to improve the dissemination of UC's scholarship,' and invite scholars 'to increase the impact and benefit of their scholarship.'" Researchers and students have easy access to a *diminishing fraction* of relevant scholarship" (emphasis added; http://libraries.universityofcalifornia.edu/libraries/).

Action to be taken: "Support sustainable scholarly communication" (http://osc.uni versityofcalifornia.edu/).

It's a heady pleasure finally to be in the reformation of scholarly communication after the early years of struggle. This strategic plan is aimed primarily at UC faculty and researchers, but given the planet-level stature of UC, this call unequivocally incites the scholarship revolution and is being heard at the most prestigious academic and research institutions in many parts of the world. Academic libraries clearly foment the revolution. I still remember Dan Greenstein's repeated call to arms: There's "a boatload of information about the repository, its policies and operating procedures" (personal e-mail, April 8, 2005).

Cornell University likewise took early action in 2003 to restore control of scholarly publication to the universities whose faculties produce new knowledge and findings, then virtually donate it to commercial publishers so they can sell it right back to the universities at prices university libraries cannot afford. Cornell has been just as vehement as the UC libraries, and clearly stated its case: "Only a fundamental change in the modes of scholarly communication will meaningfully address rising serials costs. This change has begun" (http://www.library.cornell.edu/scholarlycomm/serials/).

The Cornell Faculty Senate voted, "Recognizing that the increasing control by large commercial publishers over the publication and distribution of the faculty's scholarship and research threatens to undermine core academic values promoting broad and rapid dissemination of new knowledge and unrestricted access to the results of scholarship and research, the University Faculty Senate *encourages the library and the faculty vigorously* to explore and support alternatives to commercial venues for scholarly communication" (emphasis added; http://www.library.cornell.edu/scholarlycomm/resolution2.htm).

Who says libraries aren't in the middle of inciting a revolution in scholarly communication? Who can deny that this is a completely logical and appropriate action for libraries to take, given their mission and objectives? The UC, MIT, and Cornell libraries and many others like them should be applauded not only for coming to terms with the price gouging that has a stranglehold on scholarship and on higher education itself, but for devising clear strategies and even the tools to rectify the problems at hand. In fact, I wager that libraries themselves are the only institutions that can bring this revolution to fruition. If we don't do it, no other assemblage of academic entities, publishing conglomerates, community agencies, or central governments can (may God forbid). Despite their best intentions to control nose-thumbing publishers, attempts by various groups such as the Scholarly Publishing and Academic Resources Coalition (SPARC), JSTOR, Stanford's High Wire Press, and the California Digital Library (CDL) have had much less than spectacular results in curbing the continuing spiral of exorbitant price gouging. The publishers are standing firm.

University Presidents

In 2003, Richard Atkinson, retiring as president of the University of California system, openly and in print blasted scholarly publishers for their outrageous journal subscription costs and called for much more open access to scholarly communication and publishing. He urged faculty not to relinquish their copyrights, demanded that scholarly publishers lower their subscription rates, and stated that the best way to restore the free flow of scholarly communication is for universities to take control of scholarly processes using emergent applications of technology. He also charged other university presidents to lead their institutions into new models for scholarly communication. Yet while Atkinson sympathized with academic libraries in their budgetary predicament, he failed to envision any role for libraries (except CDL) in bringing about his proposed reformation of scholarly publishing.

Despite these vehement calls for reform and waves of digital publications emanating from libraries, scholarly communication is still in a critical state as commercial publishers have continually raised their prohibitive subscription rates and continue to impede the rapid spread of new knowledge among educators, scholars, researchers, students, and the general public.

Not much changed after Atkinson's article in 2003, and I was disappointed that he did not focus on academic libraries as the great potential for a massive scholarly communication overhaul. After all, if it makes sense for universities to assume control of scholarly communication, it would be a great oversight not to place their libraries at the center of the movement. Until very recently in their history, libraries were always at the center of scholarly communication, and they can be so again, undivided.

Many academic libraries are positioned to take leadership roles in the reformation of scholarly communication. They are mastering the new digital models, such as e-repositories, electronic dissertation collections, scholarship management software, and other e-innovations developed by digital libraries with more yet to come quite timely. These are the types of technological applications Atkinson might have had in mind to restore control of scholarly communication to the universities. These are also the technologies that are in high-speed development among digital libraries. Libraries have perennially collected and provided access to printed forms of scholarly communication, and they are uniquely suited to provide the same types of services in the digital domain.

Some older faculty vociferously argue against the move to e-publishing, open access, and institutional repositories, which certainly has been the case in Hong Kong, but that has not entirely been my direct experience. I grant that different disciplines adapt to e-journals and other digital publication options sooner than others. The early adopters have tended to be in the sciences, technology, and some others, while humanities and social sciences early on tended to be more conservative. Faculty reticence is not the flavor of the experiences at UC, Cornell, Harvard, or MIT. Similarly, my own direct experience tells me that faculty *are* ready for the e-reformation of scholarly publishing because they are chafing under the outrageous costs of research and publication processes controlled by publishing monopolies.

The Surge

The restructuring of scholarly communication will be inevitable as e-publications rise rapidly to the full measure of credibility they now deserve. These two factors — the rise of e-publications and their credibility — will affect faculty duties, recruitment, tenure and promotion review boards, and university administrations. Researchers and faculty authors must buy in.

When I was working at CSUS, for instance, we were devising methods to unhamper access and contributions to scholarly communication, and the faculty senate leaders explicitly asked me what the library could do to help new faculty research and publish while hefting their heavy teaching loads. I responded with some possibilities — a digital academic press (DAP; see Chapter 6); online applications to control their scholarly projects, IRs, e-learning, digital dissertations, and so on.

In a similar effort to overhaul scholarship processes, in this case for administrative efficiencies, the CSUS dean of graduate studies anticipated our library's preliminary investigations of ETDs, and requested that the library immediately undertake the creation of an ETD at CSUS and work with the graduate school administrators and faculty departments to develop the procedures that would allow the university to move as quickly as possible away from print submissions of theses and dissertations and into digital formats submitted electronically. Because the graduate studies administrators of all 23 CSU universities had arrived at the same conclusion in an earlier systemwide meeting, the urgency and acceptability of ETD implementation had become a CSU initiative without any campaigning or cajoling at all from the librarians.

ETDs now are huge, numerous, and international in scope, such as the Networked Digital Library of Theses and Dissertations (http://www.ndltd.org/membership/dir.html). The vast university collections of masters' theses, and especially doctoral dissertations, are a priceless body of scholarship. Due to the nature of graduate-level research, these treatises are often the only places to find very esoteric research and information. Putting these collections in online full-text resources is a major research accomplishment, and is attractive not only for easier access to the research, but also to facilitate the administrative procedures of graduate studies departments and expedite library processing and storage of these works while making them much more accessible.

It has been said that there are so many doctoral students on the planet that they need to find ever smaller and more peculiar topics to secure originality. Urban myth, perhaps, but dissertation topics can become pretty oblique. Their ready accessibility, therefore, could motivate student scholars to do more excellent work. At the very least, I hope this contributes to the freezing of microfilm collections with only selective, on-demand retrodigitization, and with no thought whatsoever given to massive retrocon projects for all those reels.

The spread of institutional repositories, e-scholarship repositories, and ETDs among academic libraries has helped restore ownership of scholarly communication to the academic community, despite the fact that their spread is hardly well organized or as pervasive as they should be across librarydom. I heartily endorse Greenstein's CDL model for institutional repositories (http://repositories.cdlib.org./escholarship). Far from being a disruptive technology, these contemporary resources springboard from older, proven digital knowledge bases such as the Conflict Archive on the Internet (CAIN), Perseus, the Schoenberg Center for Electronic Texts, Matthew Ciolek's Asian Studies Curriculum Online, the Asian Studies WWW Virtual Library, and others. E-repositories and their immediate predecessors are extremely appealing to researchers and other mainstream audiences, and are hardly upstarts of limited functionality.

A Scholarly Cascade

With the likes of UC, Harvard, MIT, NIH, Cornell, and others, we're moving forward fast and "embracing openness" (Van Orsdel and Born 2008). I never expected to see the fulfillment of OA in my lifetime, not to mention my career, but we're getting closer.

Probably the most successful e-repository is the Human Genome Database (GDB), which came to spectacular prominence in the 1990s at Johns Hopkins University. The GDB was the product of geneticists, librarians, and computer scientists (Levin 1992). The geneticists acted as the editorial boards (one board for each human chromosome). The librarians received the approved submissions from research findings, articles, papers, reports, and direct communication with genetics researchers. The librarians processed these data and passed the submissions to the appropriate editorial boards to vet the findings, then uploaded the new knowledge to the swelling database so it could be accessed immediately by genetics researchers and scientists around the world. The computer scientists designed and maintained the online systems. The equipment needed for this project was enormously expensive, but the product of the collaboration was of inestimable value in the hurtling development of genetics research over the last couple of decades.

Today's e-repositories managed by digital libraries can have the same dramatic effect on many fields of research without the exorbitant costs associated with the current commercial model of scholarly publishing. It is not possible to know exactly how much the GDB accelerated the spectacular progress that was achieved in human genetics in the 1980s and '90s, but it seems unlikely that any other previous scientific venture has progressed with such dispatch, with the possible exception of inventing the atomic bomb in the 1940s.

Punishing Publishing

Drawing on Shakespeare's line from *King Henry VI* "Let's kill all the lawyers," Rich Lowry (2003), editor of *National Review*, was eager to add, "Sure—but only if we can kill all the librarians next." Lowry was shocked at what he saw as ALA's role in fostering political leftism in the profession, "making an otherwise worthy profession seem a blight on the republic." Lowry must have been absent from libraries since his distant childhood, when he wistfully recalled reading the "Hardy Boys" novels, and saw his librarians "preside over a sanctuary of neighborhood quiet." It is plain to see that Lowry knows little about modern radicalism and even less of American librarianship. Of library radicalism, I will say nothing here, but I would almost grant Lowry his wish to kill all the librarians, but only if the librarians can kill all the publishers first.

It appears that the only goal of publishing conglomerates is to drain every last dime out of the research they acquire from the academic community to the point that libraries cannot purchase the research they need to keep their programs going. Underhanded publishers suck dry the library materials budgets of universities by inflating prices to Enronic proportions such that academic libraries cannot acquire research that their own faculty members developed, and then sold it to publishers for a mere pittance.

Still, conditions in academe, namely, the still growing OA movement, the proliferation of library-based digital collections and e-repositories, the exorbitant costs of scholarly journals, and the present uncertainty of mission in professional librarianship, may well create a very propitious moment for librarians and publishers to redraw the divisions that have existed between them, and devise new models for scholarly communication. Along with creating massive electronic collections and acquiring an ever-growing number of vendor-supplied information resources, academic libraries would be neglecting their responsibilities if they fail to assume a major role in scholarly communication and publishing, especially digital publishing.

Tin Pan Alley

In his article for *The Chronicle of Higher Education*, Steven Bell (2005) dismantles Questia's claims to be the self-said largest academic resource and research library on earth, and he decries Questia's blatant efforts to turn *students* into *customers*, while it employs no faculty member and too few full-blown reference librarians. "It's not enough just to answer reference and technical questions," Bell says. He adds that in real academic institutions, faculty work with librarians to build unique collections for unique institutional curricula. In Bell's words, Questia's result would be "so unfocused" that the collection would benefit "no one well."

I certainly believe that commercial publishing conglomerates would dearly love to make deals with the universities to sell their digital information resources directly to the students and discontinue sales to academic libraries altogether. I was told by a leading figure in SPARC that a publisher had hired the publicity firm that once worked for Enron. If true, it's hard for me to think this was just coincidence.

Similar situations arose with course pack vendors like XanEdu. Many of the articles, essays, and other texts in course pack readings, which the students must pay for, are already in the library's online resources, with subscriptions partially purchased with money from the student's tuition. In other words, campus book stores and teachers could be knowingly or unknowingly requiring their students to purchase materials for their classes that have already been purchased through student tuition. This is an outrage no less than criminal and Enronic.

There is no reason to doubt that commercial publishers would gladly sell their digital resources directly to students and take libraries right out of the scholarship equation completely. Kindle and devices like it could be the Yeatsean herald of this.

Mixing Metaphors

With some irreverence, I classify computerized library resources of digital libraries into three categories: Born Again, Born Digital, and Born Free. "Born Again" resources frequently are created in massive retrospective conversion projects reminiscent of similar projects a few decades ago when libraries began madly converting and entering all card catalog records into automated catalogs. In those ancient days (circa mid–1970s), I was a cataloger in a public library that had a state-of-the-art circulation system with a clever name: ULYSYS. These projects were undertaken posthaste, taking thousands of books at a time directly from the shelves to enter their bibliographic descriptions into the online catalog. A better and perhaps faster and less costly approach would have been to raise borrowing quotas significantly and let the patrons return the books in greater numbers back to the circulation desk where the staff could enter the book descriptions at the circ desk more efficiently.

In today's born-again digital projects, libraries convert portions of their print collections into digital formats to facilitate access for library users, especially works that are too rare or fragile to be handled.

At this moment, the largest born-again digitization projects ever conceived are underway, including the One Million Book Project (MBP), on omnivorous Google, which includes the UC libraries, the Bodleian Library, and so many others. At a 2006 conference in Hong Kong on the challenges and development of e-books, Reginald Carr, Bodleian Librarian at Oxford University, strongly and rather convincingly defended his decision to take Oxford's libraries, including the Bodleian, into a digitization agreement with Google. The object, he said, was to make the treasures of the Oxford libraries available to everyone.

I am not necessarily a champion of comprehensive digital library projects, and I also know from my public library experience decades ago that many public libraries have a tenuous hold on their community roles. I countered Mr. Carr with an observation that massive online collections may put small public libraries out of business. He admitted that he had not considered that possibility, but his Google plan went forward nonetheless.

Similarly, Dan Greenstein, the savvy futurist and director of CDL committed all the University of California libraries to a digital collaboration, not only with Google, but also with the Open Content Alliance simultaneously. He stated, "It's not about OCA, Yahoo, Microsoft, or Google. It's about what we want to do. It's absolutely essential that we would continue to push forward in these ways. We see this as the future of the academy and the future of the university" (Carlson 2003). Greenstein uses the term "discoverability" in connection with Google's voracious digitization scheme, meaning that scholars will be able to find books for their research that they might never find otherwise (Young).

"Born Digital" projects begin not with paper and paste resources but instead collect, preserve, and maintain user access to digital information on websites and other resources that exist only in electronic formats. Born-digital resources, including those with highly important contents, are notorious for disappearing from the Internet without warning, taking their unique information and documentation with them into nothingness.

The University of California at Berkeley devised an acclaimed four-level preservation strategy for born-digital resources (LC21). "Archived" websites reside permanently on Berkeley servers, where they will remain continuously accessible. "Served" digital resources, on the other hand, remain only temporarily on the servers. "Mirrored" sites are copied on Berkeley's servers to back up and increase the accessibility of important resources that also reside permanently at other institutions. "Linked" resources are notable, but do not merit collection by Berkeley at the higher collection levels — Berkeley simply links to them. Cornell University and other libraries also have preservation projects for born-digital resources.

The Library of Congress (LC), however, was severely criticized by a committee of librarians and other information experts in a report entitled *LC21: A Digital Strategy for the Library of Congress* (2001). The report stated that digitizing print collections is less urgent than archiving electronic resources because even very old print materials will still be available for digitizing many years from now. Much more urgent, the report said, is the need to archive important electronic resources because they often disappear suddenly and without warning because of funding shortages or personnel departures at the institutions that maintain these resources. The *LC21* report urged LC to take a lesson from Berkeley's born-digital resources preservation method.

The projects I call "Born Free" focus more on the present and less on the past. In born-free projects, preservation is less important than very timely dissemination of very current research, scholarship, and even raw data. Born-free resources are not necessarily connected to any existing print publication. Nor are born-free resources necessarily "free," although they may be greatly less expensive than vendor-supplied resources because they are open access collections of unique digital texts and other resources. To my way of thinking, the most impressive and portentous of the born-free resources are the open access digital research repositories that are proliferating in libraries in many parts of the world.

These e-repositories come in all shapes and sizes, but they generally are based on two different approaches, both of which were articulated by CDL at different times. Clifford Lynch saw "institutional repositories" as containing a wide variety of information formats: "intellectual works of faculty and students — both research and teaching materials — and also documentation of the activities of the institution itself in the form of records of events and performances and of the ongoing intellectual life of the institution" (2003). This approach advocates repositories that are cross-disciplinary, and archival records that document the activities of the academic institutions that sponsor the repositories. Lynch adds, "The definition I propose for an institutional repository does *not* call for a new scholarly publishing role for universities" (emphasis added).

A few years later, the thinking at the CDL under Dan Greenstein regarding online scholarly repositories became more discipline specific. CDL's "e-scholarship" repositories are designed to capture the scholarly publications of UC faculty and researchers according to departments. Each department at every UC campus was given server space at CDL, and permitted to submit digital copies of the department's scholarly output at the discretion of the department. This research was then made available as open access resources to any interested persons in the world. And unlike Lynch's institutional repositories, the CDL model of e-scholarship repositories is designed "to facilitate and support scholar-led innovations in scholarly communication ... in response to an expressed need for alternative publishing mechanisms" (http://www.cdlib.org/cdlinfo/2002/04/11/escholarship-repository-launched/).

Both types of repositories have their proper purposes — one is for active research, the other for archiving, which fosters its own important brand of research. I heartily endorse the e-scholarship repositories that follow the current California Digital Library model as the stronger candidate for reforming scholarly communication. E-scholarship repositories are all about what's happening now in all fields of serious research, scholarly investigation, and publication. These contain digital copies of faculty papers, research, articles, online journals, and other scholarly resources. These materials are submitted directly to the repository from university departments, who act as peer reviewers and editorial boards to evaluate the quality of the materials being submitted for inclusion in the e-repository. The submission process requires very little handling by librarians. Once a submission is approved by a university department for addition to the e-repository, uploading is performed by special publication software that performs the digital publishing tasks from submission to electronic distribution. This model is quite extensive, but not nearly moving fast enough to displace the commercial publishers — yet.

There is at least one smallish drawback to this model, however. Because the submission process requires no collection development strategies to be imposed by librarians, gaps in the digital collections are likely to occur. Digital academic presses (DAPs) can help alleviate this problem (see Chapter 6).

Pressing ever forward through determined R&D, CDL's evolving functionalities, scope, and vision seems to be the clear successor to GDB–type resources, and may prove to be the single most important force so far in returning control of scholarly publication to academe.

Jerry Campbell

I've never met the man face to face, but I've heard him speak, and one instance stands out in my mind. In October 1998, the library of Peking University sponsored the International Conference on New Missions of Academic Libraries in the 21st century. It convened in the striking new Peking University Library, and was probably the most invigorating librarianship conference I have attended. At that conference, Campbell, then CIO and dean of university libraries at the University of Southern California, stated, "Because of the capabilities of technology, digital libraries will increasingly focus on providing access to original materials, both those born digitally and those converted from analog formats. The effect of this will be to enrich vastly the research potential of our resources and to provide new opportunities for our institutions to benefit from the potential commercial value of such holdings. The new content paradigm for digital libraries will be *raw, source materials*" (Campbell 1998; emphasis added).

That is pretty close to what has happened. Libraries have taken on much larger roles as originators of new digital information, not simply customers of commercial electronic information vendors. Since Campbell spoke those words, many libraries have become digital publishers themselves. He also said that a digital library of the future may likely be a highly sophisticated search engine. Again he is nearly on target in the form of new catalogs that are ready to harvest data for users with the subtlety of a John Deere combine. The catalogs of today will be passé. That's good. It may change everything in librarianship, to which many of us aspire.

In that same conference, Zhang Xiaolin, then of Sichuan Union University, stated in his presentation that 21st-century university libraries should be "developers for information activities, services, systems, and products for various clients in the university," and "operators of value-added and integrating services utilizing various resources, services, and systems in and outside the campus" (1998).

These back-to-back presentations — one made in America, the other made in China — resonated with each other like no other presentations in the conference. They made me believe, well over a decade ago, that the new content paradigm was actually on the verge of coming into being, and substantiated my growing conviction that unique, online full-text resources, created not by publishers but by libraries working with researchers and faculty, were the future of scholarly communication and of libraries. Some things predicted, however, seem not to have happened, and the library profession needs to re-address those matters. The problem appears to be that librarianship is often in a position to exert a powerful influence on the IT industry and on the processes of scholarly communication, but although our profession seems always to be on the verge of something big, we seldom pull ourselves together enough to turn that "something" into a stunning achievement. This is only another demonstration of our dividedness from our mission.

We are reinventing librarianship through transformational services, and we should involve students in this learning package. For instance, librarians need to devise appropriate implementation models for Kindle readers, perhaps using the early PC methods of developing large computer labs for students; or the laptop model that encourages students to acquire their own laptops that they can take anywhere. OA and DAPS for student projects can be accessible to students as learners and participators. Enhanced blogs are popular for specific courses. New-phase catalogs such as Discovery Services from Serials Solutions and EBSCOhost stretch much farther than facets and federated searches. Likewise, these companies are buying data like crazy because "It's da data, stoopid!"

Back on Earth

My own very modest contribution to the 1998 conference in Beijing included the observation that some libraries, even then, were partnering with faculty, researchers, professionals, business firms, and government agencies to collect and electronically publish information to stimulate scientific inquiry, accelerate economic and social development, and join the revolution in scholarly communication. I added that the digital output of knowledge and information from 21st-century libraries would likely make them the most prodigious publishers in the world due to the vast information resources at their disposal.

With Google, Open Content Alliance, and others, along with OA IRs, this, too, will come about. For instance, in 2005 the British Library projected that by the year 2020, "90 percent of newly published work will be available digitally ... [and] only half of this will also be available in print form, with just 10 percent of new titles available only in print" (BBC News 2005). The press release then described the massive digitization projects the British Library planned to undertake in the next few years. Other libraries are moving in similar digital directions.

Campbell also said the "new content paradigm" for libraries would include "raw data." According to Treloar (2008), the amount of data-intensive research is rapidly increasing. Most data is now born digital, and is largely generated semi-automatically. Through cross-disciplinary research, it is now possible to answer questions that are unrelated to the reasons for which the data sets were originally collected. He adds that the means of aggregating, federating, and accessing data are becoming increasingly important. Also, data is the next great challenge for scholarly communication and for libraries.

We're seeing that the paradigm also includes very current research, gray literature, underground literature, faculty writings, and existing bodies of information that are too little known or too specialized to be of interest to conventional publishers, but which would be especially valuable for courses, programs, or research in highly specialized academic circles, if the information were made easily accessible. From time to time, almost all librarians and teachers discover unpublished and therefore "hidden" quantities of information and knowledge that would have great value to appropriate interested groups that may be scattered around the world. Such information might reside in businesses, professional organizations, information and research centers, government bureaus, and social service agencies; it might be available from community groups, ethnic associations, local historians, political action bodies, or directly from researchers and other gifted individuals. This is the kind of information and knowledge all libraries, public and academic, can strategically harvest and provide digitally to their users.

In 2005, seven years after the Beijing conference almost to the day, the International Conference on the Universal Digital Library was held at Zhejiang University in Hangzhou,

China. I had hopes that it would turn out to be a milestone follow-up meeting to the 1998 conference at the Peking University Library, and that we would hear about bold new digital research creations looking like Campbell's predictions and carrying forward the reformation of scholarly communication. Libraries of that ilk were certainly represented at the Hangzhou conference: Carnegie Mellon, Cornell, Rutgers, Zhejiang University, Peking University, Hong Kong University, Bibliotheca Alexandrina, and others that I supposed had made incursions into the new content paradigm and perhaps had even breached the walls of scholarly communication and retaken some ground that libraries had lost to commercial publishers who want to crowd libraries out of their traditional position at the center scholarship and research.

Instead, topics at the Zhejiang conference were literally and figuratively all over the map with talk of data mining, algorithms, digital library consortia, transliteration editors, and other jargons. Much of the talk was about digitizing all the books in the world. Really. Google had recently announced its plans to partner with major libraries and publishers to digitize oceans of existing texts that could be word-searched, and a high-level Googlecrat was there, self-assured, in the flesh, to reassure us all that this was a good thing to do. Another vendor from another firm promoted his company's project to digitize whole libraries of texts in such profusion that children in Africa could buy a book for "just a dollar." I have traveled and consulted in Africa, and I stifled an impulse to ask, "Where are kids in Africa going to get a dollar to buy a book? And what about the kids in the U.S. who don't have a dollar to buy a book?"

Another major topic discussed extensively was the Million Book Project, a joint effort of Chinese and American academic libraries to digitize one million books, half in Chinese, half in English. Since the project's inception, other Asian countries have joined as well. I suspect this is at least in part a showcase project to enlist numerous libraries east and west and dazzle the world with the marvels of technology and with the prospects this undertaking promises for global, "affordable" education delivery (see Xiao, Shao, and Ma). More than just a stunt, the project could certainly have admirable geopolitical impacts. China's active international academic and cultural exchange programs over the past few decades have been leaven to its development plans. Cooperation between academic libraries in China, the United States, and many other countries can certainly play a large role in improving communication between the nations.

Having said that, though, I wonder if barnstorming like this is the best way for libraries to get global attention for our digital transformations. Is this the route we want librarianship to take? Do projects like this really push back the frontiers of knowledge by facilitating research through rapid scholarly communication? I don't think undertakings and directions like the MBP quite fit Campbell's perception of the new content paradigm, nor do they highlight strongly enough our mission as educators.

It was clearly evident that an even more immense born-again project was looming: Google's snowballing collaboration with some of the largest and most prestigious libraries in the world. It would make an innumerable number of texts available cheaply worldwide, regardless of the digitization costs involved, and with complete disregard of the fact that many of these books slated for digitization are already plentifully and freely available in countless local libraries or obtainable quickly through interlibrary loan.

As for the librarians' presentations in the conference, much discussion centered on copyright issues, viz., how are we going to get access to the billions and billions of books we want to digitize? Librarians just can't seem to get beyond retrocon projects. To my mind, that's not the direction to preserve librarianship and bring our divided profession together. At this time, retrocon, especially of materials that are already accessible in print, could turn out to be a horrendously expensive boondoggle that could siphon fortunes away from the more important current task of reforming scholarly communication, and clarifying our role as educators. Nor do I think these undertakings quite fit Campbell's 1998 perception of the new content paradigm, either.

CDL and the DSpace Rush

CDL e-scholarship repositories (on the backs of bepress), ignited the rush to create online repository research projects of all types and at all levels of scholarship. DSpace, created by MIT Libraries and Hewlett-Packard Laboratories, was an early open-source digital environment to store and disseminate text, images, video, and audio files, and can be used for e-repositories, ETDs, preservation, digital publishing, and other applications. And because DSpace is an open source environment, it is available for free. Much more than a product for holding and distributing information, DSpace sees itself as a movement. The creators and users of DSpace advocate "open access to research literature," and "developing a critical corpus of content that represents the intellectual output of the world's leading research," and "ensuring the long-term preservation of scholarly work" (EndUser-Faq 2005).

DSpace, and numerous other projects like it, however, boil down to lots of labor to configure the product. The discussion here is not an endorsement of this product, but it was one of the innovations that created a turning point in the blooming of IRs. We should have done it much, much sooner.

It seems clear that e-repositories, ETDs, digital presses, DSpace, and other information-sharing digital creations are technological descendants of the Human Genome Database, and their appearance at this point in time indicates that the academic and research communities are ready for a transformation of the processes of scholarly communication. And because digital libraries have been deeply involved in the creation of these revolutionary resources, it is equally clear that libraries and librarians should take a leading role in redesign of scholarly communication and publishing, that is, if we are to survive as a profession.

Today's e-repositories managed by digital libraries can have the same effect on many fields of research without the exorbitant costs associated with the current commercial model of scholarly publishing. That these current collaborations can proceed without the direct involvement of computer scientists is because of (1) the blinding rate of technological developments, (2) the astonishing cost reductions of these developments despite constant vendor price gouging, and (3) the number and caliber of digital librarians now permeating the profession.

There are other notable efforts to mitigate the divisions between librarians and instructional faculty: Blackboard, WebCT, Moodle, and e-reserves, among others. This is a propitious moment for academic libraries. We must assume a leading role in electronic scholarly publishing, in worldwide scholarly communication, and in the IT industry or, once again, libraries will lose a crucial opportunity to assert the fitness of our profession to provide leadership in the fields of academic and information technologies, processes, and standards. We will once again lose our opportunity to influence information and knowledge delivery to some other entities.

CDL Larges

The 1960 California Master Plan for Higher Education was developed to set up a three-tiered system for post-secondary education: UCSU, and the California Community Colleges (CCC). Decades later, the CDL was established by the California Legislature as an insightful educational project to enhance all state-funded tertiary institutions at the three levels, or so it was interpreted by Dan Greenstein in my discussions with him. Because the CDL was mandated by the state government, Dan was sure that CDL did not belong just to UC. Instead, all three tiers should be brought into CDL to develop IRs that would accommodate them separately.

On the very brink of entering an agreement with CDL and bepress, however, the CSU found out a dirty little secret: bepress had quietly sold out its Digital Commons product to ProQuest. Earlier, bepress had advocated for its system to be replicated world-wide, but then it changed directions and sold itself for the PQ buy-out. A while later, bepress took back the license from ProQuest because of customer dissatisfaction with the maintenance side of the application, or so it was said. After that, the three-tier model went by the wayside with a lot of grumbling, especially from me. Dan Greenstein was promoted to a broader and higher position in the UC president's office.

OA was probably not the central issue at the time of the developments at CDL and bepress, e-scholarship IRs, and so on. Once the developments were in place, however, it was clear that CDL, IRs, and other innovations could be expressly adapted to bring down the impossible costs charged by greedy publishing firms, launching a reformation of scholarly communication.

SLAC and DES

There were other, much earlier OA forerunners of today's e-repositories. One was created at the library of the Stanford Linear Accelerator Center (SLAC). Formed in 1962 and specializing in the systematic rapid acquisition of paper preprints in high-energy physics, the SLAC library industriously gathered disciplinary research, loaded it into computer databases as they were being invented, and exploited every type of technology that would serve the purposes of SLAC. By the late 1970s and early '80s, scholar workstations were being designed and used by SLAC scientists and librarians. In 1974, the SLAC library and the library of Deutsches Elektronen-Synchrotron began collaboration to create online resources that are still in use (Addis 2002).

Librarians played indispensable roles in the conception, creation, and operation of these wondrous information inventions. Those librarians included Luisella Goldschmidt-Clermont, Louise Addis, Hrvoje Gallic, Nina Matheson, Scott Bennett, Richard Lucier, and many others. It is strange that despite the marvelous accomplishments of librarians such as these, many other librarians are now somewhat baffled about the future of librarianship, especially regarding digital libraries. To the author of this book, our future seems pretty clear, and it will spring from these earlier beacon technologies and collaborations.

OA in Hong Kong

Hong Kong is quite an interesting case study amid the sweeping change in OA and new research methods. Simply put, the government big heads, and even many of the librarians, have been hidden deep in the sand. The Hong Kong Research Grants Council (RGC) meeting notes of June 15, 2007, state, "The RGC decided not to make it compulsory for the Principal Investigators ... to allow open access of their research outputs. However, the RGC strongly encourages your institution and researchers to make available the research output via open-access repositories on a voluntary basis." Of course, no one volunteered.

The RGC wrote (August 6, 2007), "We have concerns that researchers in Hong Kong would oppose any initiatives that may compromise their IP rights ... researchers would also object to any proposal that might restrict their choice of publication venues.... We can only encourage them, but we will not be in a position to make it mandatory."

After lengthy e-mail correspondence with Michael Stone, secretary-general of the University Grants Council (UGC), I helped persuade him that open access is essential for the benefit of Hong Kong's universities. After several months of e-mail chains on OA benefits with Stone, I sent him the seminal *Library Journal* article entitled "Embracing Openness," by Van Orsdel and Born (April 15, 2008). His response was contained in a brief email of September 9, 2008, which stated his agreement that the article was indeed a balanced one. He agreed to send it on to his colleagues in the RGC to get their opinion. Later that month, Anthony Chan, assistant UCG secretary-general, emailed me to say that the RGC had decided to form a working group on public access to "examine the possibility of allowing public access to research data generated by RGC–funded project" (September 29, 2008). He went on to say that the working group was expected to give its recommendations to the RGC for discussion and consideration at the December 2008 meeting.

At Cross Cultures

Despite all the friendly words from RGC, UGC, and the eight universities themselves, I heard nothing more about the working group's recommendations in the December meeting. No real meaningful OA progress had occurred in Hong Kong universities in my more than three years of trying to budge an OA movement in Hong Kong's scholarly communication. An OA committee was created at the higher levels of the Hong Kong universities' administrations, but it was stymied by inadequate interest. That's one of the reasons I decided to leave that lovely place, as exciting as it may be, because the academics and administrators are mired in tradition and dottiness.

Even though I heard nothing else from UGC or RGC at that time, I will always be grateful for the article by Orsdel and Born. Since then, OA in Hong Kong, frozen in the academic ice, began to thaw, but the way forward has been glacial, as with the other Hong Kong universities, which was especially disappointing, for me at least. How different the Hong Kong universities are from Harvard, Cornell, the University of California, and so many others! The hands-off approach of UGC and RGC would seemingly kill OA outright. It must be a top-down as well as a bottom-up undertaking with research money and other incentives and pressure from administrators to secure buy-in from the faculty and researchers. UGC was very willing to force the faculty in 2008 to (1) adopt a vigorous, objectives-based student learning outcomes project, which I applaud, and (2) accept a new teaching quality assurance method in the form a new UGC Quality Assurance Committee initiative, which also pleased me. Yet the UGC still remained aloof to force faculty into OA. It baffled me.

At Hong Kong Baptist University, where I am writing this book, the library will join with the IT department to establish six OA research areas in cross-cultural studies, contemporary China studies, environmental science, advanced materials research, advanced e-transformation and technology, and Chinese medicine. These areas are the university's current research strengths, and the new vice president for research (VP/R) acquired an OA IR EPrints application to gather peer-reviewed research from our faculty and researchers for these six areas, and also to attract contributions from around the world. The VP/R's intention is to develop the IR into an international world-class research resource on these subjects and others in an OA environment to promote the highest quality of research for the world's scholarly community. Because the VP/R strongly favors OA and also oversees the library, the future at HKBU is much brighter. I nominated him to be the chair of the OA committee for all eight Hong Kong universities. He was appointed chair, but OA in Hong Kong remained an uphill battle all the way, and it's still not done. A recent potential breakthrough, however, might be the tipping point to adopt OA at all eight Hong Kong universities.

Springer Deal/Press Release

Hong Kong/Berlin/London, 22 February 2010: the University of Hong Kong signs Open Choice agreement with Springer's Asian open access pilot project to run for one year from March 2010 to March 2011.

If not a "cascade" as described earlier with the likes of Cornell, MIT, Harvard, UC, and the NIH, this announcement is a considerable OA surge forward in Hong Kong. This is, after all, not necessarily exactly like other OA IRs. The agreement permits HKU researchers to publish their research in Springer journals using Springer Open Choice. The program offers full, immediate, free open access to the reader for HKU articles accepted for publication after a process of rigorous peer review. The accepted articles will appear in Springer's print journals published electronically using open access on Springer-Link, PubMed Central, and the HKU institutional repository, the HKU Scholars Hub.

The pro vice chancellor for research, and director of the Knowledge Exchange Office at HKU, Professor Paul Tam, stated: "The amount of cutting-edge research done at the University of Hong Kong has increased dramatically. It is important to also increase access to this research, and thereby secure all the benefits that this research can bring to the public who funded it. The Springer Open Choice is a good first step in that direction!" He added, "Making HKU's research available to all interested parties in open access format is a key goal of our Knowledge Exchange Initiative, which holds that publicly-funded universities should return the results of their research to the communities that funded them."

Professor Jan van Aalst of the Faculty of Education added, "I usually choose a journal in which to publish by the community it serves. However, all other things being equal, I prefer to publish in an open access journal. In this case, using Springer's Open Choice, I found that my article was discovered much more quickly." And so, how quickly the limelights and senior administrators can draw the faces from the crowd when they want to.

Peter Hendriks, president of STM Global Publishing & Marketing at Springer said Springer is very pleased to have "gained such a key academic institution to carry out this pilot project. We value very highly the opportunity to further develop exciting new publishing models in close cooperation with yet another respected institution." I certainly bet he does.

The press release also said "HKU is a world-class comprehensive research-led university, with close to a hundred of its faculty ranked by the Institute for Scientific Information as being among the world's top 1 percent of scientists (http://www.hku.hk). The HKU Scholars Hub is the institutional repository of HKU, begun in 2005, and collects, preserves, and showcases the intellectual output of HKU, now numbering over 25,000 items, with over 1 million downloads in 2009. The hub is a key vehicle to enable and measure HKU's Knowledge Exchange initiative (http://hub.hku.hk).

My smallish part in this, if any at all, involved my e-mail string with Michael Stone, and tying up the VPR on the OA committee. The Hong Kong University Springer deal was sprung not too long after the CDL/Springer embrace (2010). Still, the Springer deal makes me suspicious.

A Groundswell, Not a Cascade, and Such Time Wasted

As the flagship campus of Hong Kong's public universities, HKU broadened its open access for the purposes of research, teaching, and learning in several ways. First, Professor Tsui, vice chancellor of HKU, signed the Berlin Declaration on Open Access in November 2009, thereby establishing an HKU policy to require its researchers to deposit a copy of all their published articles in an open access repository, namely, the HKU Libraries Scholars Hub (http://oa.mpg.de/).

Secondly, HKU libraries took another giant step when they recognized that HKU and its researchers have an obligation to share available knowledge with the local community, and also the world at large, to realize great economic, social, and intellectual benefits.

With this specific breakthrough, along with the understanding of the achievement of these goals, the professional staff in the HKU libraries unanimously agreed to an OA requirement to deposit their manuscripts in the HKU Scholars Hub for any authored item. These staff authors will expect the intended publisher to allow open access of the published version or the author's manuscript. The complete policy can be seen at http://hub.hku.hk/local/oaPolicy.jsp#policy.

Although the output of authored items from HKU Libraries staff is small, they hope their example will inspire and attract other HKU departments to adopt the same or similar policies. The benefits of this change in Hong Kong's scholarly communication are too important to languish any longer.

Back to Lynching

According to Lynch, in many ways, institutional repositories are "a new channel for structuring the university's contribution to the broader world" (2003). When the GDB was first created, its costs were extremely high. Fortunately, the current costs for the technology that supports e-repositories are considerably more affordable. Still, the cost over time will be high as the repositories grow and as technology changes, bringing the need to migrate data from old environments to new ones.

A new digital domain is opening for librarians that involves electronically publishing appropriate resources for easy, inexpensive access by users. And because communities of users overlap considerably, what's good for the universities is likely to be good for the general public (but see Chapter 7 in this book on the Bushmen). By making e-repositories, ETDs, and DAPS accessible to the public as an outreach mechanism, and by partnering in the creation of these resources with businesses, professionals, local information providers, and community groups so that they, too, will benefit from these knowledge bases, universities can achieve their goals and raise the proficiencies of the general community as well.

Lynch also observes that "universities need to invest aggressively ... and implement thoughtfully ... with the full understanding that they will permanently change the landscape of scholarly communication" (2003).

Yet others might say that publishers and librarians could be in the same leaking boat. Information technology is assuming a huge public presence that simply will not allow either profession to control. The people crave access and control. Consequently, publishers and librarians — once locked in a love-hate relationship — may be forced more and more closely together. David Worlock of Electronic Publishing Services, London, observed, "We are all publishers and we are all users. The power has tipped toward the users and the publishers will have to acknowledge the change in power in the future." This may be a ruse, though, because he predicted that the major scholarly and research journals would maintain their traditional subscription practices while open access would take the lead in the second-tier publications, thus creating a "dual economy" in scholarly publishing. I don't cotton to that. It's like Enron admitting it engineered the destruction of California's energy infrastructure in 2003 and then apologizing.

In the same Nelinet seminar, James Neal of Columbia University predicted that the future of libraries lies in a partnership with scholarly publishers. But how much longer can academe and academic libraries chain themselves to the usury and extortion of commercial publishing conglomerates?

In a 2006 visit to Hong Kong, Anthony Watkinson, himself a scholarly publisher, eminent faculty member at University College, London, and former librarian, agreed that there will likely be a shakeout between libraries and publishers, and if not a shakeout, at least a coming to terms between libraries and publishers. In the words of Adrian Alexander (2003), perhaps digital libraries will form a cadre of "alternative publishers," such as the University of Arizona Library and its remarkable BioOne online resource, which is an assemblage or aggregation of scholarly publications.

In short, more and more library voices are calling for libraries to become de facto digital publishers, in some cases, in collaboration with actual publishers, in other cases with publishers cum information conglomerations like Google, Yahoo, and the Open Content Alliance.

Devising new models of scholarly publication that will bring digital libraries and commercial publishers into relative collaborations may require the participation of some middle-ground entity with a sound reputation and good working relationships with publishers and libraries alike. OCLC might be suitable as such a go-between. While in Hong Kong for the e-book symposium mentioned above, Richard Rosy, then OCLC corporate vice president for content management, indicated to me that commercial scholarly publishers realize — but don't yet openly admit — that the current model of scholarly communication cannot survive indefinitely, and they are taking steps to ease into some type of new model. Because OCLC has been an active intermediary of sorts between the library community and the publishing industry, it might become a shoehorn to fit the two rivals together. It might be a tight fit, but it might also be an improvement.

Watkinson agreed that publishers can see change looming, but he intimated to me that the publishers are likely first to increase their rates even more artificially in order to make a soft landing when the existing publication model and its revenues come back down to earth. It seems increasingly certain to all parties, then, that publishers cannot maintain their robber-baron hold on scholarly communication forever. Librarians and their academic colleagues should prepare for the takeover.

For a long time, I have wondered why should we *not* establish academic libraries as scholarly publishers. As mentioned above, Lynch said in 2003 that his vision of institutional repositories does *not* call for a new scholarly publishing role for universities. But why should university libraries *not* assume a much larger and active role in scholarly publishing, given their growing involvement in institutional repositories and other massive digitization projects? Stover (1996) is correct when he argues, "[Librarians] need to support the scholarly communication process — and Web publishing is a powerful symbol of our enfranchised role. Disseminating information is a function that traditionally has been associated with librarians ... and Web publishing fits well into this traditional paradigm," and he stresses librarians' "expertise in the arena of organizing and providing access to information."

Almost a Dozen Revolutions

There was another strident voice in the 1998 conference in the Peking University Library. Jim Neal identified in his presentation no less than 11 revolutions that are transforming libraries, including (1) the personal computing revolution; (2) the electronic revolution; (3) the network revolution; (4) the push revolution; (5) the self-service revolution; (6) the partnership revolution; (7) the authorship revolution; (8) the intellectual property revolution; (9) the digital preservation revolution; (10) the information as commodity revolution; and (11) the knowledge management revolution.

A decade later, these and other revolutions are looming. He stated that "the international academic library and higher education communities are stepping forward and proposing new copperative models." At the top of these models is a move to foster "a competitive market for scholarly publishing by providing realistic alternatives to the prevailing commercial publishing options"; "enrich and expand the available means for distributing research and scholarship"; "develop policies for intellectual property management which emphasize the broad and easy distribution and reuse of material"; and "assure that new channels of scholarly communication ... contribute to promotion and tenure processes."

This is not Jerry Campbell's new content paradigm. Instead, Neal portends a sweeping revision of what lies before us. I foresee continued dividedness of libraries and a tough, long campaign to secure a reformation of scholarly communication. Jim Neal sees the challenge of the academic library as "to confront the changing information environment and scholarly landscape with creativity and commitment, and to remain focused on our primary goals: to respond to the information content and information service needs of our learning and research commuities, and to advance a climate of open inquiry and intellectual freedom. This is our mandate. This is our future." I wish he had said more clearly a few words about librarians as educators, but I'm not complaining.

Crystal Balls and Touch Pads

Hackman (2009) describes a bloody autopsy of an ill-fated faculty resolution supporting OA at the University of Maryland by a *clear defeat* (his term) among the likes of MIT, University of California, Stanford, Cornell, Harvard, NIH, and many more OA institutions. Yet, when will be the tipping point for OA? The advent of Kindle, iPad, and the numerous clones and ripoffs, in the aftermath of the inevitable industry shakeout, may cause a dam burst. It will either break under the pressure that has been holding OA back or herald the end of libraries and academe as we now know them.

If OA becomes restructured in some way, just as the CSU was shut out of CDL, what might happen in our future? What rough disruptive technology might now be slouching toward us in our lusty, lofty, ivory towers?

6

DAPS: Opening a Second Front

The Role of Scholarly Publishing in Digital Libraries

One sure remedy to end exorbitant journal subscription costs is the open access movement, which will continue to gain quickly the approval of increasing numbers of readers and researchers and raise the publishers' fear level. Another remedy is copyright reform, which now seems inevitable, too, because of Googlization, other digitization initiatives, and the discrepancies between popular and academic publishing (McCleery 2008). In her opening remarks at IFLA Milan, Claudia Lux said, "Copyright should not be used to prevent readers from obtaining and using necessary information and knowledge" (2009).

IFLA's *Limitations and Exceptions to Copyright and Neighboring Rights in the Digital Environment* (2004) is well worth reading, and support for its initiatives can help end the treason of copyright holders, most of whom are greed-laced commercial conglomerated publishing companies that grossly inflate the costs of academic content, which they probably cannot even understand, nor care about, except for the fleecing of universities, colleges, other learning institutions, and the students, faculty, and researchers, whatever the market will bear.

Cracks in the Copyrights

In 2000, I was working in the Guggenheim Library at Monmouth University, in New Jersey. The Guggenheim has a marvelous collection of 3,500 books, artworks, and personal belongings of Lewis Mumford. I was contacted by a student of Professor Song Junling of the Beijing Academy of Social Sciences to find the copyright holders of two books by Mumford. Professor Song had already translated some of Mumford's works quite successfully, and his student in Canada asked me on his behalf to find the copyright holders. I agreed to help, and it did not take long to find the copyright agent in New York City. Professor Song was urgently hoping to get the information he needed to make arrangements to obtain the permissions for the two publications, which he had already translated. I contacted the agent again and again, but after several months, he simply could not trace the living relatives who might be able to grant Professor Song's request. The agent finally stopped taking my calls.

I was very sad for the professor and angry at the copyright agent. On my next trip to Beijing, I met with Professor Song in his home. We had lunch together with his family, and a good conversation (he spoke fluent English) about Mumford. Professor Song extolled the man, and talked about how his ideas could be readily introduced into China's development. I was very sad, and the incident taught me a lot about copyright flaws.

Hence the CSUS DAP

Another promising remedy worth considering to rein in the commercial publishers and the copyright lackeys is the formation of digital academic presses (DAPs) located in academic, research, and public libraries too. They can certainly have an impact on the production of meaningful publications that can reach broad audiences that commercial publishers would not stoop to touch for the lack of income.

Members of the digital databases team in the Kapiolani Library mentioned earlier reassembled at the library of CSUS and launched a DAP there in 2003. While all 23 campuses of the California State University system were gearing up to launch institutional or scholarly repositories, the CSUS library was also engaged in launching a DAP.

The proposal for the CSUS DAP was endorsed by the CSUS president in 2003, and the vice president for academic affairs approved the establishment of the CSUS DAP in 2004. The DAP was operational from 2003 to 2007. When I left for Hong Kong in mid-2006, the DAP was taken offline due to the lack of resources for the library, and short-sightedness of some administrators, and some librarians as well. The DAP's existing publications, however, are still accessible. This chapter, therefore, is a case study from the past, but *in present tense* to provide documentation, objectives, purposes, and publications of the CSUS DAP circa 2006.

A Proposal to Launch a Digital Academic Press (DAP) at CSU, Sacramento: Restructuring the Domain of Scholarly Communication

With 23 separate universities, 30,000 faculty and professional staff, and over 400,000 students, the CSU system is the largest university in the country (Moske 2005), but CSU has precious little in the way of an academic press, conventional or digital. We at CSU, Sacramento, hope to make our DAP the official press for the entire CSU system. As such, we would be in a unique position to have an immediate, positive impact on the scholarship across the CSU system, and also become a powerful force to transform scholarly communication worldwide, if not at CSUS, then some other CSU campus. This was our thinking. A CSUS/CSU DAP would be at least one excellent skirmish line for the reformation of scholarly communication. Joining forces with UC and the CDL would make our alliance even stronger.

Creating a digital press at CSUS will provide an attractive publication option for CSU faculty, and will develop a readership of faculty, administrators, and students that is both exceptionally learned and large. Potential readership within the CSU alone amounts to nearly a half-million individuals. By virtue of its size, CSU can guarantee the critical mass of faculty and scholars to act as contributors, peer reviewers, editorial boards, and readers needed to make the press successful. The press could not fail to impact positively the processes of teaching, learning, and scholarly inquiry that are the hallmarks of CSU, while at the same time exerting an influence on the reformation of scholarly communication.

Start-up costs would be affordable, and ongoing costs manageable. A born-digital press will not incur the costs of publication and distribution that severely reduce the cost-effectiveness of other university presses. In addition, digital dissemination of scholarly information is not delayed by the lengthy processes of typesetting, printing, mailing, and so forth. Submissions will be accepted in electronic format, sent to peer reviewers and returned to the press editors electronically, formatted for publication online, and distributed to subscribers or the public at large via the Internet.

Launching the CSU digital press will also add considerable credibility and prestige to electronic publications, which are still not yet esteemed internationally as highly as paper journals and monographs. The eventual rise in the stature of e-reads is inevitable, however, and depends largely on the caliber of the editorial boards and the quality of the content. Within the CSU system, there is an abundance of high-caliber individuals who can assure the scholarship of the press's editorial personnel and of CSU publications themselves.

Scholarly communication is in a critical state as publishing conglomerates inflate the subscription rates of scholarly journals to prohibitive levels, which impedes the rapid spread of new knowledge. Attempts by academic institutions to control the rising costs have had only small impact and limited success. These efforts include Stanford's High Wire Press, SPARC (Scholarly Publishing and Academic Resources Coalition), JSTOR, UC's eScholarship initiative, and others.

Atkinson (2003) argues, however, that the way to restore the free flow of scholarly communication is for universities to take control of scholarly processes by becoming digital publishers. News that CSU plans to create a digital academic press will likely bring instant attention from the media and will enhance CSU's prominence in the scholarly community.

The CSUS library is the ideal unit to create and manage the CSU digital press. CSUS library staff have the superior technical expertise, extensive digital experience, and editorial background to organize the press, direct the formation of editorial boards, and publish electronic journals and monographs on the Internet. Placing the press under the CSUS library's direction will save time and money over creating a new and separate entity. Libraries over the centuries collected and provided access to printed instruments of scholarly endeavors. They remain today even better suited to provide the same services in the virtual domain.

About the CSUS DAP

Formation of the Digital Academic Press of California State University, Sacramento, was approved by the university's vice president for academic affairs on November 15,

2004, as an entity of the CSUS library. The press was envisioned and created by members of the library staff. It is operated by the library systems office under the direction of the library director and dean, who acts as the executive editor of the Press in consultation with advisory boards assembled to help direct the Press into a full and meaningful publication schedule. Creation of the Press was made possible by a generous grant from the Tsakopoulos Hellenic Foundation.

Strictly Digital

The mission of the Digital Academic Press of California State University, Sacramento, has several provisions:

The CSUS Digital Academic Press will publish important works exclusively in paperless formats on many subjects that might not otherwise find their way to scholarly and academic communities. In doing so, the Press will collaborate with other institutions, agencies, conventional publishers, small presses, and research and educational entities within and beyond the CSU system.

The Press will have a significant, positive impact on the scholarship of CSUS and provide an attractive publication option for CSU faculty.

The Press will help raise the excellence, stature, and prestige of digital academic and scholarly publications.

The Press will help promote the worldwide reformation of scholarly communication processes that will return oversight of those processes to the academic community.

The Press will demonstrate that academic libraries are at the center of the reformation of scholarly communication. Academic libraries possess the superior technical expertise, extensive digital experience, and editorial abilities to reorganize scholarly communication around a variety of new digital models. Libraries have perennially collected and provided access to printed forms of scholarly communication, and they are uniquely suited to provide the same types of services in the digital domain.

The Press will develop new forms of digital texts that can exploit the technological advantages of electronic formats by incorporating reader-logical features not possible in print publications. The intention is to advance the utility of electronic texts to maximum functionality.

The Press will have an immediate, positive effect on the scholarship of CSUS, and potentially on the CSU system, and will also help transform the processes of scholarly communication across the academic community.

The Press will publish scholarly journals; monographs; facsimile collections; open-access e-repositories; ETDs; proceedings of conferences held at CSU universities; lecture series and distinguished addresses by prominent guests and officials; art and historical exhibits; video recordings of important concerts and performances; and other forms of scholarly inquiry and activity. All the publications will be in digital formats only. The publications will be unique, original works obtained directly by the press or in collaboration with other institutions, agencies, small publishers, and research and educational entities on and beyond the CSUS campus, and other forms of scholarly communication and inquiry in digital format only.

Situation Critical

Scholarly communication is in a critical state as publishers inflate the subscription rates of scholarly journals to prohibitive levels, which impedes the rapid spread of new knowledge among educators, scholars, and researchers. Attempts by academic institutions to control the rising costs have had only limited success. A growing number of university presidents and other administrators are insisting that the best way to restore the free flow of scholarly communication is for universities to take control of scholarly communication processes using shrewd applications of technology.

Relationship to the University's Mission

The Press will furnish a new source of intellectual support for the university's mission to provide an excellent liberal arts education, and will also open another avenue to obtaining a depth of knowledge within the various disciplines of our students and faculty. To be successful in this, the Press will stay close to the CSUS curricula in its solicitation and acceptance of publications. Also, the Press will pay close attention to the themes of the university's detailed strategic plan. In addition, the success of the Press depends on its involvement and close collaboration with the CSUS faculty.

Administrative Reporting Line

The director and dean of the library will be the executive editor of the Press, and will report on Press activities to the vice president for academic affairs. Reports will be made regularly as described in PM 96-06.

Support

There are no plans to request university funds for the Press for the time being. For at least the first two years of operation, we will scale the Press's activities to fit the resources at hand. Resident expertise and existing equipment in the Library Systems Office are sufficient to complete initial publication projects now under consideration. Also, we have attracted external funds to acquire additional equipment and expertise that will be needed in the near term.

In the longer term, the Press will develop non-commercial, cost-recovery models like those already being used in some academic libraries, and will continue to seek additional external funding from a variety of sources.

We believe DAPs located in academic libraries can enhance the teaching, learning, and research at their institutions, and also help universities regain control of scholarly publication. We chose to develop a DAP because the brilliance of e-repositories does not preclude the need for academic presses, including DAPs. Digital academic presses located in academic libraries can better assure a proper subject balance in a university's digital collections by seeking new knowledge and information to fill gaps in acquisitions that are likely to develop in e-repositories over time. Also, a DAP can provide a variety of original scholarly exposition types, including electronic books and journals, image collections, multimedia resources, and so forth. And frankly, we think running a digital academic press is much more fun than running an e-repository. Both are necessary, however, in the reformation of scholarly communication.

Opening Access

The CSUS library is the ideal unit to create and manage the CSU digital press. Placing the press under the CSUS library's direction will save time and money over creating a new and separate entity. Furthermore, the director and dean of the library also serves as the executive editor of the press. As such, he reports to the vice president for academic affairs and sits on the Deans' Council and the President's Administrative Council. The DAP will benefit from this organizational position because it can be closely integrated into the university's curricula, which will enable the digital press to have an immediate, positive effect on the scholarship of CSUS and potentially on the CSU system. It will also help transform the processes of scholarly communication across the academic community.

We will be assisted in this by advisory committees to steer the library and the digital press in beneficial and productive scholarly directions, and editorial boards that will assure the high quality and relevance of the DAP's publications. At the present time, we are working on an initial two-year publication list that includes series in the fields of Hellenic studies, Asian studies, librarianship, and anthropology.

Of course, the success of the digital press ultimately depends on its involvement and close collaboration with the CSUS faculty. We need them to provide service to the press by serving on the editorial and advisory boards; we need them to submit their scholarship to the e-repositories; we need them to make certain that their graduate students adhere to the thesis and dissertation standards required for submission to the ETDs.

Fortunately, members of the CSUS Faculty Senate are very interested in the digital press especially on behalf of the many new faculty, who are expected to engage in scholarship and publication to receive tenure. Because they are new, however, they also have heavy teaching loads, and they have difficulty finding time for scholarship and publication. The digital press can provide assistance by offering opportunities to consult with editorial boards, publication format advisors, and even use software applications that can help faculty obtain and organize their research materials and exposition.

Several types of publications are priority targets of the CSUS digital press during its initial publication period. First, we will seek to centralize the publication of electronic journals that are already in operation in the CSU universities. Second, we will provide digital publication for existing print journals produced in the CSU system. Third, we will offer digital publication to existing non–CSU print scholarly journals that support our curricula. Fourth, we want to capture and publish the proceedings of conferences, symposia, and lecture series on CSU campuses. Fifth, we intend to collaborate with academic and scholarly conferences and symposia anywhere in the world whose proceedings are relevant to CSU curricula, but which otherwise might be too specialized or too small to be able to publish them electronically. Finally, we are very willing to collaborate with other nonprofit and even with commercial publishers that may be facing publication backlogs resulting from insufficient funds for printing or the lack of digital publishing capacity.

For example, the CSUS DAP is partnering with the Subcommittee of East Asia and the Pacific of the International Relations Committee of the American Library Association to publish the papers from "Going Digital: Experiences from East Asia and the Pacific." This session of the Association's conference in June 2005 featured speakers from China, Japan, Taiwan, Singapore, and New Zealand. This publication will become part of a dual offering in the CSUS DAP's series on Asian studies and also librarianship.

Corner Cutting

When the GDB was created, its costs were extremely high. Fortunately, the current costs for the technology that supports e-repositories and DAPS are considerably more affordable. Still, the cost over time will be high as the repositories grow and as technology changes, bringing the need to migrate data from old environments to new ones. Clifford Lynch (2003) observes that "universities need to invest aggressively ... and implement thoughtfully ... with the full understanding that they will permanently change the landscape of scholarly communication."

The beauty of the CSUS digital press is that we currently will not charge for our publications or for our service to authors. We know we cannot continue this indefinitely. Start-up costs for the DAP have been affordable, and ongoing costs manageable so far, but only because we received a grant of almost $20,000 from the California state government and a $30,000 grant from the Tsakopoulos Hellenic Foundation. This foundation has been a partner in several library events and programs, and the foundation is dedicated to the mission and publication plan of the press, which is to enhance teaching, research, and scholarship in the university. The CSUS library matched these funds by installing extra electrical wiring, data lines, air conditioning upgrades, and uninterruptible power safeguards that were needed for the new equipment in the Library Systems Department server room and to insure the protection of the new equipment and the digital publications. If the CSUS DAP is approved to become the digital press for the CSU system, more funding may likely be made available from the CSU central offices.

Resident expertise in the CSUS Library Systems Office is sufficient to complete the initial publication projects now under consideration. Also, it is probable that external funds can be attracted to acquire additional equipment and expertise that might be needed in the near term. For at least the first two years of operation, we will scale press activities to fit the resources at hand. Beyond that we will explore and implement several cost-recovery models, for instance, nominal submission fees, moderate subscription fees, institutional partnerships, grants, and other financing that will allow us to publish on a manageable budget (see Joseph and Alexander 2003).

Certain budgetary conditions are clear. First, CSUS cannot support large outlays for new equipment or personnel during California's ongoing budget difficulties. Second, much of the CSUS DAP activity for the first two years will be spent developing a full business plan, suitable publications of various types, and an extended publication list. Third, the DAP will rely on its existing staff and equipment through 2006. Although we are already feeling the need for more staff, we plan to reassign some existing positions from elsewhere in the library and the campus to DAP operations temporarily. Finally, it is probable that more external funds can be attracted to acquire equipment and basic editorial expertise that might be needed in the period 2004–06. By 2006–07, however, new equipment and personnel will be needed to undertake a more aggressive publication schedule. Here again, we expect to decrease costs by attracting external funding.

Research and Development

At the CSUS digital press, we are not anti-print. But we think that publishers need to exploit fully the technological features of digital texts. We plan to introduce new formats, such as interactive texts and "smart" books. The electronic book will likely never replace the printed book entirely. Nor will the e-book ever reach its own full potential as long as it only mimics on the screen the page-like look and limitations of print. Even multimedia-equipped e-texts fail to reach a qualitative leap in learning beyond that achievable by reading printed texts. But as e-books incorporate more powerful linking enhancements, mark-up capabilities for reader commentary, and other features that begin to exploit the full capacities of digital exposition, the popularity and educational effectiveness of e-books will soar.

A digital text that incorporates artificial intelligence will have an effect on learning and scholarship that will eclipse the capacities of printed resources and even current e-resources that are appearing. As long ago as 1992, Ann Okerson at Johns Hopkins observed, "Technically, we'll have the ability to produce information cheaper and more rapidly, without the queues for publication and delays. We'll have intelligent documents. They'll be read, searched, merged, and linked with other documents. Things will be added, accumulated without a literature search through crossfiles" (qtd. in Levin). Bruce Marsh at MIT forecasts the day when we shall say, "Can you imagine, they used to have libraries where books didn't talk to each other" (qtd. in Levin).

A printed book can be read, but an intelligent book can remember and recall for the reader passages and meanings not only within its own contents, but within the contents of all the other intelligent books in the reader's e-library. As a reader of artificially intelligent books, you can put your mind into your books. It may be possible for a new e-book you download to read and learn all the other smart books you have already read, after which your new book will know your interests and research pursuits. Such books can facilitate your assimilation of new ideas in your field. Smart books can even develop your own library by scanning and selecting additional titles for you to consider, like Jerry Campbell's very powerful search engine. And these functions will not be limited to scanning only the metadata — they will select, read, store, and analyze the full contents according to your reading research interests or literary tastes. Books that remind readers of what they have read, and even written, and that can find elusive passages the readers cannot entirely recall or locate, are the types of texts the CSUS DAP eventually hopes to publish.

Hardware, Software, and Operating Systems

Our vision for the DAP is to publish research, conference proceedings, e-journals, e-books, and other forms of scholarship in digital text formats. But we also expect to publish scholarly image bases, audio recordings, video productions, 3D portrayals, virtual reality learning environments, and other formats. We also intend to provide interactive functionalities for readers, such as the capability to annotate, insert comments, and otherwise personalize the texts, along with multilingual features and collaborative wiki-like environments. We hope to explore possible roles for artificial intelligence and game theory in digital publications. It is also necessary to keep all the publications online continuously, 24/7/365.

To reach these objectives, it is necessary for our system to meet demanding requirements. We intend to use open source software whenever possible to maximize our flexibility. We are running the Debian GNU/Linux operating system on our Dell 4400 PowerEdge server, with an Apache web server, and are exploring DSpace, Fedora, Greenstone, and other software to manage and provide access to our publications.

For our image bases, we are using CONTENTdm to manage the metadata and provide users with a very flexible interface to access and view the images using, for instance, side-by-side image comparisons, extreme zoom-in and zoom-out, and other features. Although CONTENTdm is not open source, we have used it before to create other digital collections, and found it very suitable for the DAP start-up.

To assure rapid access and reliable preservation of our publications, we store them on an Apple XServe RAID, currently with four terabytes of storage space, attached directly to the servers via fiber switches. The storage area network configuration separates the data storage devices and functions from the servers so the components can run much faster and at high capacities with each other even though the servers and data storage machines are on separate, distributed networks. In addition, the RAID includes automatic data backups, which will give us considerable peace of mind.

Our equipment includes a high-quality digitizing station using a precision 4x5 view camera with a 135mm lens, fitted with a BetterLight 6000E HS scan back that scans at 6000x8000 pixels without compression. This setup allows us to digitize oversized print documents and 3D objects at very high resolution. We also have a film scanner for easy digitizing of 35mm negatives and slides at a resolution of 5400 pixels. In addition, we use a flatbed scanner at 1600 dpi. All of this equipment is connected to a desktop computer with dual monitors, 1GB RAM, 80 GB local disk space, which is also connected to the network storage.

Because hardware and software change so rapidly, we recognize that one of the most daunting challenges of a digital press, e-repository, and any other type of virtual collection will be the need to migrate these collections and their interfaces to new formats and technologies as they appear, while keeping all publications online and accessible anytime, day and night. Such migrations, of course, have already become second nature in the digital library environment.

E-Publications

E-journals and other e-scholarship products are still not yet equal in academic stature to the many long-running prestigious scholarly print journals issued by commercial publishers. It is important to remember, however, that this prestige and stature have been achieved by their reputable authors, their outstanding editorial boards, and their peer reviewers. The "prestige" resides in these persons, many of whom, if not most, belong to the academic community.

Many voices have already objected strenuously to the current state of affairs in scholarly publishing, which is this: New knowledge and scholarship are produced mainly by university faculty and researchers who then hand over their work to appear in prestigious journals. Then the commercial publishers of these journals sell the new knowledge back to the same academic and scholarly institutions where it originated, but at such outrageous prices that the institutions cannot purchase all the scholarly publications they need. This is a very amateurish business model for universities, and it has many university administrators and librarians strongly urging scholarly authors *not* to relinquish their copyrights on their publications so they can control the distribution of their scholarship.

Similarly, the secret of endowing e-journals with the prestige of the most esteemed commercial print journals lies in persuading the persons who now serve on the editorial boards and peer review panels to return to academe and offer their excellent skills and reputations to university-based, nonprofit scholarly publications, especially digital publications. The immediate results would be scholarship that is highly prestigious and also affordable. That is the basis of the reformation of scholarly communication.

Control of scholarly publishing must revert to the universities if we are to experience these benefits, and digital collections in the form of e-repositories, electronic thesis and dissertation collections, and digital presses are the mechanism for achieving these very desirable results. Using these e-scholarship technologies, libraries can and should take over the role of scholarly publishing in close collaboration with faculty and researchers, and with university administrations for long-term budgetary support. It would be another variation on the Human Genome Database. Although that innovative data resource was launched a couple of decades ago, the GDB is the model that precisely fits our current needs in scholarly communication.

Beyond Reformation

A new digital domain is opening for librarians that involves electronically publishing appropriate resources for easy, inexpensive access by users. And because communities of users overlap considerably, what's good for the universities is likely to be good for the general public. By making e-repositories, ETDs, and DAPS accessible to the public as an outreach mechanism, and by partnering in the creation of these resources with businesses, professionals, local information providers, and community groups so that they, too, will benefit from these knowledge bases, universities can achieve their goals and raise the proficiencies of the general community as well.

CSUS DAP Publications

Librarianship

BUILDING LIBRARIES FOR THE 21ST CENTURY: THE SHAPE OF INFORMATION

T.D. Webb. An image base of photographs and other visuals assembled as a digital companion volume to *Building Libraries for the 21st Century: The Shape of Information,* by T.D. Webb, a paper publication of McFarland & Company, Inc., Publishers (2000, reprinted 2004).

Shaping 21st-Century Libraries. When *Building Libraries for the 21st Century: The Shape of Information* was published in 2000, a large number of photos, floor plans, and other visuals that were submitted by the contributors could not be included in the book. In conjunction with the reprinting of *Building Libraries*, McFarland & Company, Inc., Publishers, and the Digital Academic Press of California State University, Sacramento, are jointly publishing this digital supplement of photographs and other images that were included in the book, as well as others that were *not* included. We believe that releasing the larger collection of images will significantly increase the usefulness of the book, and that this innovative blend of print and digital formats produced by joint publishers will help set a new trend in academic and scholarly publishing.

Asia Studies

THE CHINA ABROAD ARCHIVES

D. W. Y. Kwok, Professor Emeritus of History, University of Hawaii, February 2005. An important and rare collection of unpublished, underground, and dissident literary works from the People's Republic of China. This publication is a joint project of the CSUS Digital Academic Press and the library of Kapiolani College, University of Hawaii. The China Abroad Archives are in the permanent custody of Kapiolani College.

Sinology Conference Program, February 17, 2005

PARTICIPANTS FROM TAIWAN

1. Kao, Po-yuan (head of the delegation), Vice President of Academic Affairs, Tamkang University.

2. Lu, Kuo-ping, Chair, Department of Chinese, Tamkang University

3. Chen, Shih-hua, Associate Professor, Graduate Institute of Chinese Linguistics and Documentation, Tamkang University

4. Ni, Tai-ying, Associate Professor, Department of Chinese, Tamkang University

5. Chiang, Shu-chun, Associate Professor, Department of Chinese, Tamkang University

6. Cho, Wen-chien, Chair, Department of Tourism, Hsing Wu College

7. Tseng, Shou-cheng, Associate Professor, Department of Chinese, National Chengchi University

8. Hsueh, Jung-ting, Editor, Transmission Books & Microinfo Co., Ltd.

9. Huang, Li-kai, Graduate Student, Department of Chinese, Tamkang University

PARTICIPANTS FROM CSUS

1. Shek, Richard, Professor, Department of Humanities and Religious Studies

2. Robinson, Lewis, Professor, Department of Foreign Languages

3. Wang, Ruth, Professor, Department of Management

4. Ren, Xin, Professor, Department of Criminal Justice

5. Shen, Dong, Assistant Professor, Department of Family and Consumer Sciences

Sinology Conference Program
February 17, 2005 (Thursday)

8:30–9:00	Arrivals & Greetings
9:00–9:30	Opening Ceremony: President Alexander Gonzalez (CSUS)
	Vice President Kao Po-yuan (Tamkang University)
	Prof. Richard Shek (CSUS)
9:30–9:40	Group Photo Session
9:40–10:25	First Panel (Moderated by Prof. Ren Xin)
	Shen Dong (CSUS) "Chinese Urban Clothing from 1644 to Present: A Historical Study"
	Lu Kuo-ping, Huang Li-kai (TKU) "A Dialogue Between Chinese Characters and Contemporary Visual Arts"
10:25–10:45	Refreshment Break
10:45–11:50	Second Panel (Moderated by Prof. Lu Kuo-ping)
	Cho Wen-chien (HWC) "Changes in Taiwanese Food Culture and Politics as Reflected in the Menu of State Banquets"
	Richard Shek (CSUS) "Chinese Culture and Food"
	Tseng Shou-cheng (NCCU) "Expressions of Aspirations in Han Dynasty Rhapsodies"
11:50–13:10	Lunch Break
13:10–14:15	Third Panel (Moderated by Prof. Chiang Shu-chun)
	Lewis Robinson (CSUS) "Medicine for the Spirit? A Comparison Between Chinese Filial Piety and the Sense of 'Sacrifice' in Christian Salvationism,

as Reflected in Lu Xun's 'Medicine' and Mo Yan's 'Efficacious Medicine'"

Ni Tai-ying (TKU) "A Study of Trends in 21st-Century Chinese Rhetoric as Seen in Advertising Phrases"

Ruth Wang (CSUS) "Modern Chinese Online Poetry"

14:15–14:35 Refreshment Break

14:35–15:20 Fourth Panel (Moderated by Prof. Ruth Wang)

Chen Shih-hua (TKU) "Transformations in Chinese Encyclopedia and Changes in Society"

Hsueh Jung-ting (TBMC) "An Analysis of Culture and Society in Taiwan through the Collection of Popular Morality Books"

15:20–15:40 Refreshment Break

15:40–16:45 Fifth Panel (Moderated by Prof. Chen Shih-hua)

Kao Po-yuan (TKU) "Prof. Tang Chun-i's Views of Laozi"

Ren Xin (CSUS) "Legal Protection of Women's Rights in China"

Chiang Shu-chun (NTNU) "A Perspective on the Interpretation of Laozi in the Song Dynasty — Using the *Analects* and the *Mencius* to Comprehend the *Laozi*"

16:45–17:00 Closing Ceremony: Prof. Richard Shek (CSUS)

Prof. Lu Kuo-ping (TKU)

18:30 Dinner at New Canton Restaurant

Librarianship

Going Digital: Experiences from East Asia and the Pacific

These collected papers are from the June 2005 American Library Association conference. This publication is a collaboration between the CSUS digital academic press and the ALA East Asia and the Pacific Subcommittee of the International Relations Committee. Digital library experts involved in the latest developments in China, Taiwan, Japan, New Zealand, Singapore, Thailand, and Vietnam share the experiences and lessons they have learned. Introduction by Judy Jeng.

This digital publication collects the papers presented by invited speakers at "Going Digital: Experiences from East Asia and the Pacific," the held at American Library Association Annual Conference, June 23–29, 2005, Chicago, Illinois. The topics were:

1. "Going Digital: Taiwan Experiences," Chao-chen Chen, Professor, Graduate Institute of Library and Information Science, National Taiwan Normal University, Taiwan

2. "From CALIS to CADLIS: The experience of academic libraries in China," Zhu Qiang, Professor and Deputy Director, Center for China Academic Library and Information System, Peking University, China

3. "Use of Technology in Singapore libraries," Fatt-Cheong Choy, University Librarian, Nanyang Technological University, Singapore

4. "Digital Library Software from New Zealand: Selected Experiences in East Asia

and the Pacific," Ian H. Witten, Professor, Computer Science, University of Waikato, New Zealand

    5. Japanese Journal Digitization and Portal Service GeNii," Akira Miyazawa, Professor of Library and Information Science, National Institute of Informatics, Japan

    6. "Digital Library: A Transition of Academic Libraries in Thailand," Sujin Butdisuwan, Dean, Faculty of Informatics, Mahasarakham University, Thailand

    7. "Digital Libraries in Vietnam: Developments, Issues, and Concerns," Pat Oyler, Professor of Library and Information Science, Simmons College, Boston, Massachusetts

Collected on this site are all seven speakers' powerpoint slides and four speakers' papers. Judy Jeng is head of collection services at New Jersey City University. She received her Ph.D. degree from Rutgers, The State University of New Jersey.

Hellenic Studies

The new Hellenic studies program at CSUS, is a high-priority partner with the Sacramento State Digital Academic Press because the rapid development of the Program is a joint goal of the university, the library (by virtue of the Tsakopoulos Hellenic Collection), and the Tsakopoulos Hellenic Foundation. Also, the Hellenic studies program is a ready source of original scholarly research and exposition issuing from lecture series, special events, new faculty research, and other publication possibilities beginning to emanate from the program's center. These publications will also be of interest to the Greek American community at large.

When fully operational, the DAP will fast-track two Hellenic studies projects. The first is to locate and assist small Hellenic studies scholarly journals that are facing significant publication backlogs resulting from insufficient funds for printing and/or for moving into electronic formats by themselves. A sizable amount of scholarship in Hellenic studies and related fields remains unpublished and unavailable via the Internet due to a lack of publication resources. The DAP will make the transition to digital publication easier and more affordable for journals in these predicaments.

The second urgent DAP project is to establish online connections with the many other Hellenic studies centers and associations around the world, giving the CSU Sacramento Hellenic studies program worldwide recognition and presence.

DEFENDING THE GREEKS, BY BRUCE S. THORTON

The text of the keynote address delivered at a dinner in honor of former Senator Nicholas C. Petris at California State University, Sacramento, February 28, 2005. The event also recognized the official naming of the Senator Nicholas C. Petris Room in the University Library, adjacent to the Tsakopoulos Hellenic Collection.

Pending Projects for the Digital Academic Press

John McClure's Annotated Bibliography
Bibliography on Napoleon III/Mexico

Eugenics Conference, with digital exhibit
Contact Sheila O'Neill

Namour Philosophy Symposia (Annual)
CSUS Philosophy Department

Eugene Redmond: Paul Laurence Dunbar projects
Contact Rhonda Rios Kravitz

Equadorian Anthropology/Archaeology
Contacts:
Charles Stanish
Frank Salomon
Ronald Lippi
Tamara Bray
Abya-Yala Press, Quito
Joel Wright
Terry Webb

Collaboration with Heyday Books
Contact Sheila O'Neill

JEP: eJournal of Education Policy
Contact Rosemary Papa (Center for Teaching and Learning)

Small journals in Greek studies
Contact
Terry Webb
James Reid

Digital Ethnography Project
Contact
Terry Webb
Jay Crain (CSUS Anthropology Department)

7

Open Access, Modernity and Culture Change

The Down Side of OA

Despite my abiding support for open access, we must answer for all our deeds, good ones as well as bad ones. Because we can't be sure of the future, we can't always predict the outcomes of our good intentions. It's like the uncertainty principle: locating the *position* of a subatomic particle makes the *velocity* of the particle uncertain; conversely, measuring the *velocity* of a particle makes its *position* uncertain. The observer always inserts him/herself into the experiment, which directly alters the event in an unnatural way.

Culture change can occur gradually and subtly, or abruptly in incidents of social or environmental catastrophes of climatological, biological, and geological events. Culture change in any form, especially if it is sudden and widespread, can spell disaster for unsuspecting societies.

One of the most powerful agents of culture change is cross-cultural contact. History is replete with instances of colliding civilizations that sent many societies and cultures to waste and ruin. Many cases of culture loss have been purposely inflicted by invaders. Even today, in our attempts to benefit society and culture by solving one problem, we often create another problem, like converting corn into fuel for automobiles, which forced corn prices sky high on the world markets not so long ago, and significantly raised the number of starving people in developing nations.

We can't accurately predict the position or velocity of our good intentions. Partly for this reason, cultural diversity, like biological diversity, could be perceived as a potential fall-back strategy to protect life on earth. Let's say, if some new catastrophic disease appears, such as a new strain of Ebola, a databank of local knowledge systems of numerous human populations could possibly supply answers that might hold the disease in check, or even eradicate it, unless the solutions were not discovered in time, or the databank was insufficient, or the local cultural remedies had disappeared or been replaced by other more "modern" but less effective cultural practices. Although I fully support the open access reformation, I sense that a potentially enormous culture change is looming for developing nations in the form of the OA movement.

Warren (1991) observes, "Local knowledge is unique to a given culture or society. It contrasts with the international knowledge system generated by universities, research institutions and private firms." Korten (1980) stated, "Building on local knowledge and resources reduces the likelihood that ... development intervention will 'de-skill' people or increase their dependence on external experts." For example, ethnic cultural tourist centers (which are my research specialty) are microcosms of cross-cultural contacts and good examples of "globalization glitch."

Where local knowledge is vibrant in a culture, an equilibrium holds the ethnic culture in place for the locals. Tourist outsiders, however, can cause havoc if local knowledge is demeaned by the guests, especially wealthy ones. Tourists in developing nations have been killed, as in the Lake of Thousand Isles incident of 1994, when tourist passengers and the crew of a tour boat were killed in a fire set by young locals after they robbed the tourists (Li 2002).

Even glancing at cross-cultural contrasts can reveal powerful cultural oddities. For instance, in his study of festival séances performed for tourists among the Irula culture in southern India, Neil Thin (2001) found that the performers create an ulterior signifi-cance in these performances that indirectly isolates them from the outsiders they entertain, and this allows the Irula to preserve much of their local cultural behaviors, and continue engaging and practicing their local knowledge. In the terms of Carrier's study of "market talk" (2001), ethnic tourism development ventures could conceivably become a social product to cross the gap between the locals and the tourist outsiders, but the crossing would never completely occur because the tourists are unaware of the explicit dimensions of the minority performers and their culture. In his account of carnival in the Caribbean, Skinner (2001) documents the ability of tourists to influence calypso music, but they entirely fail to grasp fully the local idiom because the social and cultural gap between the performers and the tourists is too wide for either group to bridge. Tourist outsiders with intrusive cross-cultural influences can dissipate and ridicule local knowledge, and even raise anger among the locals, even if the intrusive tourists stop coming.

Road Trip

I described in an earlier chapter that my library at UH in the mid–1990s began devel-oping online databases to support Asian-Pacific studies. We worked with several UH departments and U.S. government–funded agencies in the U.S., Asia, and the Pacific. We called our online creations "value added databases," a term we borrowed from John Haak at the Hamilton Library; *OA* and *IR* were not common terms then.

In 1995, I was invited to speak to faculty and students at the City University of Hong Kong about the UH databases. When I began talking about the GDB, however, I was literally shouted down by the faculty because the GDB was so expensive. They refused to listen when I said our UH databases cost less than US$10,000, which was provided by our clients. The CityU mob seemed unaware of the rapid development of technology of that time, and would not cotton to starting newfangled research and publishing mod-els.

In 1996, I gave a contributed paper with virtually the same information to the Inter-national Federation of Library Associations (IFLA) conference in Beijing. It was roundly applauded and was published in the *IFLA Journal* in the conference issue. I received inquiries from a number of nations, including China and Russia.

In 2004, I was again invited to City U, this time by the new university president, to speak about OA. I was not shouted down that time, but the response was lukewarm, much like now in Hong Kong. Today, all eight public-funded university libraries have some form of OA IR, but they are not the type of OA research databases described in this book, unfortunately for Hong Kong. The universities in Hong Kong at the time were far from practicing OA. The faculty were simply unmotivated to move to a new scholarly publishing environment.

Whither/Wither OA?

Even though I heard very little from UGC or RGC after the lengthy correspondence outlined in Chapter 5, I will always be grateful for the article by Orsdel and Born. Since then, OA in Hong Kong, frozen in the academic ice, began to thaw, but the way forward will be slow, very slow. How different the Hong Kong universities are from Harvard, Cornell, the University of California, and so many others! The hands-off approach of the UGC and RGC may likely smother OA here. It must be a top-down as well as a bottom-up undertaking with research money, threats, incentives, and pressure from administrators to secure buy-in from the faculty and researchers. While UGC was very willing to *force* the faculty in 2008 to (1) adopt a vigorous objectives-based student learning outcomes project, and (2) accept a new teaching quality assurance method in the form of a UGC Quality Assurance Committee initiative, both of which I endorse, the UGC was still not willing to pressure faculty into OA. They simply turned their blind eyes to anything that looks like OA. It baffled me.

An Anthropology of OA

We already know that OA will likely have a major impact on developing nations. For instance, the twofold mission of the Wellcome Trust in London is to fund research to improve the health of humans and animals, and to maximize the dissemination of this research through free, online access to create a more robust worldwide research culture. Recipients of Wellcome funds are required to provide unrestricted access to their published research as a fundamental part of Wellcome's charitable mission (http://wellcome.ac.uk/About-us/Policy/Spotlight-issues/Open-access/Policy/index.htm).

The trust provides funds for research in all aspects of biomedical science organized into five "streams," including immunology and infectious diseases; neuroscience and mental health; physiological sciences; molecules, genes and cells; and populations and public health. Funding reaches into clinical and public health research that includes improving the quality of healthcare delivered to people internationally.

Peer review by external referees, funding committees composed of independent research scientists, and a strict code of ethics assures that good science will be the hallmark of the research based on Wellcome funding.

Wellcome also encourages grant proposals from or directed at developing countries, and provides significant funding for its African Institutions Initiatives. This project seeks to strengthen Africa's research capacity by creating critical mass in the local research capacity of African universities and research institutions, and by converting research training into career pathways for the best and brightest researchers in health research, including public health research.

A Certain Uncertainty

There is no doubt that unprecedented OA advances will dramatically affect developing nations, mainly for the better, or so we must hope. I've visited a number of developing nations over the last fifteen years, including China, Vietnam, India, Micronesia, and Malaysia, but the most compelling was my visit in 2004 to Ivory Coast, in Central Africa. I was a member of a delegation of educators from CSUS participating in a U.S. State Department grant to mentor eight universities there. Administrators and faculty from Ivory Coast universities visited CSUS several times, and the CSUS delegation made focused trips to Africa toward the end of the project.

The CSUS educators arrived in the capital, Abidjan, and fanned out to visit the various universities. I was stunned by the sad condition of their library facilities and the terribly small collections of outdated books. I decided not to talk about library buildings and print collections, as the Ivorian librarians and administrators had requested, because these conditions were beyond the means of the nation to remedy. Instead, I gave the Ivorians extemporary chalk talks on the principles and benefits of OA for very rapid scholarly communication. I used CDL as the model. My hosts immediately saw that OA IRs could quickly gather research on agriculture, tourism, and other industries in the region to bolster economic and social development. They agreed that peer review was essential, and decided to put buildings and collections aside and focus on digital research for scholarly communication. Then, shortly after our return to the U.S., the civil war in Ivory Coast flared again, ending all our collaboration with sure finality. This sudden turn of affairs affected me profoundly, and it clearly portends some of the fearful measures than can curtail the potential benefits of OA in developing countries.

The Ivorians were proud to show off their IT systems to the CSUS group and, though meager, the technology worked and the technical people were very savvy. I and others in our group could see that Ivorian systems managers could quickly catch up with the much more sophisticated systems in the developed nations, if they could only raise enough money to acquire them. They did not have the infrastructure to start OA IRs, but they clearly had the technical expertise, foresight, determination, and vigor to develop such resources to promote their national economy and improve their social well-being. Although the Ivorians lacked funds and infrastructure, they did not lack insight, intelligence, or education. Many of them received their academic educations in Europe.

In Beijing ten years earlier, I gave similar workshops to reference librarians at Peking University on automation, technology leapfrogging, and the value-added databases at the University of Hawaii. And look at what has happened to scholarship, research, and information-sharing by China's academic libraries since then. They rival anything the West has to offer. Of course, this burst of advancement was certainly *not* a result of my lowly workshops. Instead, it was the readiness, drive, and motivation of the librarians and administrators, and we must certainly not overlook the role of the "211" funding package. This infusion of funds from China's central government was to move 100 of China's key universities and their libraries quickly forward. 211 implies "21st century," and "100 key universities." The 211 project allocated its funds to achieve an international level of academic quality by 2010. Too bad the U.S. and other nations do not develop such grants straightaway to libraries and educational institutions.

Technology is the great equalizer; crack open a door of an underdeveloped nation with a little training and access to a bit of information technology, and many individuals will quickly become early adopters and transform their nations. While developing nations may lack "stuff," their capital is their ambition and inquisitiveness, and OA-delivered research is perfect for them. In fact, developing nations are likely to be primary beneficiaries of open access.

By using OA to access research in any number of fields, developing nations can sidestep yesterday's information technologies, install the most current systems and strategies available, and harvest scientific breakthroughs with a very short start-up time. With OA, especially, progress in developing nations will move forward at an ever-increasing pace. Health care research may be particularly abundant.

Global Vistas

OA is certainly an important part of globalization. Globalization does not touch only on economics and business. Culture is intricately pervasive in social actions and beliefs. Change the social actions and beliefs, and culture will be affected. Globalization inculcates uniformity among disparate societies. OA may not be good in all instances or in all developing nations. Knowledge is power, and power is easily turned corrupt and destructive.

Enron, for instance, secretively (for a while) manipulated the energy crisis in California. I consider it treason and sedition when a corporation wages an economic war on a sovereign state of the United States. It is quite possible that some governments in developing nations may quarantine or embargo OA information to make their own profits. Such a case would simply transfer information from one criminal monopoly (the commercial publishers) to another (a central government).

Let me repeat from an earlier chapter that a SPARC representative told me a publisher hired the publicity firm that once worked for Enron. If a government, as in the U.S. NIH bill, can mandate that all health and medical information be free, some other governments or pseudo-governments can mandate that information must be purchased, and at exorbitant prices. If our friends the publishers go out of their monopolistic business in the developed world, they might hire themselves out to governments in developing nations at even higher costs, or follow the lead of U.S. tobacco companies that dumped extra tons of its harmful products in developing nations when the U.S. campaign against smoking was just beginning to pick up steam. Unscrupulous information companies can equally rain disaster on developing nations by withholding or tampering with needed information.

We certainly cannot prevent crooked information vendors reaching into developing or remote cultures. We must go ahead for the sake of humanity. But remember the uncertainty principle: we cannot be sure of the ultimate outcomes. We can't always predict all the results of our good intentions. These days, anything and everything is for sale.

Modernization and Globalization

Let's get back to culture change. Living in the modern age does not necessarily make an individual "modern." "Modern individuals" tend to be utilitarian, more globalized, and more readily able than others to take advantage of newly perceived features in contemporary society in order to achieve ambitions, improve their lifestyle, obtain profitable learning, and enhance their personal power and efficacy — for good or even for unsavory purposes.

"Individual," or, sometimes, "attitudinal" modernity, is a construct that has been used to gauge the effects of culture change among persons who encounter cross-cultural contact. Sociologists gather their data through very precise surveys. Anthropologists use participant observation.

Remember the Bushman in the film *The Gods Must Be Crazy*? The Bushmen, or San, are hunters and gatherers and have been on the verge of extinction for generations. Nearly 2,000 years ago, African agro-pastoralists began arriving in Central Africa, disrupting the San lifestyle and culture. In the 17th century, European settlers arrived and brought more disruptive cross-cultural contact (Marshall 2003). And in the late 20th century, an empty Coke bottle fell from the window of a passing airplane, and nearly wrecked the life of an entire San village, or so goes the story in the film.

The San culture is in shreds. In 2003, *National Geographic News* stated, "The San have largely lost their sense of community and identity by being dispossessed of their territories and becoming physically dispersed. They have suffered language loss and some of their important social institutions have become dysfunctional." Few of them hunt now. Instead, many work as farm laborers, and others are chronically unemployed.

Yet the San population also stands to earn perhaps billions of dollars by assigning their "intellectual property rights" to a gigantic pharmaceutical interest that will pay huge sums to process and market a local desert plant named *Hoodia gordonii*. The San have used hoodia for centuries as an appetite suppressant to quell their hunger on a long hunt. The pharmaceutical firm will sell hoodia to overweight people around the world. This is a rather unique instance of conglomerates willingly recognizing "intellectual property rights" of indigenous peoples, instead of simply stealing the local natural resources.

According to *National Geographic*, there is growing international recognition for the intellectual property rights of indigenous peoples. The monies that go to the San will be used, in part, to reconstruct their culture by initiating dialogues "between the elders who still have knowledge of ... the old ways and the younger generation who have lost [that knowledge].” The young people do not know about the traditional uses of hoodia, but their interest in the plant will certainly skyrocket as the money rolls in. Already the San are becoming more secretive about their plants. In other words, they are repackaging their traditional plants as commodities to sell to outsiders. I have often observed that when cultural practices, implements, and arts become objects for exchange, they merely hasten the draining of traditional culture. By diminishing the social practices once connected to their traditional plants, the San culture may likely dissipate even faster.

In 2002, the South African Council for Scientific and Industrial Research (CSIR) officially recognized the San tribespeople’s rights over hoodia, allowing them to take a percentage of the profits and any spin-offs resulting from the marketing of hoodia. Now *Hoodia gordonii* is a protected plant that may only be wild-harvested by individuals and the few companies who have been granted a license.

In short, the San are well on their way to becoming modern, globalized, materialistic, and capitalistic. Thomas Friedman (2005) can only be delighted by this. He reinterprets “globalization” as the 21st-century “flattening of the world.” He believes that “geographical boundaries will not be able to restrict the flow of information and commerce. The world is increasingly embracing capitalism. The rise of digital and broadband communications has helped bring nations and people together.”

Friedman is talking about massive cross-cultural contact and modernization, if not outright enormous losses of traditional cultures. To him, digital communications and border-neutral commerce have broken down political walls between cultures, his paradigmatic example being the Berlin Wall, and replaced the walls with windows, that is, Microsoft “windows.” Capitalism reigns, free to barrel over flatlands without portfolio. Friedman knows perfectly well that he is talking about massive cross-cultural contact. He is ushering cultures into rampant globalization, saying, “The more your culture easily absorbs foreign ideas and best practices ... the greater advantage you will have in a flat world.” I shudder to think of it. He uses terms like *globalization* and *glocalization*. I think of “gobblization” as people and nations flatten themselves together. It’s boring and it’s frightening. It reduces cultural diversity that we might desperately need in the future for much more than high finance and weight loss.

Modernity on the Malay Peninsula

In 2006, I attended a three-day family and parenting conference in Kuala Lumpur entitled Family Strengthening Workshop: Empowering the Family in Challenging Times, sponsored by the Malaysian Ministry of Women, Family, and Community Development, and the Malaysian National Council of Welfare and Social Development. Most attendees were professional family, social, and welfare officers of the Malaysian government and also NGOs. Over 400 people attended the conference, from the U.S., Middle East, China, Hong Kong, and elsewhere.

Malaysia is quickly becoming a nation of modern individuals. By that I mean Malaysians can pick and choose the social customs and practices that make the most sense to them and which embody the values they have embraced as the keys to their happiness.

Their firm hold on certain traditional values—especially the family and disciplines of worship—will be central in their accommodations to the stress of rapid economic development. In the developing nations I have visited, social development always lags far behind economic development. I know of no instance in which these two forces for change have ever progressed in step with each other. It is a propitious time for humanitarianism in Malaysia, supported by media, social services, and professional assistance directed at social stabilization and strengthening at the family and individual levels.

Modernity appears to the Malaysians as another stage of human history that can be successfully navigated using traditional family values and structures no matter what other changes might occur during their nation's social and economic progress. If social upheaval follows modernization, the rigging of traditional family operations must be tightened and reinforced as the sails of a ship are lashed for strength, control, and faster progress on a pitching, wind-driven sea. One strategy discussed in the workshop was, not simply to adapt traditional family structures to modern social and economic conventions, but instead to conform modern practices and contingencies to tried-and-true successes in family structuring and practice, with an eye to hone interpersonal skills to make family life in modern Malaysia even more resilient and effective.

Modern individuals can make good use of globally accessible mass media, high-speed travel, and border-neutral sociocultural influences to compare their native social situations with other societal systems of which they become aware. They often choose between those different value sets or blend them into personal life patterns that best satisfy their tastes and needs. Simply put, individual (or attitudinal) modernity is a matter of expanding one's range of choices by selecting from among available social options that are within reach and which matter most to modern individuals and those others they care for. I seemed to see these abilities among the participants of the Family Strengthening Workshop: Empowering the Family in Challenging Times.

The Workshop

The voices I heard at the Workshop were those of people in the process of adjusting superstructures while not necessarily uprooting infrastructures. My contacts with the Malaysian government representatives were well educated, economically stable, and forward looking. They were energetic and positive about addressing the stresses of ramping up a modern production-based economy, and doing so by holding tightly to the values of family, faith, and compassion. They may well evade Friedman's flattening of their world.

In terms of content and attendance, the Workshop was clearly a success. In terms of the unity of thought among the participants regarding family sanctity, the gathering was even more remarkable. There appeared to be a meeting of minds on the continuing importance of the traditional family structure in modern times. Most appeared to be starting from the same premise: perennial family values are a safeguard to social stability and individual happiness that can and must withstand the stresses of modernity and cultural fit in order to preserve society and humanity. This assumption was the foundation upon which the discourse, instruction, and learned reports were based. The gathering was reassuring in that a unity of thought was unmistakable from the very opening of the event despite the variety of political, ethnic, and religious groups in attendance.

These attendees were acting in a very modern way even by inviting foreign experts whose ideas harmonized with many of their own most fundamental life anchors. This unity of thought was all the more intriguing because major contributions to the Workshop dialogue were made by Christian family life experts, who were applauded roundly by the other attendees, who came from many nations and many faiths, most of them non–Christian, since Islam is Malaysia's state religion.

Like the Malaysians, I have also observed that modern individuals in India, at least for the time being, can straddle border-neutral social influences to adapt to a changing world, but not necessarily a flat one. They appear to be able to reserve or blend their choices between different value sets. Simply put, individual modernity is a matter of expanding one's range of choices by selecting from among available social options that are within reach and which matter most to modern individuals, built sometimes very much on traditional foundations.

Individual Modernity

Two classic modernization studies that affected my thinking about culture change were conducted by sociologists Daniel Lerner (*The Passing of Traditional Society*, 1958) and Alex Inkeles and David Smith (*Becoming Modern*, 1974). Lerner recounted a case study of a grocer in a small village in Turkey. While watching an American movie in Ankara, he was riveted by a scene in a U.S. grocery store that showed him wall-to-wall rows of metal shelves with uniformly labeled cans and boxes of store goods stacked high and arranged in orderly ranks "like soldiers in a parade." The grocer knew immediately that this was the future of grocery stores in Turkey. It was his personal future, too, and he set out to bring to reality that vision he had received from a foreign movie.

Almost two decades later, Inkeles and Smith likewise found in their multinational study of individuals in six developing nations that the popular media were powerful change agents that could light a spark of modernity in individuals sequestered in traditional settings and social structures. Other inculcators of modernization were also identified during the exhaustive surveys conducted worldwide. These somewhat surprising inculcators included participation in formal, hierarchical organizations, even rural cooperatives; travel; mass media contact; education, including the parents' educational levels; employment in factories; time management; and experience in urban settings. According to Inkeles and Smith, contact with these types of modern technologies, organizations, and behaviors induces individual modernity in those who participate in these activities. The process works through modeling, imagined role reversals, and empathy, that is, seeing oneself in a different, more beneficial situation. In his earlier study, Lerner called empathy *psychic mobility*, and regarded it as a prerequisite state of mind for *social mobility*.

Inkeles and Smith also claimed to have identified a "syndrome" of attitudes that characterized individual modernity, including a sense of personal efficacy; being active citizens; valuing education and technical skills; staying informed about the larger world; planning;

openness to new experiences; aspirations of economic and social advancement; acceptance of individual responsibility; freedom from automatic submission to traditional authority in family, tribe, and sect; and formulation of new non-parochial loyalties.

I do not see globalization as equivalent to individual modernity, psychic mobility, or social mobility. Globalization is compelled. Modernity is more individualized. Studies like those conducted by Lerner and by Inkeles and Smith remain controversial for many reasons, but I was persuaded by them at my first reading. And because I have visited a number of developing nations around the world over the years, and seen firsthand most of the features and transformations that correspond to the findings these sociologists documented, I remain persuaded.

In the April 2003 issue of *The Asian Journal of Social Psychology* a study conducted by three Chinese authors (Zhang, X. Gui, Zheng Xue, and Wang Lei) indicated that students from urban settings had much higher levels of individual modernity than students from the countryside. They also found that the males were more traditional than the females in the sample of 300 students. The authors predicted that traditional values will decrease and modernity will increase because of the rising educational level in rural China.

Modern individuals are optimistic and opportunistic, and are able to choose the social customs and practices that make the most sense to them and which embody the values they have embraced as the keys to their happiness, but are not necessarily hell-bent on replacing traditional values and practices. They can perceive advantages in change that accommodates, complements, or strengthens persistent values that underlie their traditions and customary behaviors. Yet there is resistance and opposition in all things, and modernization often spawns deadly violence, cultural disruptions, and culture loss.

Controversial though the term *individual modernity* might be, developing nations are soon likely to receive massive infusions of information at an astounding rate, much of which will be delivered through OA. Open access can create breakthroughs in every subject from medicine to politics, parenting and education, and much, much more, that will change the lives of people. This will also, almost of necessity, change and perhaps even erase cultural diversity.

Double Indemnity

The 1944 film *Double Indemnity* starred Fred MacMurray, Barbara Stanwyck, and Edward G. Robinson. The movie is about an insurance man and a suburban wife who conspire to trick her husband into signing a policy that pays double for accidental death — then they strangle him and plop him on a train track. It's an almost perfect crime.

There is a grocery store scene in the film; it may well be the scene the grocer saw in Ankara that moved him resolutely toward modernity. The decade seems about right. The motif of the movie *and* of open access *and* of culture change is this: you can't have it both ways. If we introduce new practices, cross-cultural contacts, and new ideas into existing cultures, some things will be overwritten, like text on a hard drive or an invisible subatomic particle we can't see, but which affects us nevertheless, and we can't always be sure what will happen, what might disappear, what will remain, and how that which remains, changes after all.

Moral

Think of massive destructions of historic landmarks, buildings, *hutongs*, villages, and cities, along with gigantic relocations of entire populations, in a mad race for globalization or Westernization, which are not the same as modernization. Remember, in developing nations social development always lags far behind economic development.

Recalling Friedman's energetic reference that digital and broadband communications will bring nations together is certainly a refrain of the prospect of the open access reformation. That's the way he sees the future as a flat world. I'm not sure I want to go there. Certainly, his flattist statements are also an aspect of the open access reformation.

About a decade ago, I heard a talk from Marshall Sahlins, perhaps the foremost cultural anthropologist in the U.S. He spoke to a large group of anthropologists at the University of Vienna on cultural anthropology in a globalized world. Then, as now, I don't think anyone at that conference, including myself, quite fully understood that Sahlins was subtly telling us that globalization will relegate anthropology, oddly enough from premises of this book, to the mere study of subcultures. And that study might bring those subcultures to ignominy.

We librarians should ask ourselves, "What rough beast is slouching to Bethlehem now?"

8

Library Management

Learning the Profession

Much of what was said in previous chapters of this book addresses selected broad aspects of library management in one form or another. More specifically, the book is intended to shed light on serious divisions in the profession and practice of modern librarianship. I hope the proposed remedies can reduce significant damage caused by divided libraries. Broadly speaking, everything stated in the chapters above revolves around basic actions that will improve library contributions to their institutions through (1) excellent teaching provided by librarians to improve student learning, (2) connecting seamlessly to the faculty to enhance their research, (3) providing maximum support to the specific missions of their institutions, (4) obtaining the finest training for library school students up to the doctoral level, and (5) assessing quantitatively the true impact of student library usage on overall student academic performance measured by their GPAs.

The Fault Line

Nothing in librarianship beats being a director. It's great to make the decisions, but I must say that one of my most productive activities is to listen to people around me. I don't know all the answers, but I know a good idea when I hear one, and I give full recognition to staff who help solve problems through initiative and a spirit of collaboration. Borrowing a line from Lucile Wilson (1996), Stueart and Moran agree (2007): "Listen more than you talk."

Unfortunately, I have encountered too many library directors who should never have been allowed to enter the profession, not to mention being promoted to director, and who rightly belong in prison for inflicting mental cruelty on their staff. I overheard one library director say to another, "Selecting new librarians is the most important and lasting task a library director can perform." In my own irascible way, I thought to myself, "What about developing the librarians and support staff who are already in the library?"

School Daze

I was one of the many graduate LIS students to cut teeth on the first edition of the textbook *Library Management* (1977), authored by Stueart and Eastlick. It was only 180 pages long, but I learned a lot at that time as a library school brat. My first in-depth encounters with Maslow and his self-actualization hierarchy of needs, McGregor's Theory X and Theory Y, the Hawthorne effect, and so on, were taught in my library management class. On Saturdays I attended an education class taught by a "road-scholar" professor from the University of Arizona graduate library school in Tucson, who traveled each week to Phoenix to teach for a couple of hours. I learned a lot from his class, but he didn't get tenure and was gone at the end of the semester like a vapor. I thought he was a good teacher, but now I suspect that being a good teacher in the 1970s was not a priority for tenure in the library profession. Too bad not much has changed in this regard.

Barbara Moran took over for Eastlick in 1987, and the book was retitled *Library and Information Center Management.* At this writing, *LICM* is in its seventh edition, totaling 492 pages. Because I was in a mood for counting, I found the 1977 index had around 250 primary entries; the 2007 edition index has over 600 primary entries. The expanding index certainly confirms the growing depth, complexity, and potential futures of librarianship. Still, many topics I searched that should be explicit in the 2007 *LICM* do not appear in the index or the book, such as the emphasis on librarians as teachers and educators; the demand for open access and the return of scholarly communication to academe; flimsy MLS or "advanced degrees"; the need for doctoral degrees for librarians; real quantitative library assessment methods that correlate students' learning with their library involvement; and other matters that have been discussed in this book and elsewhere.

In short, Stueart and Moran (2007) are still steering too closely to Stueart and Eastlick (1977) by addressing management per se instead of integrating the most current and crucial issues of library education and practice with the present dilemmas facing library management to supercharge library practice and directions. Mainly, this means the author's next edition should look at library management in terms of resolving the monumental issues dividing libraries and librarianship.

This book is in no way an attempt to match the breadth and depth of Stueart and Moran. Instead, the previous chapters herein have addressed several specific aspects of managing libraries, some of which have not been adequately addressed in the literature or discussions of librarianship, but which contribute to the detriment of library science in the 21st century. I perceive that dividing librarians from their fundamental role as educators, and the confusion of their misconstrued missions, along with the psychical distance between librarians and the faculty and administrators of their institutions, could very easily provide openings for commercial publishers and other extortionist concerns to deal directly with university administrators and the students themselves, while bypassing the libraries. Hence the vital need for closer collaboration with teaching faculty to demonstrate our instructional abilities. My aim has been to bring libraries together and librarians to their senses, and move them back to where they belong, viz., at the front of academe, not the rear.

Interpersonal Management

Among the most pressing needs to heal the divisions in library practice is the person-to-person connection between library managers and their so-called support staff. In most libraries I know of, there is an invisible line between professional librarians and support staff. I began my career as a library assistant, and I learned that the invisible line is guarded on both sides. It is in my nature to erase that line. For this purpose, the 2004 CSUS Library Self-Study created the staff group: "Library Personnel/Non-Faculty (LPNF)," and entered their levels of expertise in identical terms, skills, and performance. This innovation was praised by the faculty review team and the external evaluator. In respect for the fine work and expertise of those employees, I will use *LPNF* in this chapter in place of *support staff*. LPNF is a bit awkward, I admit, but it is a reflection of the awkward long-standing division between professional librarians and other staff that has long been the reality of library management and staffing in libraries.

Similarly, I am more than just "comfortable" with diversity. I *expect* diversity, and I am uncomfortable without it. I have conducted successful programs and professional activities in the western and eastern regions of the U.S., in central Africa, in several Asian nations, and diverse in European countries. Internationalism is one of the bright spots in the future of librarianship.

Librarians as Managers

No wonder we're divided. In almost every library I've ever directed, I found when I arrived that the LPNFs were so beaten down by the previous director, the personnel department with their overly complex calculations to minimize LPNF salary increases, and many professional librarians who were simply inhospitable to the LPNFs, that I concluded it was my personal mission to improve the working conditions of the library employees in my library, especially the LPNFs.

I have peered into numerous libraries of all types and in many countries to see that time was passing agonizingly, especially for the LPNF. I have to say that a large number of the librarians and library directors I have observed and/or worked with should be incarcerated for inflicting mental cruelty on their subordinates, and they have seemed not to realize their own capacity for harshness and discrimination against their lower-ranked partners. It's like a virulent strain of workplace abuse, and it's a double heartbreak because even after the offending persons depart, they leave the scars and discomfort in the hearts of those they hurt.

I know tyrants exist in all lines of work, but I just don't understand why so many librarians are plagued with this affliction. How did they get that way? Who are they modeling? Why do such people gravitate to librarianship? What is lacking in our professional training that would prevent such behavior, especially to our LPNFs, without whom all libraries would shut down? Maybe it's because librarians are fed up being a subculture in academe, and they're lashing out at their subordinates; but whose fault is that? Not the LPNFs, but the librarians for sure. Librarians may or may not have comparatively superior educations to faculty, so should they then turn around and dump their disfavor on the nonlibrarians to feel superior?

I have no sure answers to such questions. I'm just an aging bookworm wondering what I have accomplished, if anything, and pondering the future of the profession I've pursued for more than 30 years. And especially, what was the bottom line effect I had on those I supervised? Did I leave them better than they were before I came? Or did I at least leave them without any personal diminishment? I hope I did some good.

Crossing a Bar

At my second library position, as an assistant library director in Hawaii, I met Ed Jensen who introduced me to a new version of library management. As it was then and even now, there is no systematic pedagogy for librarianship education nor a separate management model specifically for libraries because librarians normally do not tell library users how they should apply the information librarians provide from the collections. This might change in the future as librarians become more inclined and take steps to be teaching partners with the faculty. At the same time, many librarians become managers early in their careers because they become supervisors of support staff in small libraries, or they seek higher compensation attached to managerial responsibilities.

Webb and Jensen state, "Fortunately, the ethics and philosophy that guide librarians in their duties as information professionals can also provide fundamental skills for managing the library. In this age of information technology, the librarian's philosophy of information is itself the best introduction to good management behavior."

Simply put, library ethics are founded on confidentiality and rejection of censorship. Librarians are determined to see that users have every right to learn through reading and gathering information with an expectation of privacy in what they wish to read. Our philosophy as librarians combines confidentiality with deep respect for human life and reason, and also the basic goodness of people, or at least a trust in human rationality. Our best hope for social stability is that society will continue to survive and thrive if enough people have enough information to make good decisions.

The librarian who wishes to become a successful manager can apply the same philosophical discipline to organize a suitable and stable information flow within the library, in this case, a flow that is directed toward the library staff instead of users.

Ethics, Philosophy, and Management

"The ethics and philosophy that guide librarians in their duties as information professionals can also provide fundamental skills for managing the library. In this, the age of information technology, the librarian's philosophy of information is itself the best introduction to good management behavior" (Webb and Jensen).

My friend Ed backed up the issue that I came to understand later myself, which I called in Chapter 1 of this book "leadership at all levels." Here are just a few recommendations to strengthen leadership across the library: Erase rank distinctions from management all the way to the newest or lowliest staff member. Steadily make the workplace more pleasant no matter how long it takes to do so. Applaud staff for the work they do so as to engender pride in them as they complete their work. Encourage creativity, curiosity, experimentation, and having fun. Show your staff, and remind them often, that you depend on them. Once they know that, they will more willingly commit themselves to the tasks at hand.

Since my collaboration with Ed Jensen, I've subscribed to the following principles: The manager does *not* achieve the goals of the organization. The *other* employees, those who are managed, achieve the goals of the organization, and they should have all the credit and recognition for that. It falls to the manager, then, to create the optimum environment in which the *other* employees can most effectively achieve the organization's goals, and enjoy themselves as much as possible while they are performing the tasks they were hired to complete at the highest levels possible. The manager's task is to provide the resources — staff, material, technology, training, education, organization, and so on — that may be necessary to that end, but also kindness, humor, and clear correction when needed.

Organizational communication within a library can be greatly enhanced by a manager's adapting the philosophy and ethics of librarianship, namely, free access to information and personal confidentiality for the library staff themselves. Should we not treat the employees of our libraries at least as well as we treat the library patrons?

Between and Among the Ranks

On my first day as a new dean at a library I will not identify, a group of library LPNFs came to my office to welcome me, and one of them asked, "What is your motto?" I knew what was important to me as a library manager, but I had never verbalized it as a motto. I had to think fast because I also knew that many LPNFs were disgruntled about the previous dean. After a few moments, this was my response: "Work hard, have fun, and treat each other as equals." It seemed to hit a responsive chord, and I was pleased that the motto soon appeared on placards in a number of LPNF workrooms. After many glad and successful instances of team-based advances, the placards were still there a few years later, even after I had left for another position and returned to that library for a visit. Maybe my motto should be the epitaph chiseled on my gravestone.

The dean I mentioned just above had summarily, and apparently with no prior notice, disbanded the regular monthly LPNF meetings that had given them the opportunity to meet with the dean in close quarters, and who deemed it wise in the future to get their information from their section heads, who continued to meet with the dean, who in turn apparently could no longer find the time to meet regularly with the largest staff work force in the library. Furthermore, some section heads were lax in reporting to the LPNFs the notes of their meetings with the dean. True, many LPNFs did not care what happened in the meetings with the dean, but they should have, and their section heads should have acquainted them with the meeting minutes nevertheless. It might well have benefited the section heads and the LPNFs to achieve a better togetherness.

When I arrived at that library and heard from the LPNFs that they had lost their meetings and direct consultation with the previous dean, I immediately reconstituted the regular monthly meetings and met with them each month from then on. This decision was disputed by some librarians and even a library administrator. These confused events caused me to admit to myself that I'm still a paraprofessional at heart. Even now I often behave as I did when I was an LA I and LA II, and make a spectacle of myself at times by shedding light on the absurdities we fall into as library employees of widely differing ranks. Shaking off the unfairness among library classification that arises from time to time is like taking a deep breath of air after coming up from the bottom of a diving pool.

I cannot run a library without inclusive management and respect for the sound opinions of staff at all levels. Nor can I run a library without the input from LPNFs. I must know the conditions and attitudes of all library sections and classifications. I need to know the conditions and attitudes of all staff members and classifications, up close and personal, one-on-one, eye-to-eye, but always cordial and nonthreatening.

A Slap in the Face Book

As dean at another library, I was appalled when the head of circulation told me she had asked the erstwhile dean to persuade the librarians to be more considerate to the LPNFs, including herself. His response to this effective, good-natured middle-aged veteran, who was not without authority in the library, and always courteous herself, was something like this: "If you don't like being a staff member, get an MLS. You made your choice not to get a library degree. Now live with it." The circulation head was deeply hurt. Because of her age and family responsibilities, she couldn't go for an MLS even if she had wanted to, and the dean knew it. It was a heartless affront.

Why in the world do librarians, especially library directors, get so high and mighty when so many faculty and administrators look down on librarians, including library directors? Don't librarians know how painful and shameful it is for LPNFs to be demeaned by their superiors? And I often doubt that the term *superiors* is at all appropriate for many library managers. Many bandy with the lives of others they supervise.

More Administrative Crimes

I worked closely at another university with a VP who was belabored in the deans' meetings; questions were asked repeatedly for their input week after week; and pressing issues were tabled until they became out-dated and dropped off the docket completely because new and more pressing matters were emerging. The VP was well versed, but he was under water.

Then from bad to worse, the head of IT, who was an excellent specialist, resigned under the stress of his work and all the blame went to the IT Head, for what dire reason I don't know, but there were bitter words, no doubt and misgivings, all across the university, but I knew that the IT crew was excellent. As luck would have it, I was appointed to be the Head of IT, and the only person who could stand-in with such short notice. I began working with the IT crew right away. It was a gratifying and exhilarating experience and moved the university forward quickly by undertaking the IT projects, and also the library and IT were in the right place and the right time. They were champing at the bit to get on with their projects and keeping IT on level and on time.

After a year later, the VP recognized the fine work of the IT crew, and acknowledged my management of the library, librarians, and the IT Department, then asked me to assume the post of Interim Associate Vice President for Instructional Technology when the Acting VP abruptly resigned without notice after a dispute with the university administration.

Working with those excellent friends and very capable colleagues was one of the most enjoyable experiences in my career. In the end, the IT crew brought IT out of the "shambles," as the VP, thought, but he did not know until I told him later that the IT staff were perfectly capable of completing all the projects, and were a well-adjusted and well-seasoned team. The best work I did in that IT department was to get out of the way of those eager IT experts, give them their lead, and let the team do what they knew best how to do. My main tasks were to dismantle administrative roadblocks and protect the IT folks from jealous adversaries. It all worked out quite well.

Just Because

Despite the fact that I reminisce about being an LPNF and admire their expertise and endurance, I would not want to be employed in a library as anything but a director, as I said at the beginning of this chapter. The reason? I like making the decisions for my libraries after serious planning with the staff. There is no other library job I would accept after being a director, with the possible exception of being a cataloger. I began my library career as a cataloger, and found it enjoyable because I could work with few interruptions, winnow backlogs quickly, and see the new books in my fields first; no major administrative decisions, no one to supervise, just looking out for myself and working hard for the head cataloger.

The technology of cataloging, however, is now so sophisticated and automated I would have to go back to library school to be re-educated, something very unlikely at this point in my life. And I'm sure I would not be able to exam-out of the cataloging test a second time.

The Itinerant Librarian

My first library director was the head of the Phoenix Public Library. Even though I was only a library assistant, he was happy to talk with me about whether or not I should make librarianship my career. I asked for the appointment and was a little surprised that he would take time to advise me. He gave me at least an hour of his time, as I recall, and I received some good advice on two themes. First, he said a library director has to be ready to stick to long-term change implementations. Gratification often needs to be deferred. At administrative levels, projects can go on for years, and attention to the details must be conscientious to a bitter or a sweeter end, despite the many change orders that inevitably ensue. Second, he said, "be mobile." In other words, to get a good sight on the nature of librarianship, don't stay too long in the same place. Maybe this was his cagy way of suggesting I should hit the road and find a job somewhere else. After all, I was perceived as something of a troublemaker to certain higher-ups.

Later, at my second library, another very good friend taught me that "a change is as good as a rest." I took this advice to heart so I would not get stale. I became more familiar with a number of library management styles and library operations. This was also a subtle advice to "be mobile" and learn from other libraries. Now, because I've worked in six libraries of different types, sizes, and regions, one of the most beneficial outcomes of my itinerant career is that I learned to adopt preventive strategies, especially in budgetary, personnel, and strategic matters, *before* downturns arise. Good data and experience lead to accurate planning, but only for the watchful. In such instances, my role at almost all costs is to keep the staff happy enough to stay and work hard.

One of the presenters at the Milan IFLA 2009 conference observed that the people, not books, are our primary collection. I completely agree. This same presenter also said that libraries generally have forgotten to have fun, which is needed for an exciting, dynamic environment. I couldn't agree more with this observation as well. His freshness might be due to the fact that he is not a librarian, and plainly not a typical library supervisor.

Togetherness

Here are a few words about team building, managing, staff development, and change I've picked up along the way. I am nothing if not personable and respectful toward those whom I supervise. I strongly urge all library staff to engage in professional development, educational opportunities, grants, and professional travel. I have supervised promotion and tenure processes in all the academic libraries where I have worked, except in my current institution, which grants promotion but not tenure to librarians. I treat tenure-track librarians with utmost care because as they improve their professionalism in librarianship and teaching, I can be better assured that my library will contribute more meaningfully better to the success of students, faculty, and the university mission.

Open Stacks and Services in Beijing

Zhu Qiang is the brilliant leader of the Peking University Library, an organizer of numerous national library projects in China, and a developer of several massive sophisticated electronic resources that rival libraries anywhere. In 2008 at a national meeting of Chinese librarians and members of China's Ministry of Education Academic Library Committee, he endorsed Rush Miller's view that librarians need to be service-minded and people-oriented. He applies this respectful approach to the library staff as well. The result will be better service to users, and support along with loyalty from the library staff. How nice it would be if all U.S. library leaders and managers were consistently respectful. Education's purpose is to make people better, more honest, and more caring to the human condition.

I have also learned that collaboration within the university is the lifeblood of the library and a great benefit to the students. Cooperation within the larger professional and geographic communities is a windfall for the university, including the library. While engagement with external organizations can sometimes be cumbersome because of divergent objectives and motives, much more often, involvement with community groups are quite beneficial and enjoyable. At CSUS, we worked closely with the Tsakopoulos Hellenic Foundation, the Japanese American Archival Collection Board, the Royal Chicano Air Force, museums, art galleries, schools, and donors. Difficulties can be avoided or minimized by educating constituencies clearly about the university's methods, objectives, and mission. Frequent reminders of the university's purposes may be necessary for community organizations.

These kinds of collaborations may mature into donations, grants, gifts in kind, bequests, and endowments. In my library career, I've raised over two million dollars for the libraries and institutions where I was employed.

Libraries in Their Proper Place

Library construction, expansion, and renovation, along with the study of the relationships between library functionality, purpose, and space design, are becoming more important parts of library management. Over the past two decades and up to the present day, there has been a surge in library construction, particularly of large libraries. This convinces me that the influence of libraries is healthy and growing. This is not to say, however, that libraries are not at risk: commercial publishers would be very happy to put academic libraries out of business and go straight to students and faculty, and if academic libraries cannot demonstrate empirically that they contribute directly to student learning, faculty research, and the overall mission of their universities, libraries will suffer as a result.

Every library manager should make space management, including renovation and expansion, part of his/her library's strategic thinking. Academic libraries must be more densely populated with users than ever before. An academic library must draw its users into inviting spaces, a complement of services, a team of knowing experts, and other features that involve library users in the unique brands of teaching and learning that only occur in libraries and which are a necessary complement to classroom learning.

Library Building Inside and Out

I few years ago, I edited a book entitled *Building Libraries for the 21st Century*. It was applauded by reviewers and readers, and contains case studies of newly constructed libraries from the U.S., Asia, and Europe. The book makes very clear that libraries are gaining in importance, but planning new library construction requires delicate decision making for projects, services, and technologies that will take years to implement.

Another presenter at the IFLA Milan conference fully expected to see two imperative trends in the near future. First, library service must be integrated to the point of invisibility. Second, libraries will use their large space to become "stunningly beautiful architecture in the modern design mode."

Scott Carlson in *The Chronicle of Higher Education* (2005) found that academic library attendance is rising to the point that some libraries no longer rely on circulation statistics. Instead, libraries are brimming with students as if the once staid library has become "an academic counterpoint to the student center," especially when new libraries are opened, or renovated.

It is very clear to all of us that library management has become increasingly complex and intensive since Steuart and Eastlick in 1977, and will require more accountability of library managers than ever before in all aspects of the job. U.S. universities from SUNY to CSU are plagued with uncontrolled conditions that hamper student enrollment stability, undercut budgets, and impede teaching and learning. Academic libraries must generate programs that meet current university effectiveness measures, and insure that graduates become lifelong learners via quantifiable library assessment measures.

Leadership at All Levels

I frequently follow the leadership of my "subordinates" when they have good ideas and know what they are talking about and where they are going. I like to give assignments to bright people and then get out of their way so they can take charge of those responsibilities, with myself as follower and coach. I love to acquire resources and feed motivation to smart, eager staff. Sometimes I'm disappointed but, more frequently than not, I am struck with a superb product, performance, or breakthrough. Many of these projects are appropriate for tenure and promotion, improvement of student teaching and learning, and research as well.

Last Words About Tenure and Ph.D.'s

Tenure, the time-worn issue, can certainly benefit librarians in three ways: recognition of professional well-tended responsibilities carefully reviewed; eligibility for promotion; additional compensation; leaves; research and development funds; and academic freedom. These are the same activities that most faculty undertake almost automatically for their own prestige and also for the stature of their institutions (see Murray-Rust 2005). That being the case, the institution will benefit from the academic endeavors of librarians.

In 1972, the Association of American Colleges and Universities together with the American Association of University Professors agreed, with deference, that librarians "contribute" to teaching and learning, thus meeting the "essential criterion for faculty status" (Murray-Rust 2005). A nice invitation, but hardly praise. How have we responded to the faculty? From the other camp, Carver responds, "A few librarians engage in original research, but that is not the norm. We function as knowledge providers, not knowledge creators" (2005). That's a vacuous argument that puts librarianship in a very faint academic light.

Conditions of the tenure track and advanced degrees fit together in ways that can bring librarians into a heightened state of discovery and productivity. Levels of staff education, experience, enthusiasm, and native intelligence can supercharge the effectiveness of library management projects. Library managers should not be content with low-grade employees. Instead, encourage them; build their skills and further their education, or at least cross-training. Ph.D.'s are good for librarians, libraries, and library management, not to mention the benefits that accrue to the library's clientele. That's precisely the "why" of the CLIR scholarships, but we don't have to rely on such organizations as CLIR. The rigor of education at doctoral levels can sharpen the skills of the librarian and the smoothing of the library's advancement.

Maslow–Mayo Overdrive, and Henry James

Library management is not military maneuvers; it's not a commercial venture; and normally it won't bring in much revenue. Common decency and equality should prevail among all library classifications. Supervisors should be calming and supportive; at times applying correction, and afterward restoring a non-threatening cordiality to retain or maintain good working relations. A superior should not be afraid or ashamed to apologize to a staff member, especially an LNPF staff member, when needed. It's the right thing to do.

Stueart and Moran take me back more than three decades to Stueart and Eastlick, and it made me wonder how many library managers who studied under S&M actually applied the managerial models in their careers and found them successful or lacking.

From my experience, it seems that Maslow's hierarchy to reach self-actualization, a workplace form of nirvana, is generally on track, but he's asking too much for one scale, while McGregor's theory X is too negativistic for any supervisor to manage without a sidearm. Theory Y is very close to what my friend Jensen taught me: "*Y-type* managers see themselves as responsible for creating an environment that promotes positive development of individual employees ... [and] do not try to impose external control and direction over the employees; instead [*Y-type*] managers allow them self-direction and control." Yes, OK, but only to a finite point for each employee.

Mayo and his group of psychologists in Chicago's Hawthorne plant stumbled on a conundrum that literally shed light on workers who increased their productivity when the scientists increased the brightness of the lights in the plant. When the scientists decreased the brightness, the workers' productivity increased even more. Productivity increased even when the scientists left the lights untouched. Simply put, the moral is worker morale. The sheer experimentation on the employees gave them a sense of importance to the company they had not encountered before, and they took more pride in their work. Unfortunately, it could not last forever, given human nature.

Stueart and Moran commented:

(1) Workers are more motivated by social rewards and sanctions than by economic incentives. *My view*: The motivation may last for a while until salaries are frozen or reduced.

2) Workers' actions are influenced by the group. *My view*: Of course! But it depends on the situation of each individual worker.

3) Whenever formal organizations exist, both formal and informal norms exist. *My view*: OK, but they can easily become unbalanced. Life is a roller coaster for everyone, and talk is cheap. Be ready to stay the course, stick in the batter's box, and use the appropriate management styles that will carry your library and your staff at all levels through the hard times.

I would like to throw into the motivational mix a quote from one of my favorite authors, Henry James, who famously said, "Three things in human life are important: the first is to be kind; the second is to be kind; and the third is to be kind."

Let's Get Back to the Future

... and step back from librarians as managers to librarians as educators. That's one of the starting points in this book, and we need to return to it because librarians are still not recognized at that level by campus communities. We must achieve collegial status with faculty, researchers, and administrators. One way to do this is outlined in university expectations of undergraduate learning, and a focus on a university graduate attributes.

The two statements of learning goals and graduate attributes that follow below are very different in many ways. They have different dates, and were composed on opposite sides of the Pacific Ocean. One was written by a group, the other largely by a professor with help from a number of colleagues. One furnishes a lengthy opening rationale and a statement of principles. The other is like a brief resonating solo. The point is this: each institution has its objectives. Librarians as educators are obligated to contribute to the respective learning goals of each institution, influence senates, work with departments, faculties, and administrative entities, and safeguard the overall missions of the institutions.

CSUS BACCALAUREATE LEARNING GOALS

Prepared by the Faculty Senate Working Group
on University Learning Goals
(Fall 1999/Spring 2000)

BACKGROUND/RATIONALE

Several forces, both internal and external, have led to the development of these learning goals for recipients of a CSUS baccalaureate degree. Groups and individuals we loosely define as "external stakeholders" have been the most vocal advocates of changes in the ways we conceive and evaluate our degree and the programs that support it. Our most recent WASC accreditation involved the development of broadly conceptualized student outcomes and preliminary efforts to document our institutional effectiveness through assessment. CSU system initiatives first proposed as part of the "Cornerstones" plan for reformation of the baccalaureate have metamorphosed into a system-wide proposal for key performance indicators of "continuous improvement." The language of "accountability" has entered the vocabularies of the governor, the state's legislators and the publics we serve most directly — students, parents and employers.

However, the impetus for the development of campus-based student learning goals and meaningful program assessment and evaluation has not been merely a reactive response to "outsiders'" demands. The 1994 CSUS Strategic Plan noted that in order to meet the campus' goals for high quality academic programs, the campus community needed to "revise the academic program review and evaluation process to focus on teaching, learning and improving desired student outcomes." As a result of this recommendation, the academic program review process was revised, and the Faculty Senate approved a University assessment policy. In the fall of 1998 and the spring of 1999, CSUS faculty collaborated with colleagues from a number of disciplines at CSU Chico and San Francisco State University, in a project that developed common learning outcomes for two General Education requirements — written communication and quantitative reasoning. The results of their efforts were presented to the chancellor and the statewide Academic Senate. In fall 1999, during the Senate retreat, a working group on assessment was organized. Additionally, in the fall of 1999, the Senate was asked to reconsider and revise the Academic Programs theme of the Strategic Plan and the assessment policy that underpins it. These two activities have propitiously coincided with two additional campus initiatives that are firmly rooted in the values of our campus community. One, the first program review of General Education, since 1988, has begun the collection of data about the effectiveness of this central component of the university curriculum. The second, our participation in a nationwide project to create an on-line institutional portfolio, funded by the Pew Charitable Trust, led to a faculty and outside stakeholders' survey of fundamental learning goals for the baccalaureate degree. The results of that survey and consultations with departments and individual faculty members form the basis of the proposal that follows.

Our campus is poised to undertake a major step in formalizing and making explicit the values, knowledge, skills, and expectations which are at the heart of our efforts as educators. These expectations of undergraduate learning place our common values at the center of our efforts to evaluate and improve the quality of student learning at CSUS. The implementation of these expectations across the curriculum will allow us to work together in consistent and coherent ways to embody our goal of offering "academic programs characterized by high quality, ... a commitment to life-long learning, the preparation of an educated citizenry, and a responsiveness to regional needs."

A STATEMENT OF PRINCIPLES

A baccalaureate education is focused on the premise that all students should explore how the great body of human knowledge is organized and become familiar with the methods for gaining, evaluating and extending that knowledge. Baccalaureate students should possess a range of knowledge, values, and skills that will enrich and shape their lives long after their formal education has ended.

Most of the learning expectations that follow emphasize ways of knowing and contexts for knowledge rather than specific content. More that any specific list of courses, these baccalaureate learning goals emphasize the development of knowledge, values and skills that will serve students throughout their lives, providing them with the resourcefulness and flexibility to adapt successfully to rapid social, economic and technological change, the understandings and tolerance necessary for informed citizenship and social action, and the interest and curiosity that is essential to the pursuit of learning throughout a lifetime.

EXPECTATIONS OF UNDERGRADUATE LEARNING

COMPETENCE IN THE DISCIPLINES

Definition: The ability to demonstrate the competencies and values listed below in at least one major field of study. Additionally, this learning goal requires students to demonstrate informed understandings of other fields, drawing on the knowledge and skills of disciplines outside the major.

Specific Expectations: This expectation is demonstrated by a student's ability to:

a) examine, organize, and reveal significant understanding of at least one disciplinary way of knowing

b) apply at least one discipline's knowledge and methods to specific problems and issues

c) examine, organize, and integrate a variety of disciplinary perspectives and ways of knowing to reveal a broad understanding of the relationships between disciplines and the ways they strengthen and enliven each other.

ANALYSIS AND PROBLEM SOLVING

Definition: The ability of students to identify and diagnose problems; organize and critically evaluate relevant information of a qualitative and quantitative nature; develop reasonable arguments and effective solutions.

Specific Expectations: This set of expectations is demonstrated by a student's ability, as an individual and in collaboration with others, to

a) analyze complex issues and make informed decisions

b) recognize and synthesize valid and relevant information from various sources in order to arrive at reasoned conclusions

c) diagnose and solve problems, including those which are quantitative in nature

d) evaluate the effectiveness of proposed solutions

COMMUNICATION

Definition: The ability to read, write, speak and listen effectively. The ability to respond, with understanding and appreciation to a wide variety of communicative acts.

Specific Expectations: This set of expectations is demonstrated by a student's ability to

a) express ideas and facts in a variety of written and quantitative formats and to a variety of audiences in discipline-specific, work-place, and civic contexts

b) comprehend, interpret, and analyze written and oral presentations

c) communicate orally in one-on-one and group settings

d) communicate in a language other than English

e) interpret, analyze, and evaluate ideas presented in a variety of creative formats, including written, verbal and visual.

INFORMATION COMPETENCE

Definition: The ability to make effective and ethical use of information resources and technology for personal and professional needs.

Specific Expectations: This set of expectations is demonstrated by a student's ability to

a) locate needed information using a variety of resources, including journals, books, and other media

b) use basic computer applications such as word processing software, e-mail, the internet, and electronic databases

c) learn, understand, evaluate and apply appropriate technologies to information processes, communication needs, and problem-solving in productive and sustained ways in both professional and personal settings

d) distinguish and make judgments among available information resources

CULTURAL LEGACIES

Definition: Acquisition of knowledge of human accomplishments in the creative and performing arts and the achievements of human thought.

Specific Expectations: This set of expectations is demonstrated by a student's

a) application of a broadly historical consciousness to the human condition, the social world, and human achievements in the arts and sciences

b) experience of and appreciation for the fine and performing arts

c) understanding of the development of world civilizations and the values of different cultural traditions

d) ability to apply aesthetic principles to various cultural expressions

VALUES AND PLURALISM

Definition: The ability to apply ethical standards in order to make moral judgments with respect to individual conduct and citizenship, and to recognize the diversity of human experiences and cultures, both within the United States and internationally. The development of positive social attitudes, values and behaviors.

Specific Expectations: This set of expectations is demonstrated by a student's

a) recognition of the moral dimensions of decisions and actions

b) understanding of and respect for those who are different from oneself

c) willingness to accept individual responsibility

d) ability to work collaboratively with those who come from diverse cultural backgrounds

e) ability to recognize and understand the implications of various social structures and the ways people are grouped by such characteristics as status, race, ethnicity, gender, sexual orientation

f) valuation of service as a component of active citizenship

LEARNING GOALS MATRIX

Please refer to Learning Goals for an explanation of the definitions and expectations of the following Matrix.

GE AREA	LEARNING EXPECTATIONS					
	Competencies in the Discipline	*Analysis and Problem Solving*	*Communication*	*Information Competence*	*Cultural Legacies*	*Values and Pluralism*
AREA A						
A 1 Oral Communication			X	X		
A 2 Written Communication			X			
A3 Critical Thinking		X	X	X		
AREA B						
Area B 1 Physical Science		X				
Area B 2 Life Forms		X				
Area B 3 Lab		X				
Area B 4 Mathematical Quantitative Reasoning		X				
Area B 5 Further Studies in the above, B1, 2, & 4		X				
AREA C						
C 1 World Civilizations					X	X
C 2 Introduction to the Arts					X	X
C 3 Introduction to the Humanities					X	
C 4 Further Studies in the Arts and Humanities					X	X
AREA D						
D 1 A Foundations in Social and Behavioral Sciences						X
D 1 B World Cultures					X	X
D 2 Major Social Issues of the Contemporary Era						X
D 3 American Institutions					X	X
AREA E						
E Understanding Personal Development		X				

HONG KONG BAPTIST UNIVERSITY EXPECTATIONS OF UNDERGRADUATE LEARNING

COMPETENCE IN THE DISCIPLINES

Definition: The ability to demonstrate the competencies and values listed below in at least one major field of study. Additionally, this learning goal requires students to demonstrate informed understandings of other fields, drawing on the knowledge and skills of disciplines outside the major.

Specific Expectations: This expectation is demonstrated by a student's ability to:

a) examine, organize, and reveal significant understanding of at least one disciplinary way of knowing.

b) apply at least one discipline's knowledge and methods to specific problems and issues.

c) examine, organize and integrate a variety of disciplinary perspectives and ways of knowing to reveal a broad understanding of the relationships between disciplines and the ways they strengthen and enliven each other.

ANALYSIS AND PROBLEM SOLVING

Definition: The ability of students to identify and diagnose problems; organize and critically evaluate relevant information of a qualitative and quantitative nature; develop reasonable arguments and effective solutions.

Specific Expectations: This set of expectations is demonstrated by a student's ability, as an individual and in collaboration with others, to

a) analyze complex issues and make informed decisions

b) recognize and synthesize valid and relevant information from various sources in order to arrive at reasoned conclusions

c) diagnose and solve problems, including those which are quantitative in nature

d) evaluate the effectiveness of proposed solutions

COMMUNICATION

Definition: The ability to read, write, speak and listen effectively. The ability to respond, with understanding and appreciation to a wide variety of communicative acts.

Specific Expectations: This set of expectations is demonstrated by a student's ability to

a) express ideas and facts in a variety of written and quantitative formats and to a variety of audiences in discipline-specific, work-place, and civic contexts

b) comprehend, interpret, and analyze written and oral presentations

c) communicate orally in one-on-one and group settings

d) communicate in a language other than English

e) interpret, analyze, and evaluate ideas presented in a variety of creative formats, including written, verbal and visual.

INFORMATION COMPETENCE

Definition: The ability to make effective and ethical use of information resources and technology for personal and professional needs.

Specific Expectations: This set of expectations is demonstrated by a student's ability to

a) locate needed information using a variety of resources, including journals, books, and other media

b) use basic computer applications such as word processing software, e-mail, the internet, and electronic databases

c) learn, understand, evaluate and apply appropriate technologies to information processes, communication needs, and problem-solving in productive and sustained ways in both professional and personal settings

d) distinguish and make judgments among available information resources

CULTURAL LEGACIES

Definition: Acquisition of knowledge of human accomplishments in the creative and performing arts and the achievements of human thought.

Specific Expectations: This set of expectations is demonstrated by a student's

a) application of a broadly historical consciousness to the human condition, the social world, and human achievements in the arts and sciences

b) experience of and appreciation for the fine and performing arts

c) understanding of the development of world civilizations and the values of different cultural traditions

d) ability to apply aesthetic principles to various cultural expressions

VALUES AND PLURALISM

Definition: The ability to apply ethical standards in order to make moral judgments with respect to individual conduct and citizenship, and to recognize the diversity of human experiences and cultures, both within the United States and internationally. The development of positive social attitudes, values and behaviors.

Specific Expectations: This set of expectations is demonstrated by a student's

a) recognition of the moral dimensions of decisions and actions

b) understanding of and respect for those who are different from oneself

c) willingness to accept individual responsibility

d) ability to work collaboratively with those who come from diverse cultural backgrounds

e) ability to recognize and understand the implications of various social structures and the ways people are grouped by such characteristics as status, race, ethnicity, gender, sexual orientation

f) valuation of service as a component of active citizenship

HONG KONG BAPTIST UNIVERSITY GRADUATE ATTRIBUTES

Every university hopes to inculcate in its graduates a set of intellectual and personal attributes which are consistent with its mission and philosophy of education. A list of such attributes should neither be so brief and general as to be vacuous, nor so detailed and lengthy as to lose all sense of focus, nor so idealistic and high-sounding as to be unattainable. Bearing in mind these factors, most of us would probably agree that, ideally, a HKBU graduate should possess the following attributes:

1. Have up-to-date and in-depth knowledge of an academic specialty, as well as a broad range of general knowledge

2. Have bilingual communicative competence in English and Chinese (including Putonghua)

3. Be able to think logically, critically and creatively

4. Have the necessary numeracy skills to function effectively in work and everyday life

5. Be an independent and self-directed learner, motivated by an inquiring spirit

6. Be well-developed as a "whole person" — intellectually, morally, spiritually, culturally, socially and physically

7. Be a responsible citizen with an international outlook, and willing to serve and lead.

It is easy enough to draw up a list of graduate attributes like the above, but they will all need to be justified on two grounds: a) Why are these particular attributes considered desirable or even essential? b) Are they *realistically attainable* within the context of a 3–4 year undergraduate programme? The first question is easier to answer, since there are a number of graduate attributes which are — by general consent among enlightened educators — clearly desirable or essential. They tend to fall into three or four major categories:

I. Knowledge

Since a university is traditionally a place for higher learning and the pursuit of knowledge, our graduates are expected to acquire up-to-date and in-depth knowledge of an academic specialty. At the same time, they also need to acquire a broad range of general knowledge in order to understand the world they live in and keep abreast of its developments. Our undergraduate curriculum, with its major requirements and its expanded provisions for "complementary" and "distribution" subjects, is designed to ensure sufficiently in-depth knowledge of an academic specialty as well as broad general knowledge.

II. Transferable/Generic Skills

While knowledge itself is specific and liable to be superseded, or even (in some cases) irrelevant to the future undertakings of some of our graduates, a good education should inculcate generic intellectual skills which our graduates can transfer and apply to *any* intellectual or professional pursuit (whether or not related to their original academic specialty). These include:

(i) Language and communication skills
- We have reasonably adequate provisions for basic language courses in English and Chinese (including Putonghua); what we need more of are language courses designed to develop *higher-level* communicative skills — such as public speaking, creative writing (in a broad sense), and language for specific purposes;

(ii) Critical and creative thinking
- This is an area which demands more attention and effort from most of our academic programmes. There is still too much reliance on the traditional mode of teaching as "knowledge transmission," to the neglect of getting students to think critically and creatively about what they are learning. Critical and creative thinking cannot be taught successfully in isolation — it has to be practiced and inculcated by *all* teachers in the teaching of *all* subjects (just as physical fitness is in all sports)

(iii) Numerical and problem-solving skills
- A proposed introduction of a core course on "Logical and mathematical thinking" in a 4-year curriculum in HKBU may go some way toward meeting this need. Like critical and creative thinking, this is something which every programme should try to take on board in whatever shape or form is appropriate for them

(iv) Independent and self-directed learning skills

We have our students with us for only 3 or 4 years — what are they going to do for the remaining 50 or so years of their lives? They are unlikely to develop into "lifelong learners" if we teach them mainly by transmitting ready-made knowledge to them and getting them to regurgitate it at the end of the course. If we really want them to be lifelong learners, we will have to develop a spirit of inquiry in them and help them discover knowledge for themselves instead of "spoon-feeding" them all the time. This involves a lot of re-thinking of our ways of teaching, but it can (and should) be done in all disciplines.

III. Personal Attributes

Our undergraduate curriculum, with its major requirements and its expanded provisions for "complementary" and "distribution" subjects, is designed to ensure sufficiently in-depth knowledge of an academic specialty as well as broad general knowledge. Our graduates, therefore, should be well-developed as "whole persons" — not only intellectually but also morally, spiritually, culturally, socially and physically. Living as we do in a modern "world city" like Hong Kong, they should develop into responsible citizens with an international outlook, and be willing to serve and lead.

The above attributes are attainable within the undergraduate programme in HKBU — but *only* if all academic and support units regard them as a *collective* effort and take them on board in designing and implementing their teaching and learning activities. Otherwise, the "Graduate Profile" would be no more than a mere list of good intentions. It is necessary for individual programmes and the institution as a whole must contribute to realizing the proposed graduate attributes.

"Whole person" education cannot be left to any one single unit (like CHTL) or programme (like Complementary Studies) — though they can obviously contribute a great deal. It is everybody's business (or nobody's business). The desirable values of the "whole person" can be communicated (to a greater or lesser extent) through the teaching of *any* subject, by trying to "humanize" it and relate it to real-life concerns. The teaching of Language and Medicine are two obvious examples, but there are opportunities in every academic subject to contribute to "whole person education," and to make it a real practice and not just a vogue word. Again, this requires the cooperation of all programmes, but at present many of them are not even aware of it.

AFTERWORD

Some months before finishing this book, I was thinking about its afterword, and I came across the University of San Diego website, which addressed the questions "What Are the Humanities," and "What Are the Social Sciences." Because my academic fields are the humanities, social sciences, and librarianship, I borrow from USD.

In the 15th century, Renaissance scholars championed the humanities as a "return to the classics," in particular, the literature of ancient Greece and Rome. Newly established universities such as the University of Alcalá in Spain (1499) offered an innovative liberal arts curriculum that included language, art, architecture, history, philosophy, and literature. Their aim was to produce educated "Renaissance men."

Today, the humanities remain focused on the core liberal arts disciplines: art, English, history, languages and literatures, music, philosophy, theater arts, and theology and religious studies.

USD continues: The social sciences are one of three divisions of science, along with natural science and formal science. Social science concerns itself with human aspects of the world, like the arts and humanities, although social science places more effort on experimentation and the scientific method. Because the methods used in the social sciences are often qualitative and based more on personal interpretation, they are often referred to as the "soft sciences" in contrast to the "hard" natural and formal sciences. The social sciences include anthropology, economics, education, geography, history, law, linguistics, political science, psychology, sociology, communication studies, development studies, information science, and sociobiology (http://www.sandiego.edu/cas/humanities/about_the_humanities.php).

A rather exhaustive list, I think!

I did not see "library science" on the list, however, but librarians do have a valid place for librarianship in the humanities and social sciences according to the USD list. It has to do with education, and *education* is on the list for the very good reason that librarians are educators or, as I said earlier, not "instructors" necessarily, not "teachers" in all cases, but in all cases "educators." I hope this book will better help convince our neighbors in academe of this truth, *au fur et à mesure*, little by little. I hope I have given adequate evidence from my own career experience that public service librarians and technical service librarians, along with library administrators and library personnel non-faculty (formerly "support staff") likewise are educators.

BIBLIOGRAPHY

Abell, Susan. NELINET press release. Reports on library/publishing forum: Principles, Money and Access. An Institute on Building New Scholarly Publishing (June 6, 2003).

Adams, Mignon. 1992. The role of academic libraries in teaching and learning: An interview with Middle States' Howard Simmons. *College and Research Libraries News* (July/August): 442–445.

_____, with input from Barbara Fister and Steven Bell. 2005. What do librarians do? *Library Issues* (July).

Addis, Louise. Brief and biased history of preprint and database activities at the SLAC Library, 1962–1994. Updated January 1997, June 1999, April 2000, January 2002. http://www.slac.stanford.edu/spires/papers/history.html.

Association of College and Research Libraries. 1995. Standards for college libraries, 1995 edition. *College and Research Libraries News* 56 (April): 245–257.

_____. 2004. Standards for libraries in higher education. http://www.ala.org/ala/mgrps/divs/acrl/standards/standardslibraries.cfm.

_____. 2010. 2010 Top ten trends in academic libraries: a review of the current literature. http://crln.acrl.org/content/71/6/286.full.

Atkinson, Richard C. A new world of scholarly communication. *The Chronicle of Higher Education* (November 7, 2003): 16.

Avery, Chris, and Kevin Ketches. 1996. Do instruction skills impress employers? *College and Research Libraries News* (May): 249–258.

Bacon-Shone, John. 2007. E-mail to Anthony Ferguson and David Palmer (December 28).

Barkey, Patrick. 1965. Patterns of student use of a college library. *College and Research Libraries News* (March): 115–118.

BBC News. Publishing makes shift to digital: The vast majority of UK research material will be available in electronic form by 2020. http://news.bbc.co.uk/2/hi/technology/4633423.stm. Retrieved June 20, 2005.

Bean, John P. 2003. College student retention. *Encyclopedia of Education*. 2d ed. Vol. 1. New York: Macmillan.

Becher, Melissa, and Jean Caspers. 2003. Research agenda for library instruction and information literacy: Guest editorial. *College and Research Libraries News* (November): 428–429.

Bell, Steven. 2005. Electronic libraries can't be academic. *Chronicle of Higher Education*. Section B: 14.

_____, and John Shank. 2004. The blended librarian: A blueprint for redefining the teaching and learning role of academic librarians. *College and Research Libraries News* (July/August): 372–375.

Bolger, Dorita F., and Erin T. Smith. 2006. Faculty status and rank at liberal arts colleges: An investigation into the correlation among faculty status, professional rights and responsibilities, and overall institutional quality. *College & Research Libraries News* (May): 217–229.

Breakstone, Elizabeth. 2005. Librarians can look forward to an exhilarating future: We not only participate in the information revolution, but help direct its course. *The Chronicle of Higher Education* (September 30): B20.

Brunner, Marta L. 2009. Ph.D. holders in the academic library: The CLIR postdoctoral fellowship program. Librarian Publications. UCLA Library.

Bundy, Alan. Education, education, education. *inCite* 22(6): 4.

Burger, Leslie. 2007. President's message: Changing library education: Instructional program transformation is key to the profession. *American Libraries* (April): 5.

Bush, George. President Bush signs omnibus appropriations bill: Public access mandate made law. Appropriations Act of 2007 (H.R. 2764), December 28, 2007.

Campbell, Jerry. 1998. The management and organization of digital libraries. Presentation delivered at the International Conference on New Missions of Academic Libraries in the 21st Century. Peking University Library, Beijing, October 25–28.

_____. 2006. Changing a cultural icon: The academic library as a virtual destination. *EDUCAUSE Review* 41:1 (January/February).

Carlson, Scott. 2003. New allies in the fight against research by Googling." *The Chronicle of Higher Education* (March 21): A33.

_____. 2005. Thoughtful design keeps new libraries relevant: Not everything students want and need is online. *The Chronicle of Higher Education* (September 30): B1–B5.

_____. 2006. U. of California is in talks to join Google's library-scanning project. *The Chronicle of Higher Education* (August 11).

Carrier, James G. 2001. Diplomacy and indirection, constraint and authority. In *An Anthropology of Indirect Communication*, edited by Joy Hendry and C.W. Watson. New York: Routledge.

Cawthorne, Jon E. 2003. Integrating outreach and building partnerships: Expanding our role in the learning community. *C&RL News* (November): 666–669.

Child, Maxwell L., and Christian B. Flow. Faculty meeting notebook: Motion to allow free online access to all Harvard scholarly articles. Harvard Crimson Online. February 13, 2008. http://www.thecrimson.com/article/2008/2/13/faculty-meeting-notebook-while-its-ways.

Cohen, Patricia. 2008. At Harvard, a proposal to publish free on the web. *New York Times*, February 12.

Cohen, Sarah Faye. 2008. Taking 2.0 to the faculty: Why, who, and how. *College and Research Libraries News* (September): 472–475.

Consolidated Appropriations Act of 2007 (H.R. 2764). http://www.sciencecodex.com/public_access_mandate_made_law.

Cornell University. May 17, 2005. Cornell University Faculty Senate endorses resolution on open access and scholarly communication. http://www.library.cornell.edu/scholarlycomm/resolution.html.

Covey, Denise Troll. 2002. Academic library assessment: New duties and dilemmas. *New Library World* 103 (1175/1176): 156–164.

_____. 2005. Using data to persuade: State your case and prove it. *Library Administration & Management* (Spring): 82–89.

Council on Library and Information Resources. CLIR Postdoctoral Fellowship in Scholarly Information Resources. 2006. Available at: http://www.clir.org/fellowships/ postdoc/postdoc.html.

Crowley, Bill. 2004. Just another field: LIS programs can and should, reclaim the education of academic librarians. *Library Journal* (November 1): 44–46.

Crowley, Bill, and Deborah Ginsberg. 2003. Intracultural reciprocity, information ethics, and the survival of librarianship in the 21st century. In *Ethics and electronic communication: A festschrift for Stephen Almagno*, edited by Barbara Rochenbach and Tom Mendina. 94–107. Jefferson, NC: McFarland.

_____, and _____. 2005. Professional values: Priceless. *American Libraries* 36:1 (January) 52–55.

Desai, Shevon, Marija Freeland, and Eric Fierson. 2007. Lesson study in libraries: Building better lessons, better teachers, and better teams with creativity, collaboration, and revision. *College and Research Libraries News* (May): 290–293.

DiMattia, Susan. 2003. Arizona's SIRLS gets $1.5M gift. *Library Journal* (June): 22.

Dinkins, Debbi. 2003. "Circulation as assessment: Collection development policies evaluated in terms of circulation at a small academic library. *College & Research Libraries News* (January): 46–53.

Doskatsch, Irene. 2003. Perceptions and perplexities of the faculty-librarian partnership: An Australian perspective. *Reference Services Review* 31(2): 111–121.

Double Indemnity. 1944. Screenplay: Billy Wilder and Raymond Chandler. Director: Billy Wilder.

Douglas, Gretchen V. 1999. Professor librarian: A model of the teaching librarian of the future. *Computers in Libraries* (November/December): 25–30.

Ducas, Ada M., and Nicole Michaud-Oystryk. 2003. Toward a new enterprise: Capitalizing on the faculty/librarian partnership. *College and Research Libraries News* (January): 55–74.

_____, and _____. 2004. Toward a new venture: Building partnerships with faculty. *College and Research Libraries News* (July): 334–348.

Dunmore, Helen. 2006. The digital future: Authors hold many of the cards in a future dominated by digital content, but booksellers will have a vital — if changed — role. *The Bookseller* (September 29).

Durant, David. 2005. The loneliness of a conservative librarian. *The Chronicle of Higher Education* (September 30): B12.

Educational Testing Service. "California State University Students Take New ETS ITC Literacy Assessment: New Test Measures Students' Cognitive Abilities to Process and Communicate Information in a Technological Environment." April 4, 2005. http://www.businesswire.com/news/home/2005 0404005685/en/California-State-University-Students-ETS-ICT-Literacy.

Emmons, Mark, and Wanda Martin. 2002. Engaging conversation: Evaluating the contribution of library instruction to the quality of student research. *College & Research Libraries* (November): 543–560.

EndUserFaq — DSpace Wiki. http:/wiki.dspace.org/EndUserFaq?action=print. Retrieved July 1, 2005.

Farber, Evan Ira. 1999. College libraries and the teaching/learning process: A 25-year reflection. *Journal of Academic Librarianship* (May): 171–177.

Ferguson, Anthony, Fred Nesta, and Colin Storey. 2007. Managing across cultures: The experiences of three Hong Kong academic library directors. *Library Management* 4/5: 213–223.

Forys, Marsha. 2004. The university's role in developing future librarian teachers: The University of Iowa Libraries' experience. *College and Research Libraries News* (February): 67–69, 73.

Friedman, Thomas. 2005. *The world is flat: A brief history of the twenty-first century.* New York: Farrar, Straus and Giroux.

Gilman, Todd. 2003. New movements for Ph.D.'s. *Library Journal* (June 15): 16–17.

_____. 2006. Show your librarian some love. *The Chronicle of Higher Education: Chronicle Careers* (October 3).

Gjelten, Dan, and Teresa Fishel. 2006. Developing leaders and transforming libraries: Leadership institutes for librarians. *College and Research Libraries News* (July/August): 409–412.

Gorman, Michael. 2005. One college librarian worries about "atomizing" books. Interview. *The Chronicle of Higher Education* 51(39).

Guterman, Lila. 2008. Harvard Faculty adopts open access requirement. *The Chronicle of Higher Education* (February 12).

Hackman, Tim. 2009. What's the opposite of a Pyrrhic victory? Lessons learned from an open access defeat. *College and Research Libraries News* (October): 518–521, 538.

Hardesty, Larry. 1988. Use of library materials at a small liberal arts college: A replication. *Collection Management* (October): 61–80.

_____. 1995. Faculty culture and bibliography instruction: An exploratory analysis. *Library Trends* (Fall): 339–367.

Heine, Carl, and Dennis O'Connor. 2007. Power searching: Digital fluency at your fingertips. Presentation at the Illinois Mathematics and Science Academy, June 25.

Hiscock, Jane E. 1986. Does library usage affect academic performance? A study of the relationship between academic performance and usage of libraries at the Underdale Site of the South Australian College of Advanced Education. *Australian Academic and Research Libraries* (December): 207–214.

Hisle, W. Lee. 2005. Reference questions in the library of the future. *The Chronicle of Higher Education* (September 30): B6.

Howard, Jennifer. 2008. For advice on publishing in the digital world, scholars turn to campus libraries. *The Chronicle of Higher Education* (November 21): A8.

Hutcherson, Norman B. 2004. Library jargon: Student recognition of terms and concepts commonly used by librarians in the classroom. *College and Research Libraries News* (July): 349–354.

Inkeles, Alex, and David H. Smith. 1974. *Becoming modern: Individual change in six developing countries.* Cambridge, MA: Harvard University Press.

Jackson, Miles. Regarding the relatively sudden proliferation of library doctoral and interdisciplinary programs across the U.S. E-mail exchange with the author, April 2, 2010.

Jacoby, JoAnn, and Nancy P. O'Brien. 2005. Assessing the impact of reference services provided to undergraduate students. *College and Research Libraries News* (July): 324–340.

Joseph, Heather, and Adrian Alexander. 2003. Two years after the launch: An update on the BioOne Electronic Publishing Initiative. *College and Research Libraries News* (November): 652–655.

Kelly, Maurie Caitlin. 1995. Student retention and academic libraries. *C&RL News* (December): 757–759.

Knapp, Patricia. 1966. *The Monteith College library experiment.* New York: Scarecrow Press.

Knowlton, Sean Patrick, and Becky Imamoto. 2006. Recruiting non–MLIS graduate students to academic librarianship. *College and Research Libraries News* (November): 561–570.

Korten, D. 1980. Community organisation and rural development: A learning process approach. *Public Administration Review* (September-October): 480–503.

Kramer, Lloyd A., and Martha B. Kramer. 1968. The college library and the drop-out. *College and Research Libraries News* (July): 310–312.

Kreitz, Patricia A. 2004. Librarians as knowledge builders: Strategic partnering for service and advocacy. *College and Research Libraries News* 65:1 (January) 8–15.

Kyrillidou, Martha, and Mark Young, eds. 2004. ARL Statistics 2002–2003. New Measures, then ALA, ALCTS, CMDS, Conference. Association of Research Libraries, Washington, D.C. June 27.

Lafferty, Susan, and Jenny Edwards. 2004. Disruptive technologies: What future universities and their libraries? *Library Management* 25(6–7): 252–258.

Lane, Judy. "Nation's first executive MLIS at San Jose State University." January 26, 2005. http://slisweb.sjsu.edu/classes/exec.htm.

LC21: A digital strategy for the Library of Congress. National Academy Press. http://www.nap.edu/books/0309071445/html/R1.html. January 25, 2001.

Lee, Hur-Li. 2003. Collection development as a social process. *Journal of Academic Librarianship* (January): 23–31.

Lener, Edward F., Bruce Pencek, and Susan Ariew. 2004. Raising the bar: An approach to reviewing and revising standards for professional achievement for library faculty. *College and Research Libraries News* (July): 287–300.

Lerner, Daniel. 1958. *The passing of traditional society: Modernizing the Middle East.* Glencoe, IL: Free Press.

Levin, Aaron. 1992. The log-on library. *Johns Hopkins Magazine* (February): 12–19.

Li, Y. 2002. The impact of tourism in China on local communities. *Asian Studies Review* 26(4).

Lillard, Linda L., and Barbara A. Wales. 2003. Strengthening the profession: Educator and practitioner collaboration. *Journal of Academic Librarianship* (September): 316–319.

Lowry, Rich. The ideological librarians. Townhall.com. http://townhall.com/columnists/richlowry/2003/09/22/the_ideological_librarians.

Lynch, Beverly P., and Kimberley Robles Smith. 2001. The changing nature of work in academic libraries. *College & Research Libraries* (September): 407–420.

Lynch, Clifford A. 2003. Institutional repositories: Essential infrastructure for scholarship in the digital age. *ARL Bimonthly Report 226* (February): 1–7.

Macklin, Alexius Smith. 2001. Integrating information literacy using problem-based learning. *Reference Services Review* 29(4): 306–313.

Marcum, Deanna B. 1990. For university librarians of the future, the degree in library science. *The Chronicle of Higher Education* (August 1).

Marshall, Leon. "Africa's Bushmen may get rich from diet-drug secret." *National Geographic News.* http://news.nationalgeographic.com/news/ index.html (April 16, 2003).

Matarazzo, James M., and Joseph J. Mika. 2006. How to be popular: Two prominent educators suggest ways to ensure replacement of our aging work force. *American Libraries* (September 1): 38–40.

Maves, Mark. 2005. Thoughtful design keeps new libraries relevant. *The Chronicle of Higher Education* (September): B1. Quoted in Carlson.

Mayer, Jennifer, and Lori L. Terrill. 2005. Academic librarians' attitudes about advanced subject degrees. *College and Research Libraries News* (January): 59–73.

McCleery, Alistair. Dead hands keep a closed book. *The Times Higher Education.* June 5, 2008. http://www.timeshighereducation.co.uk/story.asp?storycode=402227.

Metz, Ray. 2006. A librarian's awareness: Strengths of the profession provide a campus advantage. *C&RL News* (December): 672–674, 683.

Meyer, Richard W. 1999. A measure of the impact of tenure. *College and Research Libraries News* (March): 110–119.

Mezick, Elizabeth M. 2007. Return on investment: Libraries and student retention. *Journal of Academic Librarianship* (September): 561–566.

Miller, Jeannie P., and Candace R. Benefiel. 1998. Academic librarians and the pursuit of tenure: The support group as a strategy for success. *College and Research Libraries News* (May): 260–265.

Mitchell, W. Bede, and Mary Reichel. 1999. Publish orperish: A dilemma for academic librarians? *College and Research Libraries News* (May): 232–243.

Moske, Lisa A., Director of Systemwide Electronic Information Resources (SEIR) at California State University, Chancellor's Office. Long Beach, CA.

Mundell, Jacqueline, Coryl Celene-Martel, and Tom Braziunas. 2003. An organizational model for instructional support at a community college. *Information Technology and Libraries* (June): 61–67.

Oberg, Larry R., Mary Kay Schleiter, and Michael Van Houten. 1989. Faculty perceptions of librarians at Albion College: Status, role, contribution, and contacts. *College and Research Libraries News* (March): 215–230.

OCLC. Perceptions of Libraries and Information and Information Resources. http://www.oclc.org/reports/2005perceptions.htm.

Ontario Library Association. School libraries and student achievement in Ontario. April 2006. http://www.accessola.com/data/6/rec_docs/137_eqao_pfe_study_2006.pdf.

Overholtzer, Jeffrey, and John Tombarge. 2003. Promoting information fluency. *Educause Quarterly* 1: 55–58.

Pace, Andrew K. 2004. Dismantling integrated library systems. *Library Journal* (February 1): 34–36.

Pearson, Richard, and T. D. Webb. 1988. The new librarians: How prepared are they? *Library Journal* (September): 132–134.

Pew Charitable Trusts. http//www.csus.edu/portfolio/index.htm.

Piaget, Jean. 1971. *Structuralism*. Trans. Chaninah Maschler. New York: Harper.

Picciano, Anthony G., and George Otte. Blended learning: Issues, research, and institutional planning. Sloan Consortium Seminar, University of Hong Kong, June 22, 2006. www.sloan-c.org.

Racine, Drew. 2006. Bifurcate to survive: To today's students, libraries mean *books*, not *information*. *American Libraries* (September): 34–35.

Rettig, Jim. My presidential initiatives are about creating connections. http://jimrettig.org/content/initiatives/initiatives.htm.

Rodger, Eleanor Jo (Joey). 2004. No sacred cows. *Library Journal* (June 15) 40–41.

Roy, Loriene. Primary platform issues. May 1, 2006. http://www.ischool.utexas.edu/~loriene/prez_elect/platform/index.html.

Savery, John R., and Thomas M. Duffy. 1995. Problem-based learning: An instructional model and its constructivist framework. In *Constructivist Learning Environment: Case Studies in Instructional Design*, edited by B. Wilson. Englewood Cliffs, NJ: Educational Technology Publications.

Shank, John D. 2006. The blended librarian: A job announcement analysis of the newly emerging position of instructional design librarian. *College and Research Libraries News* (November): 514–524.

Skinner, Jonathan. 2001. License revoked: When calypso goes too far. In *An Anthropology of Indirect Communication*, edited by Joy Hendry and C.W. Watson. New York: Routledge.

Slattery, Charles E. 1994. Faculty status: Another 100 years of dialogue? Lessons from the library school closings. *Journal of Academic Librarianship* (September): 193–199.

Starr, Kenneth. San Bernardino, Fresno, Chico ... these universities save the state. Latimes.com. (October 2005). http://articles.latimes.com/2005/oct/23/opinion/op-starr23.

Stephenson, William K. 1980. Library instruction: The best road to development for faculty, librarians, and students. In *Library instruction and faculty development: Growth opportunities in the academic community*, edited by N. Z. Williams and J. T. Tsukamoto. Ann Arbor, MI: Pierian Press.

Stoffle, Carla, Robert Renaud, and Jerilyn R. Veldof. 1996. Choosing our futures. *College and Research Libraries News* (May): 213–225.

Stover, Mark. 1996. The librarian as publisher: A World Wide Web publishing project. *Computers in Libraries* (October): 40–43.

Stueart, Robert D., and John D. Taylor Eastlick. 1977. *Library Management*. Littleton, CO: Libraries Unlimited.

_____, and Barbara B. Moran. 2007. *Library and Information Center Management*. 7th ed. Westport, CT: Libraries Unlimited.

Thin, Neil. 2001. Indirect speech: Heteroglossia, politeness, and rudeness in Irula Forest Festivals." In *An Anthropology of Indirect Communication*, edited by Joy Hendry and C.W. Watson. New York: Routledge.

Treloar, Andrew. "From data to data: One version of a history of scholarly communication." Closing keynote speech at the 2008 PRDLA Conference, Singapore.

U.S. Bureau of Labor Statistics. Occupational outlook handbook, 2010-11 edition. http://www.bls.gov/oco/ocos068.htm#training.

Van Orsdel, Lee C., and Kathleen Born. 2008. Embracing openness: Global initiatives and startling successes hint at the profound implications of open access on journal publishing. *Library Journal* (April): 53–58.

Warren, D. 1991. Using indigenous knowledge in agricultural development. World Bank Discussion Paper No. 127. Washington, D.C.: The World Bank.

Watkinson, Anthony. 2006. A publisher's view of open access. Address at University of Hong Kong, September 26.

Weaver-Meyers, Pat. 2002. Conflict resolution: A case study about academic librarians and faculty status. *College and Research Libraries News* (January): 25–34.

Webb, T. D. 1987. Open systems sing a siren song: The integrated concept remains superior. *American Libraries* (April): 257–260.

_____. 1998. Publishing on the cusp: Enlarging the mission of 21st-century academic libraries. In *Proceedings of the International Conference on New Missions of Academic Libraries in the 21st Century, October 25–28, 1998.* Beijing: Peking University Press.

_____. 2000. *Re-Membering Libraries.* Jefferson, NC: McFarland.

_____, and E.A. Jensen. 1989. "Managing innovative information technology." *Journal of Library Administration* (Spring and Summer).

Welch, Jeanie M., and Frada Mozenter. 2006. Loosening the ties that bind: Academic librarians and tenure. *College and Research Libraries News* (March): 164–176.

Wellcome Trust. What we fund. http://wellcome.ac.uk/About-us/Policy/Spotlight-issues/Open-access/Policy/index.htm.

Wiberley, Stephen E., Jr., Julie M. Hurd, and Ann C. Weller. 2006. Publication patterns of U.S. academic librarians from 1998 to 2002. *College and Research Libraries News* (May): 205–216.

Wiegand, Wayne A. 2005. Critiquing the curriculum: The entrenched LIS agenda needs to change to reflect the most critical functions of the library. *American Libraries* (January): 58–61.

Wilder, Stanley. 1990. Library jobs and student retention: The library can contribute to the university's goal of retaining students and enhance its own mission at the same time. *College and Research Libraries News* (December): 1035–1038.

Wong, Rebekah Suhn Han. Uncovering Meaningful Correlation between Student Academic Performance and Library Material Usage. 2011. *College and Research Libraries News* (July): 361–370.

Xiao, Xiao-bo, Jing Shao, and Xuan-li Ma. Thoughts on the Million Book Project practice: Building universal digital library project collections. In *Universal Digital Libraries: Universal Access to Information. Proceedings.* pp. 6–8. First International Conference on Universal Digital Library, Hangzhou, China, October 2005.

Young, Jeffrey R. 2006. U. of California system's 100 libraries join Google's controversial project. *The Chronicle of Higher Education* (August 9).

_____. 2006. U. of California will provide millions of books to Google's Digitization Project. *The Chronicle of Higher Education* (September 1).

Young, Sheila, and Julia C. Blixrud. 2003. Research library involvement on learning outcomes assessment programs. *ARL Bimonthly Report* 230/231 (October/December).

Zhang, Xiaolin. Rebuilding university library mechanisms for the 21st century. Presentation delivered at the International Conference on New Missions of Academic Libraries in the 21st Century, Beijing, Peking University Library, October 25–28, 1998.

Zhang, Xing-gui, Zheng Xue, and Wang Lei. 2003. Comparative research on individual modernity of adolescents between town and countryside in China. *Asian Journal of Social Psychology* 13 (April): 61–73.

Zhu Qiang, Sponsor of the Sixth Annual Meeting of the China Ministry of Education, Summer 2009, Ning Xia, China.

INDEX